Characteristics of Those Who Await

Shaykh Ḥabīb al-Kāẓimī

AL-BURĀQ

Copyright

ISBN: 978-1-956276-67-1
Printed and published by al-Burāq Publications.
Translated and annotated by al-Burāq Publications. Where needed, context and transliterations were added. Some minor edits were made to the translated Arabic text.

Ordering Information
We offer discounts and promotions for wholesale purchases, non-profit organizations, and other educational institutions. Contact us at the email below for further information.

www.al-Buraq.org
publications@al-Buraq.org

First Edition | August 2025

Dedication

The publication of this book was made possible through the generous support of our donors.

Please recite *Sūrat al-Fātihah* and ask God for the Divine reward (*thawāb*) to be conferred upon the donors and also the souls of all the deceased in whose memory their loved ones have contributed graciously towards the publication of *Characteristics of Those Who Await.*

We begin by giving all praise and thanks to God ﷻ for giving us the *tawfiq* to translate this book. He has guided us and without Him, we would not have been guided to the straight path embodied by the Prophet Muḥammad ﷺ and the Ahl al-Bayt عليهم السلام.

This book is dedicated to all the scholars, martyrs and believers who worked tirelessly to promote the pure Muḥammadan path.

We want to also give our thanks and appreciation to all believers from around the world and acknowledge the team which helped al-Burāq Publications complete this work, spending countless hours to make its publication possible. Please recite Sūrat al-Fātiḥah on behalf of them, their families, and their marḥūmīn.

This book is dedicated in honor of the following individuals. Please remember them in your prayers and may God ﷻ have mercy on them and their loved ones.

Duʿāʾ al-Ḥujjah

اللهم كن لوليك الحجة بن الحسن صلواتك
عليه وعلى آبائه في هذه الساعة وفي كل
ساعة وليا وحافظا وقائدا وناصرا ودليلا
وعينا حتى تسكنه أرضك طوعا وتمتعه فيها طويلا

O God, be, for Your representative, the Ḥujjat (proof), son of al-Ḥasan, Your blessings be upon him and his forefathers, in this hour and in every hour: a guardian, a protector, a leader, a helper, a proof, and an eye—until You make him live on the Earth, in obedience (to You), and cause him to live in it for a long time.

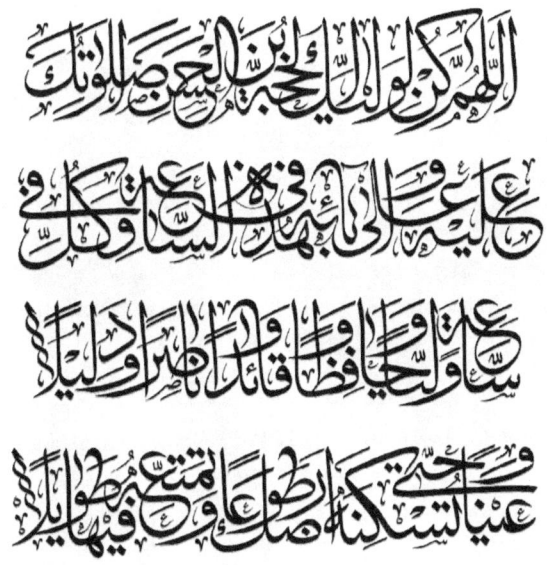

Terms of Respect

The following Arabic phrases have been used throughout this book in their respective places to show the reverence which the noble personalities deserve.

عزّ وجلّ

Used for God, meaning:
Exalted and Sublime (Perfect) is He

صلى الله عليه وآله

Used for Prophet Muḥammad, meaning:
Blessings from God be upon him and his family

عليه السلام

Used for a man (singular) of a high status, meaning:
Peace be upon him

عليها السلام

Used for a woman (singular) of a high status, meaning:
Peace be upon her

عليهما السلام

Used for men/women (dua) of a high status, meaning:
Peace be upon them both

عليهم السلام

Used for men and/or women (plural) of a high status, meaning:
Peace be upon them all

عجل الله تعالى فرجه الشريف

Used for Imām Muḥammad al-Mahdī, meaning:
May God hasten his return

قدس سره

Used for a deceased scholar, meaning:
May his resting [burial] place remain pure

Transliteration Table

The method of transliteration of Islamic terminology from the Arabic language has been carried out according to the standard transliteration table below.

ء	ʾ	ر	r	ف	f
ا	a	ز	z	ق	q
ب	b	س	s	ك	k
ت	t	ش	sh	ل	l
ث	th	ص	ṣ	م	m
ج	j	ض	ḍ	ن	n
ح	ḥ	ط	ṭ	و	w
خ	kh	ظ	ẓ	ه	h
د	d	ع	ʿ	ي	y
ذ	dh	غ	gh		
Long Vowels					
ا	ā	و	ū	ي	ī
Short Vowels					
ـَـ	a	ـُـ	u	ـِـ	i

Table of Contents

Preface 1

Believing in Him and Establishing a Connection 7

1. Measures of the Transparency of the Soul 7
2. Being Attentive to His Compassionate Heart 7
3. Standing when Hearing his Name 9
4. Seeking Refuge during the Occultation 10
5. Leadership Connection 11
6. Caring for the Affairs of the Believers 12
7. The Imām and misfortunes 12
8. Overseeing Destined Matters 13
9. The Guardian of Our Affairs 14
10. The Purpose of Creation 15
11. The Effect of Duʿāʾ in Hastening the Reappearance 15
12. Paths of Knowledge 16
13. The Imāms pray for the Reappearance 18
14. Deniers of the Imām's Birth 18
15. The Revealing Satisfaction 20
16. Ensuring the Satisfaction of the Beloved 20
17. Celebrating the Imām's Occasions 21
18. Divine Wisdom 21
19. The Significance of His Existence 22
20. Fulfilling Hopes 23
21. The Manifestation of Divine Names. 24
22. The Power of Hope 25
23. Circles Around Imām al-Mahdī 26
24. Establishing a Monotheistic State 27
25. Types of Greeting 28

26. Interpreter of the Noble Qur'ān 30
27. The Continuous Salām 31
28. The everlasting blessing of God ﷻ 32
29. The Divine Promise 34
30. The Rule of Reason 35
31. Claims of Special Affiliation 36
32. Developing Inner Maturity 36
33. The Imām's Excellence in Worship 37
34. Not Denying His Existence 38
35. His Impact on the Universe 39
36. The Acceleration of Events 40
37. The Reappearance Following the Natural Course 41
38. The Favor of God ﷻ upon His servants 43
39. Types of Reappearance 45
40. The Private Reappearance 46
41. The Trials of the End Times 46
42. Theoretical Knowledge 49
43. Claiming Representation 50
44. References for the Ummah 51
45. Channels of Divine Will 53
46. His Supplication at Birth 54
47. Supplication in the Month of Ramaḍān for the Awaited Imām's Reappearance 55
48. The Death of pre-Islamic Times 56
49. God's ﷻ Special Selection 57
50. Awaiting a Dear Friend 58
51. The Deception of Setting Time for the Reappearance 59
52. The Blind in the Presence of the Sulṭān 60
53. Those who Know His Status 61
54. Prohibition of Predicting the Imām's Reappearance 63

55. A Manifestation of Divine Retribution..................................65

56. With them in Heaven..66

57. The Decisive Word...67

58. Revival of the Religion 69

59. Avenging Imām al-Ḥusayn 🕮 71

60. Attending Ḥajj 72

61. Ibn Ṭāwūs Seeing the Imām 73

62. The Confusion of the Shīʿah 74

63. The Effect of Certainty...75

64. The Path Towards Him is Open 76

65. Unveiling the Riches 78

66. The Downfall of the Enemies Through His Prayers..............79

67. The Wonder at Those Who Deny Him 80

68. The Deep-Rooted Mahdī Idea 81

69. The Apparent and Hidden Blessings 82

70. Emerging When Necessary 84

71. His Supplication for Offspring......................................85

72. His Presence in Ḥajj 86

73. One of the Principles of Islam 88

74. The Prophet's Glad Tidings 89

75. Knowledge of the Qurʾān and Sunnah..............................91

76. Granting Him Dominion Over the Earth 92

77. Knowing Their Right 94

78. Characteristics of the Companions of the Imām 96

79. Like a Sheep Separated From The Flock...........................97

80. A Miraculous Birth...99

81. Two Similar Speeches..100

82. Avenging His Forefathers 101

83. Prayers Against the Oppressors.....................................102

84. The Virtue of Living in the Time of the Occultation 103

85. Al-Khiḍr as a Companion 105

86. Bad Outcome 106

87. The Joy of the Departed at His Return 107

88. The Fateful Role 108

89. Addressing the Occultation...................................109

90. Addressing the Imām's Long Life 110

91. Offspring in Paradise..111

92. Etiquettes of Ziyārah and Servitude....................112

93. Comprehensive Awareness of Events...................113

94. Sayyidah Fāṭimah ☺ as an Example 114

95. Known in the Heavens 117

96. Guardians of Blood...118

97. The Measure of Acceptance 119

98. The Signs and the Companions............................120

99. The Position of An Infallible in the Eyes of Another...........121

100.Building the Earth through Remembrance 122

101.The Wish of the Companions 123

102.Distinction Since Birth 124

103.Supplication for Various Groups..........................126

104.The Five Calls..127

105.Description of the Companions............................128

106.The Extension of Prophets 130

107.Revival of the Heavenly Scriptures......................131

108.Correcting the Narrations 132

109.Confronting the Deviants 134

110.The Interpretation of the Qurʾān 136

111.Their Inseparability from the Truth.....................138

112.Showing Displeasure 140

113.The Imām's ☺ Affection for His Companions 141

114.The Qualities of the Special Deputy 142

115.Authentication of Deputies....144
116.Proof of Agency....144
117.The Footsteps of Shayṭān....146
118.Exposure by the Deputies....147
119.The Depths of Lowliness....148
120.Deception and Capturing the Hearts....149
121.The Extent of Communication....151
122.His Prayers against the Oppressors....152
123.Diverse Letters....154
124.Forgetting him as a Punishment....155

During the Occultation 159

1. Following the Imām's Methodology....159
2. Provisions (rizq) through His Representative....159
3. Overseeing the Deeds....160
4. The Continuity of the Line of Martyrdom....162
5. Constant Remembrance....163
6. Sincerity in Asking....163
7. Changing the Hearts....164
8. Benefitting from him during the Occultation....166
9. Not Following other than the Imām....167
10. Reviving the Religion....168
11. Continuous Justice....169
12. Preparing for his Reappearance....170
13. Praying for him Specifically on Fridays....172
14. The Most Important Groups in the Ummah....173
15. Enduring Roughness in Life....175
16. Repentance before the Reappearance....176
17. True Awaiting....177
18. Magnetic field of The Mahdī....178
19. Allocating Time for Supplication....179

20. Among the Characteristics of the Awaiters 180
21. Praying for a Pure Heart 181
22. Hand Tied 182
23. The Best Deeds of the Ummah 183
24. Paying the Religious Dues 184
25. Financial Accounting 185
26. Praying for Righteous Offspring 186
27. Resistance to Temptation 187
28. Financial Obligation Towards the Imām 188
29. Forty Days for the Imām 188
30. Rushing to Fulfill Needs 189
31. Establishing Universal Justice 190
32. Bringing People to God ﷻ 190
33. The Mahdī-centered Family 192
34. Praying Behind the Imām 194
35. Seizing the Night of Mid-Shaʿbān 194
36. The Closest to His Noble Heart 195
37. The Neglected Duty 197
38. Achieving Sincerity in Worship 197
39. Women's Role in the Occultation and Reappearance 198
40. Supplicating to Hasten the Reappearance 198
41. Seeking Intercession 199
42. The Reason for the Setback 200
43. Unlocking our Hidden Potential 201
44. The Traits of the Awaiting Believer 202
45. Group Worship Acts 203
46. Relieving the Distress of the Believers 203
47. Group Supplication 204
48. Self-Development 205
49. Emulating Him in All Aspects 206

50. Signs of the Reappearance....207
51. Superficial Love....208
52. Practical Closeness to Them....209
53. Responding to Spiritual Needs....210
54. Praying for the Strength of His Companions....211
55. Praying for the Reappearance in the Middle of the Night...212
56. Ziyārah on his Behalf....213
57. Dispelling Adversity Through the Awaiters....214
58. Prayers as a Gift....215
59. Gifting Good Deeds....216
60. Gifting them the Qur'ān Recitation....217
61. Spiritual Sponsorship of Orphans....218
62. Being with Them in Paradise....219
63. Patience During the Occultation....220
64. The Greatest Patience....221
65. The Reason Behind the Community is Straying....222
66. The One Despised by God ﷻ....223
67. Spiritual Proximity to Them....224
68. The Prayer of Imām al-Mahdī....225
69. Fulfilling the Needs of Those Who Love the Imām....226
70. Preparing, even with just an arrow....227
71. Perfection of Intellect and Morals....228
72. Character like the Prophet's....229
73. Steadfastness on the Path of the Imāms....230
74. Circles of Companions Around the Imām....231
75. Praying for his Protection....233
76. The Importance of Ziyārah Āl Yāsīn....234
77. Physical Strength....235
78. Seeking His Intercession....236
79. The Example of the Lovers of the Imām....238

80. Signs of the End of Time 238
81. Swift Gathering 240
82. Striving while Awaiting 241
83. Gloomy Signs 242
84. Waiting is the Relief 244
85. The Honor of Correspondence 245
86. Changing the Course of Events 246
87. The Ultimate Victory 247
88. The Best People of the Time 248
89. Fulfillment of Rights 249
90. Ignorance of Some Shīʿah 250
91. Guiding Those Who Stray 253
92. The Basis of Actions 255
93. The Imām's Representatives 256
94. The Money Test 257
95. Absolute Submission 259
96. Loyalty 260
97. The Money Test 261
98. Positive Endings 263
99. The Criteria for Acceptance 265
100. The Blessings of the Soil of Karbalāʾ 266
101. A Profound Supplication in the Holy Month 267
102. Piety as a Prerequisite for Service 268
103. Supplication Near Imām al-Ḥusayn's Grave 269

Emotional Connection 273

1. Reflecting on the Imām's Difficulties 273
2. The Concern for the Ummah 273
3. The Works of God ﷻ and the Imāms 274
4. Love for their Followers 276
5. The Works of God ﷻ 277

6. Not Harming the Imām 278
7. No Fear or Sorrow 279
8. The Tragedy of al-Ḥusayn ﷺ...280
9. Submission and Devotion 282
10. The Imām's Complaint to his Grandfather.........................283
11. The Agony of Imām al-Ḥusayn's Martyrdom.....................285
12. A Prayer Filled with Anguish 287
13. Wishing to Meet Him..288
14. Awaiting is a Branch of Longing...289
15. Feeling the Weight of his Occultation.................................290
16. Gathered Under his Banner..291
17. Showing Genuine Longing 292
18. The Imāms' Grief..293
19. The Sign of Closeness...294
20. Practices for Deepening the Love 294
21. Expressing Grief..295
22. The Prayer of the Desperate 297
23. The Essence of Hosting and Hospitality 297
24. Commitment to Du'ā' al-'Ahd 298
25. Sensing the Loss 299
26. The Barrier of Worldly Pleasures...300
27. Sincerity in Supplication 301
28. Intermediaries in Supplication 302
29. Traits of the Sincere Lover...303
30. The Manifestation of Mercy 304
31. Recharging the Ummah's Spirits 305
32. Prioritizing the Interests of the Ummah.............................306
33. Praying for His Release...307
34. Defending the Imām...307
35. Prayers of the Believers for their Imām 308

36. Emotional Connection 310
37. A Private Moment with the Imām 311
38. Conversing with the Imām 311
39. Divine Retribution 312
40. Reasons for Wishing to Meet the Imām 313
41. The Involuntary Remembrance of the Beloved 314
42. Distressing News 315
43. Supporting the Vulnerable 316
44. The Impact of Loss 317
45. The Bond of Love 318
46. Supplication After Every Obligatory Prayer 318
47. His Supplication in Qunūt 319
48. The Qunūt of Amīr al-Mu'minīn 320
49. Not Feeling Gracious 322
50. Supplication on Friday Eve 323
51. Praying for him When Crying 324
52. His Prayer by The Kaʿbah 325
53. Prayer During Ziyārah 326
54. The Prayer of ar-Riḍā for al-Mahdī عليه السلام 327
55. Intense Longing 329
56. ʿĪd of Sorrows 330
57. Presenting Needs to The Imām 331
58. Praying for The Manifestation of His Authority 332
59. Compassion of the Infallible 334
60. His Prayers for His Helpers 336
61. The Position of Fatherhood 337
62. An Emotional Expression 338
63. Two Qualities of the Awaiters 339
64. Affiliation to His Banner 340
65. Gentleness in Interaction 342

66. The Imām is the one in Dire Need..343
67. The Comprehensive Du'ā'..344
68. Compassion for the Awaiters..345
69. Feeling for their Tragedies..346
70. The Aspiration for Participation..347
71. The Imām's Compassion for our Needs..348
72. Prayers for the Awaiters..350
73. The Approach of His Grandfather..351
74. Intense Longing for Him:..352
75. The Imām's Compassion Towards His Followers..354
76. He is Not Too Distant from Us..356
77. His Prayers for his Supporters..357
78. The Depth of Relationship..358
79. The Imāms' Longing for him..359

Preface

بسم الله الرحمن الرحيم

In the Name of God, the Beneficent, the Merciful

May God's blessings be upon Muḥammad ﷺ and his immaculate Household عليهم السلام.

The discussion surrounding Imām Muḥammad al-Mahdī عجل الله تعالى فرجه الشريف blends external necessity with internal affection. On one hand, we believe that the efforts of the prophets عليهم السلام throughout history must culminate in the joyful return of Imām al-Mahdī عجل الله تعالى فرجه الشريف. As God's عز وجل vicegerent, he will establish justice against tyranny.

On the other hand, the discussion about the one whose memory should reside in the hearts of his awaiting followers is a source of joy for those who genuinely love him. And who is more deserving of this love than our Imām? He represents the divine link between Heaven and Earth in our time, and under his leadership, we will gather on the Day of Judgment.

Books discussing Imām al-Mahdī عجل الله تعالى فرجه الشريف occupy a significant space in Islamic literature. Indeed, there are enough titles to warrant a dedicated dictionary or catalog covering his biography, teachings, and everything related to him from his Occultation to the present.

These works can be categorized as follows:

1. Narrative: Such as the four main books and collections of ḥadīth, serving as our primary source for understanding his teachings.

2. Analytical: Addressing misinformation, discussing signs of his Reappearance, and detailing the features of his government in the blessed era.

However, we recognize the need for another category: works that appeal to the emotional side of his followers, fostering a deeper connection to his presence. This combination of literature serves as both an internal reminder and an external tribute to the Imām, guiding believers to fulfill his commands and adhere to Sharīʿah as elucidated by scholars.

In this book, we aim to provide glimpses into the life of the Imām, igniting a longing for his blessed existence—a longing expressed by his honorable forefathers with words of yearning and anticipation.

By the grace of God, we have included approximately 275 Qurʾānic verses and narrations in many of these passages, grounding our insights in authoritative sources. Thus, this book aims to serve as a comprehensive overview of key content in this field, akin to renowned works in the genre.

Our ultimate goal is to instill a deep love for Imām al-Mahdī عجل الله تعالى فرجه الشريف, particularly in a world filled with distractions. Those who cultivate such love, embodying divine affection, will experience the Imām's special care during his Occultation. For them, the time until his Reappearance becomes inconsequential, as they have forged a profound inner bond with him. In the realm of devotees, it is the connection of souls that matters most, transcending physical distance.

We have structured the book into three chapters to enhance clarity:

1. Believing in Him and Establishing a Connection: Exploring the revered persona of al-Mahdī, his significance in relation to the Prophet and Islam, the Wisdom behind his Occultation, and the anticipation of his eventual return.

2. During the Occultation: Explores how to navigate this period of waiting, the relationship between our efforts to hasten his Reappearance, and the proper understanding of awaiting.

3. Emotional Connection: Exploring the nurturing of an emotional bond with the Imām, actions to earn his affection and avoid his displeasure, and highlighting his profound love for those eagerly awaiting his return.

In conclusion, we beseech God ﷻ to accept and bless our endeavor. Through this work, we aspire to play a humble role in preparing for the blessed Reappearance of our Imām عجل الله تعالى فرجه الشريف. Even if death, an inevitable decree from God, should intervene before that glorious day, we pray for the opportunity to witness the return of our beloved Imām.

Ḥabīb al-Kāẓimī

17 Rabīʿ al-Awwal 1440

Believing in Him and Establishing a Connection

1. Measures of the Transparency of the Soul

The liveliness and transparency of the soul are unveiled through three key indicators: a humble prayer, feeling sorrow for the misfortunes that befell the Prophet's family عليهم السلام, and the heartfelt connection to the Imām of the Time عجل الله تعالى فرجه الشريف. The first indicates closeness to the ultimate goal (nearness to God عز وجل), the second to the general means of achieving the goal, and the third to the specific means to the goal, as each group of people will be called under the banner of their Imām.

As such, a believer should test themselves in these three areas to see their closeness to God عز وجل and His vicegerent. There is a positive correlation between the two, meaning the more one is influenced by the aforementioned, the closer they are drawn to the circle of attraction of God عز وجل and His vicegerents. It is not necessary to be in a constant state of remembrance, as those who have attained the highest spiritual states may experience. However, believers should aim to maintain it as a general state in their lives, recognizing that human souls have moments of ebb and flow.

2. Being Attentive to His Compassionate Heart

Love sometimes requires sacrifice, as one may deeply care for someone but opt not to pursue a relationship due to parental disapproval. Similarly, the Imām عجل الله تعالى فرجه الشريف embodies the compassionate spirit of a father to the entire community, and it is essential to consider his noble heart in our actions. We must avoid anything that may cause him harm or add to his burdens, even if it means setting aside our desires. After all, isn't he already burdened enough with tribulations that dampen his joyous occasions?

It was reported that Imām Muḥammad al-Bāqir عليه السلام said to 'Abdullāh b. Thabyān:

> O 'Abdullāh! There is no 'Īd for the Muslims, whether Fiṭr or Aḍḥā, but it increases the grief of the Household of Muḥammad. He was asked,
>
> > Why is it so?
>
> The Imām replied:
>
> > Because they see their right in the hands of others.[1]

Considering this, can we doubt that the Imām عجل الله تعالى فرجه الشريف will reciprocate the kindness of the believer who frequently prays for his awaited Reappearance? He is likely to alleviate their worries and distress, thus repaying their devotion in equal or greater measure.

---

[1] Ṣadūq, Shaykh Muḥammad b. 'Alī, *Man Lā Yaḥḍuruh al-Faqīh*, Vol. 1, p. 511.

3. Standing when Hearing his Name

It is customary among devotees of the Imām ﷽ to stand up and place their right hands over their heads when his name is mentioned, signifying their respect for him and their submission to his command. It is as if they are saying:

> O master! Your name alone compels us to rise and show our respect, so how would it be when you are in front of us in person? And if your name alone moves us to stand in reverence, how will it be when we start seeing the signs of your awaited government?

It had been narrated that when Diʿbil reached the following part of his famous poem:

> No doubt an Imām will rise—an Imām who will govern according to the name of God and the [divine] blessing.

Imām ʿAlī ar-Riḍā stood up, lowered his head, placed his right hand on his head, and said:

> O God! Hasten his relief and reappearance, and grant us through him a mighty victory.[2]

[2] Amīnī, Shaykh ʿAbdul Ḥusayn, *al-Ghadīr fī al-Kitāb wal-Sunnah wal-Adab*, Vol. 2, p. 361.

4. Seeking Refuge during the Occultation

During the Occultation, it is our duty to seek refuge in God ﷻ, and to pray for steadfastness in faith and protection from the trials of the tumultuous end times. That is why we were instructed to recite certain duʿāʾs during the Occultation of the Imām ﷺ. One of those duʿāʾs is called Duʿāʾ al-Gharīq.

It has been narrated that Imām Jaʿfar aṣ-Ṣādiq ﷺ said:

> After this, a time of such doubt will befall you that you will be without the visible signs and a guiding Imām. And no one shall be able to achieve salvation from this except those who recite *Duʿāʾ al-Gharīq* (supplication of the drowning man). The narrator asked what this Duʿāʾ was. Imām ﷺ replied,
>
> اللَّهُمَّ! يَا رَحْمَنُ! يَا رَحِيمُ! يَا مُقَلِّبَ الْقُلُوبِ! ثَبِّتْ قَلْبِي عَلَى دِينِكَ!
>
> O God! O Beneficent! O Merciful! O the One Who transforms the hearts! Make my heart steadfast upon your religion![3]

It is crucial to note that, like any supplication, its acceptance is contingent on believers striving for spiritual,

[3] Ṣadūq, Shaykh Muḥammad b. ʿAlī, *Kamāl al-Dīn wa Tamām al-Niʿmah*, Vol. 2, p. 352.

intellectual, and ideological perfection, akin to asking God ﷻ for sustenance while working hard to attain it.

5. Leadership Connection

Our relationship with the Imām of our times ﷻ mirrors that of a flock to its leader. Just as Ādam ﷺ served as God's ﷻ vicegerent on Earth, Imām Muḥammad al-Mahdī ﷻ holds that role in our time. He is the link between the heavens and the Earth, and the one upon whom the Angels descend during Laylat al-Qadr (the night of power). It is known that the Earth cannot be without a representative of God ﷻ at all times, and all the favors and benefits that reach human beings are due to the blessings of the presence of the Imām of the Time, as he is the conduit for the flow of bounties between the Creator and the creation.

Hence, believers must acknowledge the Imām's leadership over them. When communicating with him, they should address him with the reverence and deference befitting a follower toward their leader, recognizing the immense right that the Imām and his esteemed forefathers ﷺ hold over the community. As Imām aṣ-Ṣādiq ﷺ once stated:

> Through our worship God is worshipped. And if we had not been there, God ﷻ would not have been worshipped.[4]

---

[4] al-Baḥrānī, Hāshim al-Tūbilī, *al-Burhān fī Tafsīr al-Qur'ān*, Vol. 4, p. 294.

6. Caring for the Affairs of the Believers

One of the duties of the Imām at all times is to look after the affairs of the believers, especially those striving for closeness to God ﷻ. Even if the Imām is not visibly present among the people, he is like the sun behind the clouds, as it still benefits the plants, even if the eye cannot see it.

We believe that Imām al-Mahdī عجل الله تعالى فرجه الشريف recognizes and nurtures the exceptional individuals in our time. He is much like a farmer who selects a plant distinguished by its fruit, then takes it out of the ground and places it in a special orchard, giving it special care so that its potential does not go to waste among useless crops. Therefore, wouldn't it be great if we were like those plants that the Imām sees potential in and gives special care to? This aligns with the Imām's Wisdom, ensuring that the flow of care reaches those who are capable of receiving it.

7. The Imām and misfortunes

A believer can be so moved when hearing about one of the calamities affecting the muslims, that they would lose sleep that night. Consider our Imām عليه السلام who feels all the calamities and pains in this era? It is said that God ﷻ has not created anyone since the creation of Ādam عليه السلام who bears pain in terms of duration and intensity like our Imām عليه السلام.

To strengthen our connection with the Imām, we should focus on actions that draw us closer and avoid anything that harms him or might delay his Reappearance. Regular prayers for him are important because his happiness with our efforts contributes to blessings in our lives. It is also worth considering that some of the challenges and disappointments we face in life might be a result of repeatedly causing sadness to his honorable heart.

8. Overseeing Destined Matters

Believers are urged to beseech God ﷻ through the Imām of their time to fulfill their spiritual and material needs. We read in Duʿāʾ al-Nudba:

> Where is the ultimate [Divine] source of plenty and prosperity?

and

> Where is the divine aspect the God-fearing may look up to?

On the Night of Destiny, the Imām عجل الله فرجه الشريف sees what is written for us for the year and intercedes on our behalf with God ﷻ. So, why do we not turn to him with all our requests and concerns? Imām al-Mahdī عجل الله فرجه الشريف is a manifestation of the fulfillment of the Divine Will as mentioned in the Ziyārah for his grandfather, Imām al-Ḥusayn عليه السلام, where we read:

> The will of the Lord regarding the decrees of His affairs comes down to you

Hence, any decree from God ﷻ concerning our affairs reaches us after being presented to the Imām

9. The Guardian of Our Affairs

Believers should approach their hidden Imām just as past believers interacted with their present Imāms. They lived with their Imāms and submitted to the Imāms' leadership of this nation. Even if they lived far away from the Imām and did not get the opportunity to meet him in person, they believed the Imām cared for all their matters, big or small.

This should also apply to us, especially when we remember the Imām's reassuring message:

> None of your news is hidden from us. We are not negligent in your protection, nor are we forgetful of your remembrance. Had it not been so, calamities would have descended upon you and enemies would have annihilated you.[5]

This care from our Imām ﷺ is why the path of Ahl al-Bayt ﷺ remains intact during the Occultation despite the tyrants' efforts to destroy it.

---

[5] Ṭabrisī, Shaykh Aḥmad b. ʿAlī Ṭabrisī, *al-Iḥtijāj ʿalā Ahl al-Lijāj*, Vol. 2, p. 497.

10. The Purpose of Creation

Believing in the awaited movement of Imām al-Mahdī ﷺ is a crucial aspect of our faith. God ﷻ did not create the universe without purpose. Just as the sun follows a fixed path, humanity follows a predetermined course, aiming to reach the pinnacle of justice in line with the purpose of creation.

Undoubtedly, monotheism is central to our existence, as both the beginning and end belong to the Creator. The ultimate goal is for the entire universe to unite under the banner of submission to the One God. This goal finds fulfillment at the time of Imām al-Mahdī's Reappearance, which is what Imām al-Ḥasan al-ʿAskarī ﷺ referred to when he said:

> and I hope, my son, that you will be one of those whom God has prepared to spread the truth, eradicate falsehood, uphold religion and extinguish misguidance[6]

11. The Effect of Duʿāʾ in Hastening the Reappearance

Some may think that making duʿāʾ for the hastening of the Imām's Reappearance is futile, assuming that the time of

---

[6] Ṣadūq, Shaykh Muḥammad b. ʿAlī, *Kamāl al-Dīn wa Tamām al-Niʿmah*, Vol. 2, p. 448.

his Reappearance is fixed and unalterable. However, this matter could fall in the realm of things that can be erased and substituted, which is in the hands of God ﷻ.

Certainly, the multitude of supplicants to God ﷻ during the Occultation has the potential to change the Divine Will, as God ﷻ promised to answer the calls of those who call upon Him. Some narrations suggest that God ﷻ intended ease for the nation, had it not been for their involvement in the martyrdom of Imām al-Ḥusayn ؑ, showing that our collective actions influence our destiny. Of course, all of this does not negate the need for the sure signs of the Reappearance; however, their timing can also be changed by God ﷻ.

12. Paths of Knowledge

Knowledge is of two types: one is acquired, which is gained by reviewing books and listening to scholars, and the other is illuminative, where one receives a divine ray of knowledge that enlightens their heart and mind, directs their thoughts, and relieves their fear. Didn't God ﷻ calm the hearts of the people of the cave and guide them without sending a revelation to them? Isn't He the One who inspired the mother of Mūsā, despite her not being a prophet or an imām?

This special knowledge can only be attained by asking God ﷻ for it through the Imām عجّل الله تعالى فرجه الشريف.

Zurārah b. Aʿyan narrated that he asked Imām aṣ-Ṣādiq about the time of Occultation:

> May I be sacrificed for you, if I reach that time, what should I do?

The Imām said:

> O Zurārah, if you reach that time, recite this duʿāʾ:
>
>> O God! Make me know You, because if You do not make me know You, I will not know Your Messenger. O God! Make me know Your Messenger, because if You do not make me know Your Messenger, I will not know Your Ḥujjah [The Imām of the Time who is God's authority upon us]. O God! Make me recognize Your Ḥujjah, because if You do not make me recognize Your Ḥujjah, I will deviate from my faith[7]

This demonstrates that seeking knowledge of God and His prophets is also a means of seeking knowledge of God's representatives, the Imāms.

---

[7] Kulaynī, Shaykh Muḥammad b. Yaʿqūb, *al-Kāfī*, Vol. 2, p. 149.

13. The Imāms pray for the Reappearance

Our Imāms ﷺ experienced profound sorrow and sadness over the Occultation long before the birth of Imām al-Mahdī ﷺ.

An emotionally impactful narration that reflects this is the account of Imām aṣ-Ṣādiq's ﷺ grief over the Occultation. It is recounted that he was seen sitting on the floor, draped in a Khaybarī cloak made of hair, with his neck exposed and sleeves rolled up. He wept like a mother mourning the loss of her only son, his face showing signs of deep sorrow, tears had moistened the hollows of his eyes, and he was saying:

> My Master, your Occultation has taken away my night's sleep, it has narrowed my bed for me, and has snatched away the solace from my heart. My Master, your Occultation has turned my tragedies into the atrocities of eternity! The loss of one after the other perishes a crowd and a multitude.[8]

14. Deniers of the Imām's Birth

Those who deny the birth of Imām al-Mahdī ﷺ are essentially denying the Messenger of God ﷺ, even if they are unaware of it. The Messenger himself explicitly stated this, saying,

---

[8] Ṭūsī, Shaykh Muḥammad b. Ḥasan, *Kitāb al-Ghaybah*, p. 168.

> Whoever denies any of them [the Imāms] has denied me, and whoever denies me has denied God ﷻ[9]

The Messenger equated the People of the Household ﷺ with the Noble Qur'ān; they are inseparable from it until they reunite with the Messenger at al-Kawthar. Therefore, belief in Imām ʿAlī's Imāmate necessitates belief in Imām al-Mahdī's birth, as each Imām announced the successor who would come after them.

It is crucial for believers to defend the Imām of their time against those who deny his existence. This, of course, necessitates gaining the required knowledge to engage with them effectively. Here, we must emphasize that the rational person must ensure that their knowledge of matters is acquired through well-thought-out priorities.

Consider the following narration, which prioritizes knowledge over worship and then establishes the beginning and conclusion of knowledge as the understanding of the Imām's position in existence.

It was narrated that Imām aṣ-Ṣādiq ؑ said:

> There is nothing after knowledge that equals prayers, and there is nothing after knowledge and prayers that equals Zakāt, and nothing after that equals fasting, and

---

[9] Ṣadūq, Shaykh Muḥammad b. ʿAlī, *Kamāl al-Dīn wa Tamām al-Niʿmah*, Vol. 1, p. 262.

nothing after that equals the pilgrimage, and the beginning and the end of all of that is knowing us[10]

15. The Revealing Satisfaction

Just as the happiness of Sayyidah Fāṭimah az-Zahrā' ﷺ reveals the happiness of God ﷻ with us, as indicated by many narrations, the satisfaction of Imām al-Mahdī ﷺ also reveals God's ﷻ satisfaction with us. Drawing closer to God ﷻ naturally brings us closer to our Imām ﷺ.

It is a misconception to think that awaiting the Reappearance allows one to act as they please, banking solely on the Imām's intercession, especially if they neglect prayers. The Imāms ﷺ, upon whose intercession we rely, epitomized piety and worked diligently to please God ﷻ. Therefore, emulating their example is key to attaining salvation.

16. Ensuring the Satisfaction of the Beloved

When someone loves another for who they are or the benefits they bring, they often go to great lengths to ensure their happiness, sometimes becoming overly preoccupied with this desire. Similarly, a believer who loves their Imām is constantly mindful of actions that might sadden the Imām, as they seek his continuous satisfaction.

[10] Ṭūsī, Shaykh Muḥammad b. Ḥasan, *al-Amālī*, p. 694.

The awareness that our deeds are presented to the Imām adds a layer of responsibility, as we understand that these actions can either bring joy or sadness to the Imām. The occasional sadness felt by a believer who neglects their connection with the Imām might be a result of their deeds that cause distress to the Imām's heart.

17. Celebrating the Imām's Occasions

Followers of Imām al-Mahdī عجل الله فرجه الشريف commonly commemorate him on two significant occasions: his birthday, which falls in the middle of the month of Shaʿbān, and the day he assumed the position of Imāmate after the martyrdom of his father, Imām al-ʿAskarī عليه السلام.

> It is crucial to commemorate these events with special attention, striking a balance between the emotional and intellectual aspects. We should celebrate with joy, spreading happiness among fellow believers, while also reflecting on the Imām's pivotal role in reforming our community. Moreover, we should contemplate how we can align ourselves to support his goals for our nation, drawing closer to him in the process.

18. Divine Wisdom

Divine Wisdom necessitated the Occultation of our Imām عليه السلام in order to achieve the goal of creation, which is the absolute servitude and submission to God عز وجل throughout the Earth. Divine Power will be even more apparent in the world with the Imām's Reappearance at the height of the spread of disbelief and corruption, and when humanity reaches the pinnacle of cultural and scientific advancements. At that time, the Imām's followers and supporters would have also reached the highest levels of Wisdom and maturity in the personal and scientific fields. Subsequently, they would be able to communicate with the Imām with ease, as Imām aṣ-Ṣādiq ﷺ said:

> Whilst the Imām is in his place and they are in other parts of the world, they will be able to see and hear him without any intermediary[11]

19. The Significance of His Existence

It was mentioned in the noble ḥadīth that:

> If the earth remains without an Imām from among us for a day, it will cave in on itself with all its inhabitants[12]

Another narration states:

> Whoever dies without knowing the Imām of their time dies the death of the people of Jāhilīyyah (pre-Islamic time of ignorance)[13]

---

[11] Kulaynī, Shaykh Muḥammad b. Ya'qūb, *al-Kāfī*, Vol. 8, p. 241.

[12] al-Ṭabarī, Muḥammad b. Jarīr, *Dalā'il al-Imāmat*, p. 436.

[13] Kulaynī, Shaykh Muḥammad b. Ya'qūb, *al-Kāfī*, Vol. 3, p. 53.

Therefore, knowledge of the Imām عجل الله فرجه الشريف becomes the decisive factor distinguishing between belonging to the time of ignorance and Islam. He is the Imām under whose banner we will unite on the Day of Judgment.

As nations assemble under the banner of their respective Imāms, we will have the honor of standing beneath the banner of our Imām, the Master of the Time عجل الله فرجه الشريف. However, those gathered under this banner will fall into two categories: those who were merely present during the time of the Imām, whether in his Occultation or after his Reappearance, even if they had displeased the Imām, and those who promptly submitted to his will and followed his directives. Hence, we must ponder which type we would prefer to be.

20. Fulfilling Hopes

Imām al-Mahdī عجل الله فرجه الشريف is the fulfiller of hopes for all the prophets. There is no prophet, not even the final Prophet ﷺ, who has fulfilled his hopes for his nation in this world throughout history. Take Prophet Nūḥ عليه السلام for an example, a prophet with a great deal of patience and perseverance in calling people to God ﷻ we see the Noble Qur'ān describes him by saying:

﴿وَلَقَدْ أَرْسَلْنَا نُوحًا إِلَىٰ قَوْمِهِ فَلَبِثَ فِيهِمْ أَلْفَ سَنَةٍ إِلَّا خَمْسِينَ﴾

﴾*wa-la-qad arsalnā nūḥan ilā qawmihī fa-labitha fīhim alfa sanatin illā khamsīna*﴿

⟨Certainly We sent Nūḥ to his people, and he remained with them for a thousand-less-fifty years⟩[14]

Despite the lengthy duration of his message, only a few believed in and followed him!

Thus, it is natural that the prayers of the prophets and imāms were for God ﷻ to hasten the Reappearance of our Imām, who embodies all their messages. Imām Muḥammad al-Jawād ؑ showed the significance of Imām al-Mahdī's mission to purify the Earth of all impurities when he said:

> Every one of us is a Qā'im with the Command of God, and a guide to the Religion of God. However, the Qā'im through whom God will cleanse the Earth of the people of disbelief and denial, and who will fill the Earth with equity and justice, is the one whose birth will be hidden from the people, and whose personality will be concealed from them[15]

21. The Manifestation of Divine Names.

The Imāms ؑ exhibit the Names of God ﷻ. They represent the Beauty and Majesty of God ﷻ in human form. Just as God ﷻ is Merciful and Most Loving,

---

[14] Sūrat al-ʿAnkabūt, Verse 14.

[15] Ṣadūq, Shaykh Muḥammad b. ʿAlī, *Kamāl al-Dīn wa Tamām al-Niʿmah*, Vol. 2, p. 378.

managing the affairs of His servants with care, the Imām appointed by Him assumes this responsibility with God's ﷻ guidance.

Therefore, believers should strive to receive this care by endeavoring to emulate the virtues of God ﷻ, each according to their potential. Our capacity to ascend the ladder of moral and spiritual perfection surpasses our current status, as we have not yet fully tapped into our treasures and potential energies. With each step we take towards moral improvement, we draw closer to the one who attained the highest level—the Imām of our time عجل الله تعالى فرجه الشريف.

22. The Power of Hope

Hope is a crucial force in the lives of individuals and nations. Without hope, a farmer would not plant a tree, and a mother would not care for her child. Unfortunately, enemies have opposed the concept of Imām al-Mahdī عجل الله تعالى فرجه الشريف despite its prevalence in Islamic teachings. The Prophet ﷺ left no room for doubt on this matter.

Neglecting this belief has deprived the Muslim community of the uplifting hope that could have served as a stabilizing force and a source of success for all Muslims. This, in turn, contributed to the historical setbacks and the current state of division and loss among Muslims. The Prophet ﷺ foresaw this condition from the early days of Islam when he warned:

> The nations will soon gather against you, just as those invited gather around a dish.

They asked,

> Will we be few in number on that day?

He ﷺ replied,

> No, you will be many, but you will be like the foam on the surface of a flood. God will remove awe of you from the hearts of your enemies, and He will cast wahn into your hearts.

They asked,

> What is wahn?

He ﷺ replied,

> Love of the world and dislike of death.[16]

23. Circles Around Imām al-Mahdī

In the time of the Occultation, followers of Imām al-Mahdī عجل الله فرجه fall into different categories. First, there are the select few, his close companions, whom he guides directly and sends to assist those who seek his help. Then, there are the general followers, who believe in him and pray for his

[16] Sayyid b. Ṭāwūs, *at-Tashrīf bil-Minān fī at-Taʿrīf bil-Fitan*, p. 377.

return. Lastly, there is a group whom the Imām cares for from a distance, subtly guiding their lives even if they are unaware.

Being a manifestation of Divine Will, the Imām has the ability to influence this special group, shaping their determination and praying for their success. Our advice is not to settle for general following, as it represents the weakest form of faith. Conversely, one need not aspire to join the close circles, but should aim to be among those receiving the Imām's special care.

24. Establishing a Monotheistic State

We pray for the Reappearance of our Imām عليه السلام because he will establish the principles of monotheism on Earth and seek justice from those who oppressed his forefathers عليهم السلام. Highlighting the importance of his role in establishing justice, we recall what has been narrated about Imām ar-Riḍā عليه السلام when he asked someone:

> What do you recite in the qunūt of Friday Prayer?

I replied:

> That which other people recite.

The Imām said,

> Do not recite what they recite. Recite as follows:

> O God! Reform the conditions of Your servant and caliph with those means by which You have reformed the conditions of Your messengers and prophets. Surround him with angels and support him with the Holy Spirit. Appoint protectors from the front and behind him, (those) who will guard him from all troubles and calamities. Convert his fear into security. He worships only You and does not associate anyone with You. Do not make any of Your creatures an authority over Your vicegerent. Permit him to fight against Your enemies and his enemies, and include me among his helpers. Surely You possess power over everything.[17]

25. Types of Greeting

Greetings (salām) come in two forms: the first is exchanged with a living person whom we see physically present, body and soul. When greeting someone asleep, we do not expect a response because although their body is here, their soul is with their Lord, as mentioned in the Qur'ān:

﴿اللَّهُ يَتَوَفَّى الْأَنفُسَ حِينَ مَوْتِهَا وَالَّتِي لَمْ تَمُتْ فِي مَنَامِهَا﴾

---

[17] Ṭūsī, Shaykh Muḥammad b. Ḥasan, *Miṣbāḥ al-Mutahajjid wa Silāḥ al-Muta'abbid*, Vol. 1, p. 368.

﴾*allāhu yatawaffā l-'anfusa ḥīna mawtihā wa-llatī lam tamut fī manāmihā*﴿

﴾*God takes the souls at the time of their death, and those who have not died in their sleep*﴿[18]

The second type of greeting is directed towards the essence of the person we are greeting, even if we cannot see their physical form. It is known that the light of the infallibles was seen by angels while Ādam was still being created. In the Ziyārat Jāmiʿah Kabīrah, a comprehensive prayer for all the Imāms, we recite:

> God created you as lights; He then made you observe from His Throne, until He endued us with the favor of your existence (among us)and placed you in houses that He allowed to be raised and to have His Name mentioned therein.[19]

This greeting is aimed at the divine essence created by God before their physical birth and continues after their passing. Therefore, the essence of the greeting remains the same whether directed towards them before birth, during life, or after death. Similarly, when we greet the Imām of Time, it is directed towards his essence, just as it is towards

---

[18] Sūrat az-Zumar, Verse 42.

[19] Ṣadūq, Shaykh Muḥammad b. ʿAlī, *Man Lā Yaḥḍuruh al-Faqīh*, Vol. 2, p. 613.

his predecessors عليهم السلام. We believe this greeting is reciprocated, as expressed in the Ziyārah:

> I testify that you witness my position, hear my words, and respond to my salām[20]

26. Interpreter of the Noble Qur'ān

Even if someone recites the Noble Qur'ān without understanding Arabic or the meaning of its words, they still receive rewards for their recitation. Certain phrases in the Qur'ān, such as the broken letters, hold meanings understood only by the infallibles عليهم السلام.

We read in Ziyārah Āl Yāsīn, attributed to Imām al-Mahdī عجل الله تعالى فرجه الشريف:

> Peace be upon you, O reciter of the Book of God and its interpreter.[21]

Meaning that the Imām عجل الله تعالى فرجه الشريف is the one who comprehends the secrets of the Noble Qur'ān and interprets its meanings. He is like the translator who transfers the meaning from a language the addressee does not know to one they do. It is possible that one of the Imām's roles upon his Reappearance is to address this issue, either directly or

[20] Sayyid b. Ṭāwūs, *Iqbāl al-Aʿmāl*, Vol. 2, p. 610.

[21] Majlisī, ʿAllāmah Muḥammad Bāqir, *Biḥār al-Anwār*, Vol. 53, p. 171.

through his chosen companions, by teaching the true meanings of the Qur'ān. This underscores another aspect of the Imām's importance in relation to God ﷻ and His final message.

27. The Continuous Salām

In the Ziyārah Āl Yāsīn, we offer various greetings to Imām al-Mahdī عجل الله تعالى فرجه الشريف. One greeting stands out: if its meaning were realized, we would be among the greatest beneficiaries. It is when we say:

> Peace be upon you at the hours of Your night and the two ends of Your day.[22]

When you greet the Imām عجل الله تعالى فرجه الشريف with this, ask God ﷻ to make it continuous as long as days and nights endure, just as we do when we send our salāms to Imām al-Ḥusayn عليه السلام.

Consider the possibility that God ﷻ might appoint someone, perhaps one of His angels, to greet the Imām عجل الله تعالى فرجه الشريف on your behalf at every moment and place. If this continuous salām reaches the Imām, rest assured that he will respond with an equally benevolent salām or one that is even better.

---

[22] Majlisī, 'Allāmah Muḥammad Bāqir, *Biḥār al-Anwār*, Vol. 99, p. 93.

28. The everlasting blessing of God ﷻ

Imām al-Mahdī ﷽ is often referred to by the title mentioned in Ziyārah Āl Yāsīn:

> Peace be upon you, O the everlasting blessing of God on His earth.

This unique term is found in the Noble Qur'ān, attributed to Prophet Shuʿayb ﵇. In the Qur'ān, he instructs his people not to manipulate scales or devalue others' possessions, stating:

﴿بَقِيَّتُ اللَّهِ خَيْرٌ لَكُمْ إِنْ كُنْتُمْ مُؤْمِنِينَ﴾

﴾*baqiyyatu llāhi khayrun lakum in kuntum mu'minīna*﴿

﴾*What remains of God's provision* is better for you, should you be faithful*﴿[23]

This implies that what remains after fulfilling people's rights, as mandated by God ﷻ, is a blessed sustenance. Money left after fulfilling rightful obligations is considered superior to wealth mingled with ill-gotten gains, regardless of its abundance.

---

[23] Sūrat Hūd, Verse 86.

* That is, of your lawful earnings.

Just as this leftover money is blessed because it is linked to God 🕮, likewise, Imām al-Mahdī 🕮, as God's vicegerent on Earth, can be regarded as the divine result (everlasting blessing), left by God 🕮 to govern the world under His guidance. He represents the continuation of his forefathers 🕮, echoing Lady Zaynab's 🕮 description of Imām Zayn al-'Ābidīn 🕮:

> You are the everlasting blessing of the bygone ones and the last of the survivors.[24]

Imām al-Mahdī 🕮 himself reinforces this notion by quoting the same verse:

$$\text{﴿بَقِيَّتُ اللَّهِ خَيْرٌ لَكُمْ إِن كُنتُم مُّؤْمِنِينَ﴾}$$

⟨*baqiyyatu llāhi khayrun lakum in kuntum mu'minīna*⟩

⟨*What remains of God's provision* is better for you, should you be faithful*⟩[25]

---

[24] Bāslūm, Majdī Muḥammad Sarūr, *Mawsū'at Āl al-Bayt*, Vol. 2, p. 267.

[25] Sūrat Hūd, Verse 86.

* That is, of your lawful earnings.

29. The Divine Promise

It might sound surprising to some when it is suggested that the Imām of the Time achieves what the prophets could not. But if we look closely, no prophet departed from this world without a heavy heart, filled with sadness and disappointment about what their people would do in their absence.

Consider Mūsā, who endured much hardship from the Banī Isrā'īl. Or 'Īsā, who faced countless trials until God ﷻ raised him to Heaven. Even Nūḥ witnessed his son drowning after years of trying to guide his people. And the final Messenger, Muḥammad ﷺ, endured immense suffering until his departure.

In light of this, God ﷻ, in His greatness, would not abandon the Earth to the tyrants of the time, as stated in the Noble Qur'ān:

﴿وَلَقَد كَتَبنا فِي الزَّبورِ مِن بَعدِ الذِّكرِ أَنَّ الأَرضَ يَرِثُها عِبادِيَ الصّالِحونَ﴾

﴾*wa-la-qad katabnā fī z-zabūri min ba'di dh-dhikri anna l-'arḍa yarithuhā 'ibādiya ṣ-ṣāliḥūn*[a]﴿

﴾*Certainly We wrote in the Zabūr, after the Tawrāh: 'Indeed My righteous servants shall inherit the earth'*﴿[26]

---

[26] Sūrat al-Anbiyā', Verse 105.

Hence, it is a divine promise that the righteous will pave the way for the Imām's ﷺ Reappearance and his righteous rule over the Earth.

30. The Rule of Reason

Reason dictates that there must be someone who will fill the Earth with equity and justice, just as it was filled with injustice and oppression. Imagine a believer constructing a home for their family, only for it to be unjustly seized by a deceitful oppressor before they can even move in. In such a scenario, reason and law demand that the homeowner seek assistance to reclaim their rightful property.

Similarly, God ﷻ intended this Earth for the believers, yet it has been overrun by oppressors who have seized its riches and resources. Surely, God ﷻ did not create humanity and send messengers only for the Earth to fall into the hands of tyrants. Thus, there must come a time when righteousness prevails and the Earth is rejuvenated according to God's ﷻ will.

It is the Divine Will that justice will prevail over Earth, just as the Prophet ﷺ informed us:

> Even if a day remains for the Earth, God ﷻ will prolong this day till my son, Mahdī, reappears and ʿĪsā b. Maryam descends to the Earth and recites prayer behind His Eminence. The Earth shall be illuminated

from the east to the west and his rule will reach the east and the west[27]

31. Claims of Special Affiliation

One unfortunate consequence of the occultation period is the emergence of individuals who falsely claim to have special communication with the Imām عجل الله فرجه الشريف, or even worse, claim to be appointed as his deputies. Exploiting his absence, they propagate lies with impunity, knowing that if the Imām were to return, their deceit would be exposed. However, God ﷻ has not yet granted permission for his Reappearance.

Those who propagate such egregious falsehoods should realize that their deception will be exposed, both in this life and the hereafter. This includes those who claim a special affiliation with the Imām, falsely asserting themselves as his deputies. Numerous teachings from the Imāms عليهم السلام, including Imām al-Mahdī himself, caution against believing or legitimizing such claims beyond the established four deputies.

32. Developing Inner Maturity

As humans, we naturally engage with the tangible world around us, finding comfort in its familiarity. Transitioning

[27] Ṣadūq, Shaykh Muḥammad b. ʿAlī, *Kamāl al-Dīn wa Tamām al-Niʿmah*, Vol. 1, p. 289.

to the realm of the intangible is often challenging unless we elevate ourselves above our inherent inclinations and attain a level of intellectual and emotional maturity. At this stage, we begin to navigate the unseen world with the same ease, if not more, than we do with the physical world.

In Sūrat al-Baqarah, it is emphasized that one of the primary traits of believers is their belief in the unseen. This encompasses things beyond our senses, such as the existence of the Divine and angels, as well as things absent from our immediate perception, like the revered presence of the Imām of our time عجل الله تعالى فرجه الشريف. Our ability to engage with the concept of Imām al-Mahdī hinges on this internal maturity. Without it, individuals may struggle to connect with their Imām and his mission effectively.

33. The Imām's Excellence in Worship

Imām al-Mahdī عجل الله تعالى فرجه الشريف, who assumed the position of leadership after the martyrdom of his father, Imām al-ʿAskarī عليه السلام, stands out from his predecessors due to the remarkable length of his Imāmate. Unlike the earlier Imāms such as Imām al-Jawād عليه السلام, Imām ʿAlī al-Hādī عليه السلام, and Imām al-ʿAskarī عليه السلام, who were martyred in the prime of their youth, the leadership of Imām al-Mahdī has endured for over a thousand years.

This extended period surpasses even the time of Prophet Nūḥ's عليه السلام mission, who spent a thousand and fifty years among his people. We are uncertain about the remaining duration of his Occultation. It surpasses the timelines of any other prophets who called towards God ﷻ for such an extended period.

Thus, the leadership of Imām al-Mahdī عجل الله تعالى فرجه الشريف is a blessed Imāmate unparalleled in both quantity and quality. One can only imagine the elevated spiritual state he has attained through continuous worship. If his noble predecessors had the opportunity to live his extraordinary life, they too would have undoubtedly followed the same divine path.

34. Not Denying His Existence

Throughout history, various sects have disputed the Imāmate of different Imāms عليهم السلام. For instance, the Zaidis recognized the Imāms up to Imām Zayn al-ʿĀbidīn عليه السلام, the Ismailis up to Imām aṣ-Ṣādiq عليه السلام, and the Wāqifīs up to Imām Mūsā al-Kāẓim عليه السلام. However, Shīʿah Muslims have consistently acknowledged the Imāmate of Imām al-Mahdī عجل الله تعالى فرجه الشريف, despite his young age and his Occultation. Interestingly, no Shīʿah sect stops at the eleventh Imām.

The exchange of letters between the four ambassadors of the Imām and the Shīʿah community was well-documented during their time. These correspondences, along with letters from the Imām himself عجل الله تعالى فرجه الشريف, highlight the intellectual maturity of the people of that era. Their unwavering faith in the Imām, despite his young age and absence, reflects their profound reverence for the virtues demonstrated by his noble predecessors عليهم السلام.

35. His Impact on the Universe

One of the aspects that deeply connects us to the Imām ﷻ is reflecting on the profound influence he exerts over the universe, acting with the permission of God ﷻ. The Noble Qur'ān illustrates the authority of the successor of Prophet Sulaymān ﷺ:

﴿قَالَ الَّذِي عِندَهُ عِلْمٌ مِنَ الْكِتَابِ أَنَا آتِيكَ بِهِ قَبْلَ أَن يَرْتَدَّ إِلَيْكَ طَرْفُكَ﴾

﴾qāla lladhī ʿindahū ʿilmun mina l-kitābi ana ātīka bihī qabla an yartadda ilayka ṭarfuka﴿

﴾The one who had knowledge of the Book[1] said, 'I will bring it to you in the twinkling of an eye'﴿[28]

Suppose God ﷻ made the Earth and its contents, such as the throne of the Queen of Saba', obedient to the successor of Prophet Sulaymān. In that case, it is logical to believe the same for the successor of the Final Messenger, Prophet Muḥammad ﷺ, and the Imāms who followed.

Additionally, God ﷻ spared this nation from punishment due to the presence of His noble Messenger ﷺ, as mentioned in the Noble Qur'ān:

---

[28] Sūrat an-Naml, Verse 40.

* He is said to have been Sulaymān's vizier and successor, Āṣif b. Barkhiyā.

﴿وَما كانَ اللَّهُ لِيُعَذِّبَهُم وَأَنتَ فيهِم ۚ وَما كانَ اللَّهُ مُعَذِّبَهُم وَهُم يَستَغفِرونَ﴾

﴿wa-mā kāna llāhu li-yuʿadhdhibahum wa-ʾanta fīhim wa-mā kāna llāhu muʿadhdhibahum wa-hum yastaghfirūn[a]*﴾*

﴿But God will not punish them while you are in their midst, nor will God punish them while they plead for forgiveness﴾[29]

Contrary to the divine precedent of punishing disobedient nations, our Prophet ﷺ was a source of protection. Therefore, it is logical to believe that the Earth is shielded from divine punishment by the blessings of the Imām, who is an extension of the Prophet's presence. After all, it is through the Imām that God ﷻ provides sustenance, maintains the stability of the Earth and sky, and prevents the Earth from collapsing with all its inhabitants. The Imām's عجل الله تعالى فرجه الشريف presence also averts calamities as he said:

> and through me, God shall remove all the troubles and calamities from my household and my devotees and followers (Shīʿah).[30]

36. The Acceleration of Events

In the past, changes in the world and among people were often reported as news. However, today it feels like an

---

[29] Sūrat al-Anfāl, Verse 33.

[30] Ṭūsī, Shaykh Muḥammad b. Ḥasan, *Kitāb al-Ghaybah*, p. 246.

unexpected event is unfolding every morning and evening. Surprises and potential earthquakes that could reshape our world are no longer out of the realm of possibility.

Given that we have not yet reached a boiling point, it is crucial to maintain self-awareness and strengthen our connection with God ﷻ. The best individuals during the Occultation will continue to be the best after the Reappearance. If you hope to stand by the Imām's عجل الله فرجه side, it is essential not to live in a state of heedlessness or keep a distance from God ﷻ. Work on fortifying your relationship with God ﷻ to cultivate the resilience needed to navigate the challenges and surprises that may arise both during the Occultation and the eventual Reappearance.

37. The Reappearance Following the Natural Course

Imām al-Mahdī عجل الله فرجه is waiting for us, just as we are waiting for him. This feeling that the Imām is also waiting for us serves as a driving force in our lives. Undoubtedly, if the Imām عجل الله فرجه wanted to reappear using miracles, drawing strength from God, he would have done so years ago. However, he follows the example of his great-grandfather, Prophet Muḥammad ﷺ, relying on patience and adhering to natural laws when confronting oppressors.

Consider the challenges faced by the Prophet ﷺ during his years of preaching in Makkah. Despite facing immense cruelty, he chose patience over retaliation through miracles.

Similarly, Imām ʿAlī b. Abī Ṭālib ﷺ, the Commander of the Faithful, remained patient in the face of oppression and said:

> and I remained patient, with sadness in my eyes, and pain in my heart[31]

Imām al-Ḥasan al-Mujtabā ﷺ faced betrayal from his companions, even his wife, yet he endured with patience, seeking solace in supplication to God ﷻ. The same can be said for Imām al-Ḥusayn ﷺ, who endured unimaginable trials in the Battle of Karbalāʾ. Despite having the power to obliterate his enemies with a single prayer, he chose patience over swift divine intervention.

It was reported that Imām al-Bāqir ﷺ said:

> Indeed, God ﷻ has made us capable of what we will, and if we willed to move the earth, we could[32]

However, the Imāms desired only what aligned with the will of God ﷻ, choosing to guide people through conventional means while using miracles sparingly to validate their message.

---

[31] Ṣadūq, Shaykh Muḥammad b. ʿAlī, *ʿIlal al-Sharāiʿ*, Vol. 1, p. 151.

[32] Majlisī, ʿAllāmah Muḥammad Bāqir, *Biḥār al-Anwār*, Vol. 46, p. 240.

38. The Favor of God ﷻ upon His servants

God ﷻ has bestowed two great favors upon humanity, as mentioned in the Noble Qur'ān. Firstly, He sent His noble Messenger, Muḥammad ﷺ, to guide us, and purify our hearts, as stated in the verse:

﴿لَقَد مَنَّ اللَّهُ عَلَى المُؤمِنينَ إِذ بَعَثَ فيهِم رَسولًا مِن أَنفُسِهِم يَتلو عَلَيهِم آياتِهِ وَيُزَكّيهِم وَيُعَلِّمُهُمُ الكِتابَ وَالحِكمَةَ وَإِن كانوا مِن قَبلُ لَفي ضَلالٍ مُبينٍ﴾

﴾la-qad manna llāhu ʿalā l-muʾminīna idh baʿatha fīhim rasūlan min anfusihim yatlū ʿalayhim āyātihī wa-yuzakkīhim wa-yuʿallimuhumu l-kitāba wa-l-ḥikmata wa-ʾin kānū min qablu la-fī ḍalālin mubīnin﴿

﴾God certainly favoured the faithful when He raised up among them an apostle from among themselves to recite to them His signs and to purify them, and to teach them the Book and wisdom, and earlier they had indeed been in manifest error﴿[33]

Secondly, God ﷻ promises favor upon the oppressed with the rising of Imām al-Mahdī عجل الله تعالى فرجه الشريف to lead and inherit the land, as stated in the verse:

33 Sūrat Āl ʿImrān, Verse 164.

﴿وَنُرِيدُ أَن نَّمُنَّ عَلَى الَّذِينَ اسْتُضْعِفُوا فِي الْأَرْضِ
وَنَجْعَلَهُمْ أَئِمَّةً وَنَجْعَلَهُمُ الْوَارِثِينَ﴾

﴿wa-nurīdu an namunna ʿalā lladhīna stuḍʿifū fī l-ʾarḍi wa-najʿalahum aʾimmatan wa-najʿalahumu l-wārithīn[a]﴾

﴿And We desired to show favour to those who were abased in the land, and to make them imāms, and to make them the heirs﴾[34]

These two favors are deeply intertwined. The full fruition of the prophetic mission, initiated by Prophet Muḥammad ﷺ, hinges on the emergence of Imām al-Mahdī عجل الله فرجه. The Prophet ﷺ did not witness the complete realization of his mission during his lifetime, leaving this world saddened by the denial of his request to pen a will safeguarding the Muslim community from deviation. As narrated by Ibn ʿAbbās:

> Thursday! And how tragic that Thursday was! Then Ibn ʿAbbās cried severely so that his tears flowed to his cheeks.[35]

Hence, there will come a day when God ﷻ fulfills the hope of the prophets by bestowing the favor of Imām al-Mahdī's عجل الله فرجه appearance upon the believers.

---

[34] Sūrat al-Qaṣaṣ, Verse 5.

[35] Bukhārī, Muḥammad b. Ismāʿīl, *Ṣaḥīḥ Bukhārī*, Vol. 4, p. 31.

39. Types of Reappearance

Imām al-Mahdī ﷻ is believed to have two types of Reappearance: a general one and a private one. The general Reappearance is solely in the hands of God ﷻ; it occurs when He deems it appropriate and is tied to conditions known only to Him.

At times of great calamity, like the Mongol invasions of Muslim lands, many anticipated the Imām's return, thinking it to be the ultimate catastrophe. However, despite subsequent disasters that befell Muslim nations, the Imām still awaits divine permission to reappear. While we may perceive our current trials as the worst, history shows us that greater atrocities have occurred. God ﷻ, however, does not act hastily in response to the impatience of His servants, as expressed in the supplication:

> He alone hurries who fears to miss, and only the weak needs to wrong[36]

Additionally, there is a unique reappearance that precedes the general one. This occurs when the Imām ﷻ bestows his special attention upon those devotedly awaiting him, empathizing with their longing and sorrow for his absence, even though they may be few.

---

[36] Imām Zayn al-ʿĀbidīn ﷺ, *al-Ṣaḥīfah al-Sajjādīyyah*, Duʿāʾ 48.

40. The Private Reappearance

God showers His mercy in two distinct ways. He is ar-Raḥmān, showing boundless compassion to all His creations, and ar-Raḥīm, expressing special mercy to the believers. Just as God selects those whom He blesses with His mercy, the Imām, as the embodiment of Divine Mercy, offers special attention to those who sincerely love and await his return during his Occultation. For these devoted souls, the time of his Occultation holds no distinction from the time of his Reappearance!

Though veiled from our sight, the Imām shelters some under his protection; he prays for them and implores God for their forgiveness during his prayers. It is said that the Imām is even seen praying for those among the Shīʿah community who have strayed from the righteous path.

41. The Trials of the End Times

It is crucial to recognize the trials that await us in the end times, for they will bring about immense turmoil and test our faith like never before. It is said that one could wake up as a devout believer and, by nightfall, find themselves swayed into disbelief due to the trials and temptations that will arise. The Noble Qur'ān recounts tales of those who stood steadfast in their faith despite adversity, yet many of us struggle even with minor hardships that are part of life's natural course. God warns us:

﴿أَم حَسِبتُم أَن تَدخُلُوا الجَنَّةَ وَلَمّا يَعلَمِ اللَّهُ الَّذينَ
جاهَدوا مِنكُم وَيَعلَمَ الصّابِرينَ﴾

﴿am ḥasibtum an tadkhulū l-jannata wa-lammā yaʿlami llāhu lladhīna jāhadū minkum wa-yaʿlama ṣ-ṣābirīna[a]﴾

﴿Do you suppose that you would enter paradise, while God has not yet ascertained those of you who have waged jihād and not ascertained the steadfast?﴾[37]

Imām al-Jawād ﷷ shed light on the gravity of these trials when he revealed:

> The Imām after me is my son Imām al-Hādī ﷷ whose command is my command, whose speech is my speech, and obedience to whom is obedience to me. And the Imāmate after him has been placed in his son, Imām al-ʿAskarī ﷷ. His command is his father's command, his word is his father's word, and obedience to him is obedience to his father.

The narrator says that after that, the Imām fell silent. He was asked:

> O son of the Messenger of God, then who is the Imām after al-Ḥasan ﷷ?

[37] Sūrat Āl ʿImrān, Verse 142.

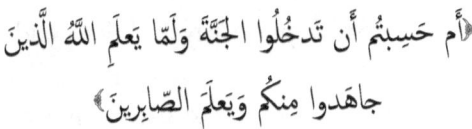

The Imām ﷺ, at first, wept greatly and then said,

> After al-Ḥasan, his son is the Establisher of Truth (al-Qā'im), the Awaited (al-Muntaẓar).

[The Imām ﷺ was asked:]

> O son of the Messenger, why has that personage been named Qā'im (The Riser)?

The Imām ﷺ replied:

> Because after his name and remembrance are forgotten and most of the believers in his Imāmate turn back from their creed, he shall rise.

[The Imām ﷺ was asked:]

> Why has he been named Muntaẓar (The Awaited)?

He ﷺ replied:

> Because he has an occultation with a very long duration, such true believers will wait for his advent and appearance, but people of doubt and uncertainty will deny, and rejecters will ridicule him. Those who specify a time for it will become many, and those who are hasty during that Occultation will be destroyed, but

> the Muslims—those who submit—will achieve salvation.[38]

42. Theoretical Knowledge

The journey towards God ﷻ begins with knowledge, a light that guides our steps in the right direction. It is often said:

> Those who act without insight are like wanderers lost on the wrong path; the faster they move, the farther they stray.[39]

To attain the position of servitude to God ﷻ, one must first grasp the teachings of Sharīʿah, which can only be achieved through a deep understanding of the Noble Qur'ān and the teachings of the Prophet ﷺ and his noble Household ؑ. While the Noble Qur'ān teaches the broad rules, it is the Prophet and his Household who explain the intricate details, for they are the second of the two weighty things (*al-Thaqalayn*) we have been instructed to cling to.

It was reported from the Prophet's Household:

---

38 Ṣadūq, Shaykh Muḥammad b. ʿAlī, *Kamāl al-Dīn wa Tamām al-Niʿmah*, Vol. 2, p. 378.

39 Kulaynī, Shaykh Muḥammad b. Yaʿqūb, *al-Kāfī*, Vol. 1, p. 106.

> Whoever dies without knowing the Imām of their time dies the death of the people of Jāhilīyyah (pre-Islamic time of ignorance)[40]

And:

> Those who truly know God ﷻ and worship Him are those who know Him, and know their Imām from among us Ahl al-Bayt, and those who do not know God ﷻ and do not know the Imām from among us worship other than God ﷻ, and they have gone astray[41]

Hence, one should not be deceived by those who worship through other than the path of the Prophet's Household ﷺ, for their actions and approach have always caused repulsion from Islam and its followers.

43. Claiming Representation

Some of what bothers the Imām of the Time عجل الله تعالى فرجه الشريف is the deceitful claims made by those who assert exclusive connections to him. Picture this: a father, unfairly banished to a distant land, leaving his family vulnerable and without support. Then, along comes an imposter who declares himself to be the father's representative. By exploiting their needs and showering them with kindness, he gains their trust, and eventually, he starts issuing commands and

---

[40] Ibid., Vol. 6, p. 123.

[41] Ibid., Vol. 1, p. 444.

prohibitions according to his whims, leading them astray. Now, imagine the anguish the father would feel, unable to alert his family to the lies of this imposter.

Yet, we affirm: the Imām عجّل الله تعالى فرجه الشريف appointed trustworthy representatives during his Occultation for us to refer to when needing to know the religious rulings. These trusted representatives are jurists renowned for their dedication to resisting personal desires and adhering to God's commands. Despite this, some people exploit the Imām's Occultation, claiming false authority in his name, leading astray the innocent and the gullible. It is not beyond the realm of possibility that the Imām عجّل الله تعالى فرجه الشريف prays against such deceivers, wishing upon them the shame and disgrace they deserve in this world before the hereafter.

44. References for the Ummah

It was narrated that Imām al-Mahdī عجّل الله تعالى فرجه الشريف said in one of his letters:

> But as for the problems which will occur in the future, you should refer to the narrators of our traditions for their verdicts as they are my proofs to you, and I am God's proof to them.[42]

Here, a narrator refers to a jurist (mujtahid), one who deduces Islamic rulings from the Noble Qur'ān and the

---

[42] Ṣadūq, Shaykh Muḥammad b. ʿAlī, *Kamāl al-Dīn wa Tamām al-Niʿmah*, Vol. 2, p. 484.

teachings of the Prophet and Imāms ﷺ. This narration underscores the importance of obeying the jurist, equating disobedience with a breach of allegiance to the Imām. To honor this guidance, follow the jurist's rulings after choosing one to follow. Failing to do so may hold you accountable on Judgment Day, as jurists serve as the Imām's representatives, and the Imām, in turn, stands as God's testimony over them.

To truly connect with the Imām ﷺ, we must follow his prescribed path, which begins with adhering to the guidance of the scholars (taqlīd). Imagine visiting someone's home; if you enter through any door but the main one, you risk being turned away, regardless of the gifts you bring. God ﷻ says:

﴿وَأْتُوا الْبُيُوتَ مِنْ أَبْوَابِهَا﴾

﴾*wa-ʾtū l-buyūta min abwābihā*﴿

﴾*and come into houses from their doors*﴿[43]

Likewise, during the Imām's Occultation, the door to his guidance is through the scholars. Those who do not follow this path, whether by adhering to a scholar, practicing precaution, or becoming a jurist themselves, stray from the path of the Imāms.

---

[43] Sūrat al-Baqarah, Verse 189.

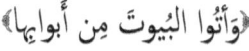

45. Channels of Divine Will

It was reported that Imām al-Mahdī ﷺ said in one of his letters:

> Our hearts are the vessels for the Will of God ﷻ If God ﷻ Wills something, we will it [44]

The Imām ﷺ shares this attribute with his noble predecessors, who stand as the epitome of God's ﷻ creation. They serve as evidence of His presence over His creation and guide us to His divine plan. Thus, it is no wonder that seeking their intercession brings about blessings; their will is harmonized with God's, and they desire only what He desires.

Moreover, consider this: if a believer's actions align with the teachings of Sharī'ah, God ﷻ may grant them the power to manifest His will, even if to a small extent. A sacred ḥadīth illustrates this promise:

> My servant, obey Me. [If you do so] I will make you an example of Myself; you will command anything to be and it will be[45]

---

[44] al-Ṭabarī, Muḥammad b. Jarīr, *Dalā'il al-Imāmat*, p. 506.

[45] an-Najafī, Āyatullāh Muḥammad Ḥasan Muẓaffar, *Dalā'il aṣ-Ṣidq li-Nahj al-Ḥaqq*, Vol. 5, p. 181.

This implies that believers wield a creative will in this world, a precursor to the autonomy they will enjoy in the hereafter. In paradise, God ﷻ grants them their every desire, as He promises:

﴿لَهُم فيها ما يَشاءونَ خالِدينَ﴾

﴿*lahum fīhā mā yashā'ūna khālidīna*﴾

﴿*There they will have whatever they wish*﴾[46]

46. His Supplication at Birth

From the moment of his birth, the weight of awaiting the blessed Reappearance has rested on our Imām ؑ. His mission, the greatest Divine endeavor in human history, is destined to unfold through him. It is no wonder, then, to hear the remarkable accounts surrounding his birth, reminiscent of the stories we have heard about the infant ʿĪsā ؑ, who spoke from the cradle and is foretold to pray behind Imām al-Mahdī ؑ upon his Reappearance.

Lady Ḥakīmah, the aunt of Imām al-ʿAskarī ؑ, recounted a miraculous sight she witnessed at his birth:

> Suddenly, as I stood before Lady Narjis ؑ, a radiant light enveloped her, blurring my vision. Then, I saw the

[46] Sūrat al-Furqān, Verse 16.

infant ﷺ bowing in prostration, lifting his index finger, and declaring:

> I testify that there is no god but God! I also believe in a single, unique God, and there is no partner for Him. I testify that my ancestor is the Messenger of God, and I testify that my father, the Commander of the believers, was the Proof of God!

Then he named the Imāms, one by one, until he reached himself, and said:

> O God ﷻ! Please, fulfill Your promise for me and help me finish my duty! Make my steps steadfast and sure, and spread Your justice and equity all over the world at my hand![47]

47. Supplication in the Month of Ramaḍān for the Awaited Imām's عجل الله تعالى فرجه الشريف Reappearance

In the sacred month of Ramaḍān, a time known for the granting of prayers, believers turn to God with heightened hopes. Fasting individuals, aware of the special divine atmosphere, intensify their supplications, seeking fulfillment for their most challenging needs, just as others delay their supplications until Friday Eve, hoping for a higher chance of acceptance. It is customary during the

---

[47] Ṣadūq, Shaykh Muḥammad b. ʿAlī, *al-Imāmah wa at-Tabṣirah min al-Ḥīrah*, Vol. 1, p. 3.

month of Ramaḍān to pray for success in fulfilling important tasks, like embarking on the pilgrimage, as highlighted in many of our Ramaḍān prayers.

What is truly remarkable, however, is witnessing the Imāms ﷺ themselves pray during the month of Ramaḍān, long before the awaited Imām's birth, for his imminent return! It was narrated that Imām Zayn al-ʿĀbidīn and Imām al-Bāqir ﷺ used to recite daily during the Month of Ramaḍān the following supplication:

> O God, this is the month of Ramaḍān. I ask You to help the vicegerent of Muḥammad, the successor of Muḥammad, and the one who will establish justice from the successors of Muḥammad. Your blessings be upon him and them. Bestow Your help to them. O You, beside whom there is no god, bless Muḥammad and the Household of Muḥammad and include me among them in this life and the hereafter.

48. The Death of pre-Islamic Times

The narrations confirm that whoever does not know the Imām of their time will die as if they died during the time of Ignorance, Jāhilīyyah. In simpler terms, during this period of Occultation, we must acknowledge the current Imām, understand his significance as one of the twelve Imāms prophesied by the Prophet ﷺ.

And it is known that this recognition comes with responsibilities, among them: pledging loyalty to him, following the path of his grandfather, the Messenger of God ﷺ, and preparing to support him. Among what confirms the necessity of recognising the Imām of the Time عجل الله تعالى فرجه الشريف is what has been narrated by Imām al-Kāẓim عليه السلام when he said:

> Whoever doubts four things, then he has disbelieved in everything that God ﷻ has revealed. One of them: knowing the Imām of each time in person and name[48]

49. God's ﷻ Special Selection

Delving into the attributes of the Imām of the Time عجل الله تعالى فرجه الشريف, one discovers a profound distinction separating him from the rest of creation. This unique quality, which positions him as the Imām and final reformer of humanity, is that God ﷻ has chosen him for Himself, shielded him from sin, and purified him from impurity. This divine designation is a testament to the Imām's worthiness and his triumph over various trials, akin to the challenges faced by Prophet Ibrāhīm عليه السلام, thus earning him the esteemed role of Imām for humanity.

When Imām ar-Riḍā عليه السلام describes Imām al-Mahdī عجل الله تعالى فرجه الشريف, he says:

---

[48] Ṣadūq, Shaykh Muḥammad b. ʿAlī, *Kamāl al-Dīn wa Tamām al-Niʿmah*, Vol. 2, p. 413.

> Your servant whom You have set aside for Yourself, chosen among Your creatures, appointed to Your servants, entrusted with Your unknown, preserved from sins, cleared from blame, purified from impurities, and freed from filth[49]

The practical lesson derived from this is profound. Those aspiring to be companions and supporters of the Imām ﷺ should strive to emulate his purity and righteousness, striving to rid themselves of flaws so they too may be among those whom God ﷻ has reserved for Himself.

50. Awaiting a Dear Friend

Living in constant anticipation and readying oneself to support the Imām of the Time ﷺ is fueled by the belief that his Reappearance may happen suddenly. The events leading up to this moment may unfold rapidly, catching those who believed the Reappearance was distant by surprise.

When discussing this, Imām aṣ-Ṣādiq ﷺ said:

> Await the reappearance of your master (*ṣāḥib*), day and night, as God ﷻ is doing something every day and one work does not prevent Him from doing another[50]

---

[49] Ṣadūq, Shaykh Muḥammad b. ʿAlī, *Kamāl al-Dīn wa Tamām al-Niʿmah*, Vol. 2, p. 514.

[50] Sayyid b. Ṭāwūs, *Iqbāl al-Aʿmāl*, Vol. 1, p. 201.

In using the Arabic term *Ṣāḥib* to describe Imām al-Mahdī عجل الله تعالى فرجه الشریف, Imām aṣ-Ṣādiq علیه السلام evokes a profound sentiment. It mixes the anticipation of his Reappearance with the warmth of awaiting a dear friend's visit. Just as one eagerly prepares for the arrival of a close friend, those sincerely awaiting the Imām عجل الله تعالى فرجه الشریف should likewise ready themselves for his return.

51. The Deception of Setting Time for the Reappearance

Numerous narrations emphasize the prohibition of making claims about presuming to know and set a specific time for the Imām's Reappearance. Such actions amount to unfounded claims and contradict the teachings of the Noble Qur'ān, which forbid us from acting on mere suspicions. Moreover, the aftermath of a failed prediction leads to disappointment and disheartenment among believers, providing an opportunity for enemies to gloat.

One such cautionary tale involves a man named Muhzim al-Asadī, who sought answers from Imām aṣ-Ṣādiq علیه السلام. He asked the Imām:

> May I sacrifice myself for you! Please, enlighten me on when this awaited event will come to pass?

To which the Imām ‹a› said:

> O Muhzim! Those who set timelines are liars, and those who act hastily will face ruin. Only those who surrender to the Will of God ‹swt› will find salvation![51]

52. The Blind in the Presence of the Sulṭān

In our daily lives, we confront many invisible forces of nature with utmost seriousness and caution, just as we handle tangible objects. Consider our approach to electricity and radiation – we treat them with respect and caution. Shouldn't we extend the same level of reverence and certainty when it comes to our guardian, Imām al-Mahdī ‹aj›?

Despite receiving numerous authentic narrations from our previous Imāms ‹a› about the existence of Imām al-Mahdī ‹aj›, why don't our hearts feel as connected to him as they do with the Imāms who walked among their companions?

The author of *Mikyāl al-Makārim* illustrated this beautifully:

> Imagine a blind person who cannot see anything. Yet, in the presence of a Sulṭān, he behaves with utmost respect, following all the protocols one should observe. Why? Because he is certain he is in the presence of the

[51] Ṭūsī, Shaykh Muḥammad b. Ḥasan, *Kitāb al-Ghaybah*, p. 426.

Sulṭān, even though he cannot see him. He knows the Sulṭān can see him. Similarly, during the period of Occultation, a believer's faith assures them that Imām ﷺ sees them, and they act accordingly.[52]

53. Those who Know His Status

The traditions of the Prophet's Household ﷺ provide evidence that understanding the importance and status of the Imām will lead one to pay attention to what others overlook and to act in ways that others may not conceive. Thus, someone who comprehends the stature of Imām al-Mahdī ﷺ as an infallible Imām will alter their conduct and devise means to support and serve him.

Consider the account narrated by Sulaymān b. Jaʿfar:

'Alī b. 'Ubaydullāh b. al-Ḥusayn b. 'Alī b. al-Ḥusayn b. 'Alī b. Abī Ṭālib said to me:

I would like to enter the house of Imām ar-Riḍā ﷺ and greet him.

I said,

What prevents you from doing so?

---

52 Iṣfahānī, Sayyid Muḥammad Taqī Mūsawī, *Mikyāl al-Makārim*, Vol. 2, p. 280.

He said:

> the respect and the prestige due to him and piety towards him.

Then Imām ar-Riḍā ﵇ fell ill with a mild illness, so people visited him. So when I met ʿAlī b. ʿUbaydullāh, I said,

> What you wished for has come to you, Imām ar-Riḍā ﵇. He became ill, and people are visiting him. If you want to visit him, then today is the day.

He went to visit Imām ar-Riḍā ﵇, who greeted him with love and respect:

ʿAlī b. ʿUbaydullāh became very happy. Later, ʿAlī b. ʿUbaydullāh fell ill, so Imām ar-Riḍā ﵇ visited him, and I was with him. So he sat until whoever was in the house left, and when we left, a servant of ours told us that Umm Salamah, the wife of ʿAlī b. ʿUbaydullāh, was behind the curtain looking at Imām ar-Riḍā ﵇. When he left, she came out and leaned over the place where Imām ar-Riḍā ﵇ was sitting, kissing it and wiping her hands on it. Sulaymān added that when he saw ʿAlī b. ʿUbaydullāh, he also told him what Umm Salamah had done. Later, I told Imām ar-Riḍā ﵇ about it, and he said,

O Sulaymān, 'Alī b. 'Ubaydullāh and his wife and children are among the people of Paradise.

Indeed, the children of 'Alī and Fāṭimah ![], if God ![] makes them aware of this matter, they would not be like the rest of people[53]

54. Prohibition of Predicting the Imām's ![] Reappearance

The teachings of the Imāms ![] passionately warn against attempting to predict the exact time of the Imām al-Mahdī's Reappearance ![]. This act is likened to attempting to unveil the timing of Judgment Day, a knowledge reserved solely for God ![]. Those who speculate about such matters are seen as challenging God's exclusive knowledge. Furthermore, becoming overly fixated on the timing, even unintentionally, might divert one's attention from the essential preparations required for the Imām's Reappearance. In turn, a person may find themselves stuck in a state of passive waiting, contrary to the proactive steps needed to ready oneself for the imminent return of the Imām ![].

An illuminating narration recounts Mufaḍḍal's inquiry to the Imām about the signs of Judgment and the related verse:

---

[53] Mufīd, Shaykh Muḥammad, *al-Ikhtiṣāṣ*, p. 89.

﴿يَستَعجِلُ بِهَا الَّذِينَ لا يُؤمِنونَ بِهَا وَالَّذِينَ آمَنوا مُشفِقونَ مِنهَا وَيَعلَمونَ أَنَّهَا الحَقُّ أَلا إِنَّ الَّذِينَ يُمارونَ فِي السّاعَةِ لَفِي ضَلالٍ بَعيدٍ﴾

﴿yasta'jilu bihā lladhīna lā yu'minūna bihā wa-lladhīna āmanū mushfiqūna minhā wa-ya'lamūna annahā l-ḥaqqu a-lā inna lladhīna yumārūna fī s-sā'ati la-fī ḍalālin ba'īdin-i﴾

﴿Those who do not believe in it ask [you] to hasten it, but those who have faith are apprehensive of it, and know that it is true. Look! Indeed those who are in doubt about the Hour are surely in extreme error!﴾*[54]

Mufaḍḍal asked the Imām:

> O Master! What does *in doubt about the Hour* [or 'dispute the Hour'] mean in this verse?

The Imām ﷺ explained,

> They question when Qā'im (Imām al-Mahdī) was born, who has seen him, where he is presently, where he will be in the future, and when he will reappear. Such impatience with Divine affairs stems from doubts about Divine decrees, leading to loss in both this world and the hereafter. Infidels will face dire consequences.

---

[54] Sūrat ash-Shūrā, Verse 18.

* Or 'dispute the Hour.'

Mufaḍḍal then asked if the Imām could specify a time for these events. The Imām ﷻ responded,

> O Mufaḍḍal! Never attempt to predict a time, as doing so claims partnership in God's knowledge and falsely asserts that God has disclosed His secrets.[55]

55. A Manifestation of Divine Retribution

When Imām al-Mahdī ﷻ reappears, the divine proof and the argument against humanity will be complete, after the long period of the Occultation. Hence, it is natural for the Imām to be a source of resentment for some, especially those who stand against his mission.

Reflecting on this, we can draw parallels with the early days of Islam when the disbelievers of Quraysh were pardoned by the Prophet ﷺ. Their newness to Islam played a role in their willingness to forgive. In contrast, those who persistently reject guidance despite prolonged exposure might face divine retribution.

Therefore, when we yearn for the Imām's Reappearance, let us couple our wish with a prayer for well-being in one's faith, seeking exemption from divine punishment. It has been narrated from Imām aṣ-Ṣādiq ؑ:

[55] al-Ḥillī, Ḥasan b. Sulaymān, *Mukhtaṣar al-Baṣā'ir*, p. 434.

> If one of you wishes for the Qā'im, let him wish for him in a state of well-being [in his religion], for God sent Muḥammad as a mercy, and He will send the Qā'im as a punishment.[56]

It is crucial to recognize that while the Imām represents divine justice, he is also a manifestation of mercy, akin to his compassionate grandfather ﷺ. However, this mercy is reserved for those who embrace and support his cause, distinguishing themselves from active adversaries.

56. With them in Heaven

On Judgment Day, a believer's ultimate wish is to be with the infallible ﷺ, in their rank in Heaven. The infallible ones have ascended to heavenly heights through unwavering devotion and servitude to God ﷻ in this world. It is a divine act of kindness and generosity that allows believers to share in their exalted status.

This blessed privilege was highlighted in the teachings of Imām al-Kāẓim ؑ, who spoke of the rewards awaiting those who steadfastly support Imām al-Mahdī ؑ. He described how those who persevere in their faith and aid the Imām will find themselves elevated to the same heavenly level.

Imām al-Kāẓim ؑ was asked:

[56] Kulaynī, Shaykh Muḥammad b. Yaʿqūb, *al-Kāfī*, Vol. 15, p. 532.

> O son of the Messenger of God, are you the Qāʾim bi al-Ḥaqq (The Establisher of the Truth/the Riser/the One Standing with the Truth)?

He ﷺ said,

> I am the Qāʾim bi al-Ḥaqq; however, the Qāʾim who will clean the Earth from the enemies of God and will fill it with equity, as it will be full of injustice, is the fifth from my sons. He will have an occultation the length of which will be much longer due to his fear for his life. Many nations will apostatize in that period, and the rest will remain steadfast.

Then he ﷺ said,

> Blissfulness be for the Shīʿah, the adherers to our love during the Occultation of our Qāʾim, who will remain steadfast in our adoration and the detestation of our enemies. They are ours and we are theirs. They are pleased with us as Imāms, and we are pleased with them as Shīʿah. Bliss be for them! They are, by God, with us in our rank on the Day of Judgment.[57]

57. The Decisive Word

We must combine our belief in the guardianship of the Imāms ﷺ with their full implications, and strive to reach a

---

[57] Ṣadūq, Shaykh Muḥammad b. ʿAlī, *Kamāl al-Dīn wa Tamām al-Niʿmah*, Vol. 2, p. 361.

state of absolute monotheism in our devotion to God ﷻ. Straying from this balance, whether by attributing excessive power to the Imāms or diminishing their status, leads one astray from the true path.

There is a narrative that serves as the final word on this matter. It unfolds in a letter from Imām al-Mahdī عج to one of his ambassadors, addressing a group of Shīʿah who were divided on whether God had delegated the authority of creation and sustenance to the Imāms.

Some argued:

> It is inconceivable and impermissible for Him to do so, as only God ﷻ can create physical forms.

Others contended:

> God, the Mighty and the High, has bestowed upon the Holy Imāms the ability and authority to carry out this task, thus they create and sustain by His permission.

This disagreement sparked a heated debate.

Amidst the confusion, someone proposed seeking guidance from Abū Jaʿfar Muḥammad b. ʿUthmān ʿĀmarī, a special deputy[58] of the Imām, as he served as a direct link to Imām

---

[58] The second of the Four Deputies of Imām al-Mahdī عج during the Minor Occultation.

al-Mahdī ﷺ. Unanimously, they agreed to consult Abū Ja'far for clarity.

The question was penned and dispatched to him, awaiting the Imām's response. The reply came swiftly:

> Indeed, it is God, the Mighty and the High, who has fashioned physical forms and apportioned sustenance. He is neither a body nor has He transmigrated into a body... Nothing resembles Him; He is the Hearing, the Wise. As for the Imāms, they beseech God ﷻ, who then creates and provides sustenance. Their entreaties are answered, and God ﷻ fulfills their requests due to the greatness of their right.[59]

In these words lies the definitive resolution, affirming the supreme authority of God while acknowledging the pivotal role of the Imāms, who, through their righteousness, serve as conduits of divine mercy and sustenance.

58. Revival of the Religion

Among the greatest blessings promised during the awaited Reappearance is the restoration of the pristine teachings of Islam, as originally delivered by the Prophet ﷺ, guided by God ﷻ. That is why he is titled al-Mahdī, the guided one, and al-Qā'im, the one who rises with the truth. Yet, this prospect may pose challenges for some who struggle to

[59] Ṭūsī, Shaykh Muḥammad b. Ḥasan, *Kitāb al-Ghaybah*, p. 294.

accept the unadulterated rulings of God ﷻ that will be reinstated by Imām al-Mahdī ﵊.

Imām ar-Riḍā ﵊ beautifully expresses this aspiration in his supplication for Imām al-Mahdī ﵊:

> O God! Put back, through him, in original form that which has been uprooted from Your religion, put in order again through him the confusion created in Your Book. Make clear, through him, the distortions made in Your commandments, so that Your religion regains its true spirit, on his hands, blooming and full of tenderness[60]

Moreover, Imām aṣ-Ṣādiq ﵊ said:

> When our Qāʾim arises, he will call people anew to Islam, guiding them to the old thing from which people have turned away. He will be called Mahdī because he will guide people to that from which they have been separated. He will be called Qāʾim because he will be commanded to establish the truth[61]

Similarly, Imām al-Bāqir ﵊ said:

---

[60] Ṭūsī, Shaykh Muḥammad b. Ḥasan, *Kitāb al-Ghaybah*, p. 279.

[61] Fayḍ Kāshānī, Mullā Muḥammad b. Murtaḍā, *al-Wāfī*, Vol. 2, p. 469.

> Al-Qā'im will rise with a new task, new principles and new judgements that will be heavy on the Arabs[62]

59. Avenging Imām al-Ḥusayn عليه السلام

One of the most prominent tasks awaiting Imām al-Mahdī عجل الله تعالى فرجه الشريف upon his return is to seek justice for Imām al-Ḥusayn عليه السلام. The tragic martyrdom of Imām al-Ḥusayn عليه السلام shook the very foundations of the heavens, causing even the angels to cry out in anguish before the throne of God عز وجل. It is understandable, for they witnessed the epitome of righteousness facing the gravest injustice, prompting their pleas to God عز وجل for retribution. Their sorrow only eased when they were assured of an avenger who would arise to avenge the blood of Imām al-Ḥusayn عليه السلام.

Imām al-Bāqir عليه السلام said:

> When my grandfather, al-Ḥusayn عليه السلام was martyred the angels voiced their lamentations of protest in the court of God, the Mighty and the Sublime, and they said:
>
>> O God, Will you ignore the one who has killed Your chosen one, son of Your chosen one and the best of the creation?

62 Nu'mānī, Muḥammad b. Ibrāhīm, *Kitāb al-Ghaybah*, p. 233.

God ﷻ revealed to them:

> O My angels, rest assured. By My Might and Glory, I will indeed take revenge on them — even if it be at a later time.

After that God ﷻ removed the veil from the faces of the Imāms from the progeny of al-Ḥusayn عليه السلام. The angels rejoiced and noticed that one of them was standing in prayer.

God said:

> I will take revenge from them through this Qā'im (the standing one).[63]

In these profound words, we notice the divine promise of justice, awaiting fulfillment through the emergence of Imām al-Mahdī عجل الله تعالى فرجه الشريف, who will stand as the beacon of righteousness and the champion of Imām al-Ḥusayn's عليه السلام cause.

60. Attending Ḥajj

One of the great blessings of Ḥajj is the presence of Imām al-Mahdī عجل الله تعالى فرجه الشريف among the pilgrims. It was narrated on the authority of Muḥammad b. 'Uthmān al-'Amrī that he said:

---

[63] Majlisī, 'Allāmah Muḥammad Bāqir, *Biḥār al-Anwār*, Vol. 37, p. 294.

> By God I swear, Imām al-Mahdī witnesses the season of Ḥajj every year. He can see and know people, and they can see him but cannot know him.[64]

In light of this, the divine blessings of his honorable presence in Ḥajj reach the pilgrims, even if they are not consciously aware of it, and his supplications for them are answered. Yet, it is disheartening to acknowledge that despite their longing to meet their Imām, the pilgrims are unable to fulfill this desire. They recognize his rightful authority over them, yet are deprived of his visible guidance and leadership.

61. Ibn Ṭāwūs Seeing the Imām

Despite numerous narrations that negate the possibility of seeing the Imām عجل الله تعالى فرجه الشريف during his Occultation, they mainly refer to being officially appointed as his deputy or meeting him as was the custom with his esteemed forefathers, where followers could meet him at will. However, although rare, there are instances of sincere and devout followers meeting him during this period. Such was the case with Ibn Ṭāwūs قدس سره, whose unwavering sincerity and faith are beyond doubt. He recounted:

> I was in Sāmarrā' when I heard his prayer عجل الله تعالى فرجه الشريف at dawn. From his supplication for those who remembered him

[64] Ṣadūq, Shaykh Muḥammad b. 'Alī, *Kamāl al-Dīn wa Tamām al-Ni'mah*, Vol. 2, p. 440.

> among the living and the dead, I memorized: and keep them- or he said make them alive- in our days of power, dominance and rulership[65]

62. The Confusion of the Shīʿah

The distress over the disunity and confusion among the Shīʿah community during the Occultation weighed heavily on the hearts of the Imāms ﷺ. This anguish intensified their yearning for the time of his Reappearance, as they envisioned it as the era when the cloud of confusion and disunity would finally dissipate from the Muslim community. Remarkably, this concern has persisted since the days of Imām ʿAlī ﷺ, despite the considerable time that has passed between him and his grandson, Imām al-Mahdī ﷺ.

Aṣbagh b. Nubāṭah, a reliable companion of Imām ʿAlī ﷺ, narrates:

> I presented myself before Imām ʿAlī ﷺ. I saw that he was engrossed in thought, marking the Earth with his finger. I queried,
>
> > O Amīr al-Mu'minīn! What is the matter? I find you today in some perplexity, making signs on the Earth. Do you love this Earth?

[65] Sayyid b. Ṭāwūs, *Muhaj ad-Daʿawāt wa Manhaj al-ʿIbādāt*, p. 296.

He ﷺ replied:

> I swear by God that it is not so. I have never befriended this world; rather, I was reflecting on that son, the eleventh one from my progeny. He is the Mahdī, who will fill the Earth with justice and equity as it was filled with injustice and tyranny. There is an occultation for him in which some people will deviate while others will be guided.

I asked:

> O Amīr al-Mu'minīn, would this come to pass?

He replied:

> Yes, just as they are created[66]

63. The Effect of Certainty

What draws those eagerly awaiting the Imām closer to God during the Occultation is their unwavering belief in the unseen and their profound connection with their Imām, despite not seeing or hearing him. This stems from their absolute conviction that the Earth cannot be left without an Imām and that twelve Imāms are destined to follow the Prophet ﷺ.

In this regard, it was narrated that Imām aṣ-Ṣādiq said:

66 Kulaynī, Shaykh Muḥammad b. Ya'qūb, *al-Kāfī*, Vol. 2, p. 151.

> The most proximate servants of God and those with whom God is pleased are those who when the proof of God (Imām al-Mahdī) disappears from sight and they do not know about his whereabouts, yet they continue to have faith that the Proof of God can never be invalid, and day and night they continue to wait for him[67]

It becomes evident that the stronger a believer's certainty is in this matter, the nearer they draw to the circle of the Imām's ﷺ special care.

64. The Path Towards Him is Open

Being unable to see the Imām ﷺ physically does not equate to being deprived of his benevolent presence, cultivating a deep emotional connection with him, and sensing his watchful care over us.

Consider the words Sayyid b. Ṭāwūs ؒ shared with his son:

> ...the path to your Imām ؑ is open for anyone whom God ﷻ considers deserving of the grace of His Eminence and for whomsoever God completes his favor upon.[68]

---

[67] Ibid., p. 137.

[68] Majlisī, 'Allāmah Muḥammad Bāqir, *Biḥār al-Anwār*, Vol. 53, p. 306.

Similarly, Sayyid Murtaḍā قدس سره said:

> If it is asked what is the difference between the fact that [the Imām عجل الله تعالى فرجه الشريف] exists, but he remains in occultation; and no one can meet him and no person gets any benefit from him, and on the other hand he does not at all exist, and according to terminology he is non-existent. And whether it is not allowable that he should remain in non-existence till the time God knows that it is the time for his coming into existence? Because just as you consider it lawful for him to be kept hidden till He knows the obedience and submission of the people for him, and at that time He brings him out?
>
> In reply, it would be said:
>
>> Firstly, we do not consider it lawful and possible, as many of his devotees, followers, and those who believe in his Imāmate have had the honor of meeting him. They have benefited from him, as have those who were not from his Shīʿah community and his friends. When they visited him, they also derived the same benefits. Because they believed in the existence of His Eminence and considered his obedience incumbent and necessary upon themselves, they compulsorily feared committing sins and those acts disliked by him. They were fearful that he would punish and chastise them and make them pay for all such

things. Therefore, they committed the fewest sins.[69]

65. Unveiling the Riches

Besides the establishment of justice, the time of the Imām's ﷻ reappearance promises a flood of blessings upon the Earth. It is the sins of humanity that act as a barrier, hindering these blessings from descending upon us. God ﷻ addresses this in the Noble Qur'ān:

﴿وَلَو أَنَّ أَهلَ القُرىٰ آمَنوا وَاتَّقَوا لَفَتَحنا عَلَيهِم بَرَكاتٍ مِنَ السَّماءِ وَالأَرضِ﴾

﴿*wa-law anna ahla l-qurā āmanū wa-ttaqaw la-fataḥnā ʿalayhim barakātin mina s-samā'i wa-l-'arḍi*﴾

﴿*If the people of the towns had been faithful and Godwary, We would have opened to them blessings from the heaven and the earth*﴾[70]

Regarding the missing blessings in our time, Imām ʿAlī ؑ said:

> When our Qā'im rises, the sky will send down its drops, the earth will grow its plants, enmity will leave from the servants' hearts (in order that they live in peace and

---

[69] Sharīf Murtaḍā, ʿAlī b. al-Ḥusayn, *Rasā'il al-Sharīf al-Murtaḍā*, Vol. 2, p. 297.

[70] Sūrat al-Aʿrāf, Verse 96.

brotherly love), and savages and beasts will live together peacefully...[71]

66. The Downfall of the Enemies Through His Prayers

The downfall and humiliation of those who oppose the Ahl al-Bayt ﷺ, even if they reign for ages like the Umayyads and the ʿAbbāsids, is a direct result of Imām al-Mahdī's ﷺ heartfelt prayers against them. If the prayers of the oppressed are answered, then how much more so for the one most oppressed and closest to God ﷻ?

To that effect, Muḥammad b. ʿUthmān al-ʿAmrī said:

> I saw Imām ﷺ near Bāb al-Mustajār clutching the cloth of Kaʿbah, beseeching God:
>
> > O my Lord, take my revenge from my [Your] enemies[72]

We are urged to emulate his example, for believers should frequently pray against the enemies of the Ahl al-Bayt ﷺ. Imām aṣ-Ṣādiq ﷺ advises us to do this as a will from his great-grandfather, the Prophet ﷺ. He narrates that the Prophet ﷺ said:

---

[71] al-Ḥarrānī, Ibn Shuʿba, *Tuḥaf al-ʿUqūl*, p. 115.

[72] Ṣadūq, Shaykh Muḥammad b. ʿAlī, *Kamāl al-Dīn wa Tamām al-Niʿmah*, Vol. 2, p. 440.

> Blessed be those who are fortunate to live during the time of Qā'im of my Ahl al-Bayt; those who would believe in him during his occultation and before his advent; who would love his friends and remain aloof from his enemies. Such people would be my closest ones and my friends on Judgment Day, and the most respected creatures of God in my view.[73]

67. The Wonder at Those Who Deny Him

It is perplexing how some deny the existence of Imām al-Mahdī عجل الله تعالى فرجه الشريف simply because of the peculiarity of his extended life! Yet, if we ponder, prolonged life is not inherently implausible; without hindrances, longevity could indeed be commonplace. Shaykh aṣ-Ṣadūq رحمه الله sheds light on this, remarking:

> Most of our opponents accept the traditions about Khiḍr عليه السلام; they believe that he is alive but cannot be seen, and that he is present where he is remembered. Neither the opponents deny his long life nor say that these traditions are illogical. However, they object to the long life of the Qā'im عجل الله تعالى فرجه الشريف. These people believe that it is within the power of God to keep a person alive till the blowing of the horn. They agree to the life and occultation of the accursed Iblees till the known time. But they do not accept the longevity and occultation of the Proof of God even though authentic traditions

[73] Ṭūsī, Shaykh Muḥammad b. Ḥasan, *Kitāb al-Ghaybah*, p. 456.

have come down from the Messenger of God ﷺ regarding his name and clarifying his genealogy and origin.[74]

68. The Deep-Rooted Mahdī Idea

The belief in the Mahdī and the anticipation of his arrival have been deeply ingrained in the minds of the companions of the Imāms عليهم السلام since ancient times. Whenever they witnessed any sign hinting at the reappearance, their thoughts immediately turned to the emergence of Imām al-Mahdī عليه السلام, or the possibility that he had already appeared. This enduring belief suggests that the concept of Imām al-Mahdī has been deeply rooted in the minds since the era of the Prophet Muḥammad ﷺ.

To illustrate this point further, consider the following narration:

The narrator said:

> I expressed to Imām ar-Riḍā عليه السلام that we hope you are the awaited figure, and that God may facilitate your emergence peacefully, without the need for conflict. Homage is being paid to you, and currency is being minted with your name.

---

[74] Ṣadūq, Shaykh Muḥammad b. ʿAlī, Kamāl al-Dīn wa Tamām al-Niʿmah, Vol. 2, p. 392.

He replied,

> None of us to whom letters have been sent, who has been pointed at with fingers, who has been consulted on religious matters, and to whom legal religious rights have been sent, has escaped being killed or dying in his bed until God sends for this matter a boy from our progeny. His birth and early life will be unknown, but his lineage will not be concealed.[75]

69. The Apparent and Hidden Blessings

Among the greatest divine blessings lie the gift of existence, followed by the blessing of Islam, and then the invaluable privilege of being under the guardianship of the Imāms. Furthermore, there is the profound blessing of being associated with a specific Imām, gathering under his banner.

Imām al-Kāẓim explained the concealed blessing as his son, Imām al-Mahdī. He emphasized that God provides unwavering support and victory to His representative and urged believers to nurture a special bond with Him, ensuring His remembrance never fades from their hearts. As narrated:

I asked my master Mūsā b. Jaʿfar regarding the verse:

[75] Nuʿmānī, Muḥammad b. Ibrāhīm, *Kitāb al-Ghaybah*, p. 168.

﴿وَأَسبَغَ عَلَيكُم نِعَمَهُ ظَاهِرَةً وَبَاطِنَةً﴾

﴾*wa-'asbagha 'alaykum ni'amahū ẓāhiratan wa-bāṭinatan*﴿

﴾*and He has showered upon you His blessings, the outward and the inward*﴿[76]

He replied:

> The apparent bounty is the Imām who is seen, and the hidden bounty is the Imām who is in occultation.

The narrator says: I asked:

> Is there any among the Imāms that shall go into occultation?

He replied:

> Yes, his person would be unseen by the people, but his remembrance would remain hidden in the hearts of the believers. And he is the twelfth one of us. For him, God ﷻ would make every difficult thing easy and tame every disobedient one. He would open up the treasures of the Earth for him and make every remoteness a proximity. He would

[76] Sūrat Luqmān, Verse 20.

destroy every disobedient sinner and eliminate
every transgressing satan at his hands.[77]

70. Emerging When Necessary

Despite the Imām's ﷺ obligation to adhere to the rules of
occultation, there are moments when necessity calls him to
reveal himself, albeit while concealing his identity. One
such instance occurred during the restoration of the black
stone to its rightful place after the Qaramations decided to
bring it back, a task traditionally reserved for the Imām.

Jaʿfar b. Muḥammad b. Qulawayh ☆ closely monitored this
event, aware that only the Imām could perform this sacred
duty, much like Imām Zayn al-ʿĀbidīn ☆ did in the past.
Determined to witness this momentous occasion, Jaʿfar
planned to make a pilgrimage to Makkah. However, illness
hindered his plans, compelling him to send Ibn Hishām in
his stead, bearing a letter and a crucial question for Imām
al-Mahdī ﷺ regarding the sender's age. Upon reaching the
Kaʿbah, Ibn Hishām witnessed a remarkable scene:

A young handsome man with a wheatish complexion
took the stone and put it in its original place. People
started shouting and saying,

God is the greatest, and there is no god except God.

---

[77] Ṣadūq, Shaykh Muḥammad b. ʿAlī, *Kamāl al-Dīn wa Tamām
al-Niʿmah*, Vol. 2, p. 368.

The young man got out of that place, and I started following him, pushing the people until some people thought that I was insane. They opened the way for me while I was walking fast. My eyes were fixed on the young man until he reached the street. The young man was walking slowly, but even though I was walking fast, I could not catch up to him. When we arrived at a place with no one around, he stopped, turned around, and looked at me, then said,

> Give me the letter you have brought.

I took the letter out of my pocket and gave it to him. Without reading the letter, he said:

> Tell the writer of the letter not to be afraid of his illness. He will die after thirty years.[78]

71. His Supplication for Offspring

One of the most cherished blessings of Imām al-Mahdī's ﴿عجل الله فرجه﴾ presence is his heartfelt prayers for those who hold him dear, especially those who implore him for his intercession, particularly for matters that contribute to preparing for his awaited return.

A touching illustration of this is recounted by Shaykh aṣ-Ṣadūq ﴿رحمه الله﴾. It is said that ʿAlī b. Bābawayh [the father of

[78] al-Irbilī, ʿAlī b. ʿIsā Hakkārī, *Kashf al-Ghummah fī Maʿrifat al-Aʾimmah*, Vol. 2, p. 502.

Shaykh aṣ-Ṣadūq] penned a letter to Imām al-Mahdī ﷺ, entrusting it to al-Ḥusayn b. Rūḥ. In his letter, he beseeched the Imām ﷺ to pray for him to be blessed with a son. In response, the Imām assured him that God ﷻ would grant him two righteous sons.

True to the Imām's words, ʿAlī b. Bābawayh was soon blessed with two sons, whom he named Muḥammad and Ḥusayn. Muḥammad went on to become an accomplished author, penning renowned works like *Man Lā Yaḥḍuruh al-Faqīh*. Meanwhile, Ḥusayn's lineage flourished with scholars.

Muḥammad often reflected with pride on being the fruit of the Imām's supplication, and his mentors would remark,

> It is befitting for one born from the Imām's prayer to excel in such a manner.[79].

72. His Presence in Ḥajj

The Imām's occultation does not negate the possibility of seeing him in some sacred sites, such as around the Kaʿbah and Karbalāʾ, without his true identity being revealed. Thus, it is possible that many would recognize him at the time of his reappearance, because his face would be familiar to them.

---

[79] Ṭūsī, Shaykh Muḥammad b. Ḥasan, *Kitāb al-Ghaybah*, pp. 309–310.

This text, narrated by al-Kulaynī in his book, serves as evidence of that. He relays that a man told him:

> I was on pilgrimage with a companion of mine. When we arrived at the stopping point, a young man sat there wearing an Izār and a cloak, with yellow sandals on his feet. The Izār and cloak were worth a hundred and fifty dinars, and there was no sign of travel on him. A beggar approached us, and we turned him away. Then, the beggar approached the young man and asked him. The young man picked up something from the ground and handed it to him. The beggar prayed for the young man, exerting effort in his supplication and prolonging it. Then the young man stood up and disappeared from us. We approached the beggar and asked him:
>
> > What did he give you?
>
> He showed us a gold-studded stone, which we estimated to be twenty Mithqāls. I said to my companion,
>
> > Our master is among us, and we are unaware.
>
> He said:
>
> > Then we went in search of him, we searched the entire place and could not find him. We asked everyone around, from the people of Makkah and Madīnah, and they said:

> There is a young ʿAlawī who performs Ḥajj every year on foot.[80]

73. One of the Principles of Islam

Islamic literature is rich with writings about Imām al-Mahdī ﷽, making his role a fundamental aspect of the religion, even amid debates surrounding the specifics of his life. However, these debates do not diminish the belief that he represents the culmination of divine messages.

One compelling narrative illustrates this belief:

> I entered upon the Messenger of God ﷺ during the illness which caused him to pass away, and Fāṭimah ﷺ was beside him at his head, weeping until her voice rose. The Messenger of God turned to her and said,
>
> > My beloved Fāṭimah, what troubles you?
>
> She replied,
>
> > I fear loss after you.
>
> He said,
>
> > O my beloved, did you not know that God surveyed the Earth, choosing your father and sending him with His message, then surveyed again

[80] Kulaynī, Shaykh Muḥammad b. Yaʿqūb, *al-Kāfī*, Vol. 2, p. 314.

and chose your husband, revealing to me that you should marry him? O Fāṭimah, we, the household, have been blessed by God with seven qualities not given to anyone before us or after us. I am the Seal of the Prophets, the most honored by God, the most beloved to Him among His creatures. I am your father, and my successor is the best of successors, loved by God, and he is your husband. O Fāṭimah, by the One who sent me with the truth, there will be from among us a Mahdī from this nation when the world is in turmoil, trials become rampant, paths are cut off, and people turn against one another, where neither the elder has mercy on the young nor the young respect the elder. God will send from among us one who will breach the forts of misguidance and soften hardened hearts, establishing the religion at the end of time as I have established it at its beginning.[81]

74. The Prophet's Glad Tidings

Prophet Muḥammad ﷺ foresaw, guided by divine wisdom, the trials that would befall his community after him. He also knew that the ultimate salvation lay in the emergence of his son, Imām al-Mahdī عجل الله تعالى فرجه الشريف. He emphasized the close connection between the Imām and himself, urging us to go to great lengths to serve him, even if it meant enduring hardship to reach him.

---

[81] Majlisī, ʿAllāmah Muḥammad Bāqir, *Biḥār al-Anwār*, Vol. 51, p. 79.

Muḥammad al-Tirmidhī narrated in *Sunan al-Tirmidhī*:

> While we were with the Messenger of God ﷺ, a group of young men from the Banū Hāshim approached. When the Prophet saw them, his eyes welled with tears, and his complexion changed. We asked,
>
> > Why do we continue to see something displeasing in your face?
>
> He replied,
>
> > We, the people of the Household, God chose for us the Hereafter over the worldly life. Indeed, my family will face trials, displacement, and persecution after me until a group comes from the East with black banners. They will seek goodness, but it will be denied to them (he repeated it three times). They will fight and be victorious, yet they will not accept what they sought until it is handed over to a man from my family. He will fill it with justice, just as it was filled with oppression. Whoever among you reaches that time should go to them even if it means crawling on snow.[82]

[82] al-Ṭabarī, Muḥammad b. Jarīr, *Dalā'il al-Imāmat*, p. 442.

75. Knowledge of the Qur'ān and Sunnah

In the age of Imām al-Mahdī's ﷺ reappearance, one of his most profound responsibilities is to unveil the sacred wisdom of the Qur'ān and the teachings of the Prophet ﷺ. Firstly, he is addressed by the Qur'ān, much like his forefathers ﷺ, who possessed an intimate understanding of God ﷻ's intentions within its verses. Secondly, he carries the mantle of the Prophet's knowledge ﷺ, reminiscent of his great-grandfather Imām 'Alī ﷺ, who was a gateway to the Prophet's knowledge. Thirdly, he holds the knowledge bestowed upon all the prophets of God ﷻ ﷺ, utilizing the original, unaltered heavenly scriptures as his evidence.

In this context, it was narrated that Imām al-Bāqir ﷺ said:

> Knowledge of the book of God, the Mighty and Sublime, and the Sunnah of His Messenger develops in the heart of our Mahdī, just as a plant grows to perfection. Thus, whosoever of you survives till he sees him, when you meet him, you must greet him by the words:
>
>> Peace be on you, O folks of the house of mercy and prophethood and the mine of knowledge and the abode of messengership.[83]

[83] Ṣadūq, Shaykh Muḥammad b. 'Alī, *Kamāl al-Dīn wa Tamām al-Ni'mah*, Vol. 2, p. 453.

This narration shows that the Imām's extensive knowledge is ever-increasing, like the growth of a flourishing plant. Undoubtedly, the longing to access this spring of pure knowledge intensifies the anticipation of the Imām's reign and fuels our yearning for him, our Mahdī, as Imām al-Bāqir lovingly referred to him —a symbol of pride in his mission to establish global justice.

76. Granting Him Dominion Over the Earth

The era of Imām al-Mahdī's reign promises a way of life beyond our wildest dreams, especially as we have grown accustomed to injustice and oppression. In this extraordinary time, God ﷻ will unveil some of His hidden wonders, such as the speech of the animals, reminiscent of the miraculous communication between Prophet Sulaymān ؑ and creatures like the ant and the hoopoe. Moreover, the Imām عجل الله تعالى فرجه الشريف and his companions will be endowed with authority over the very Earth itself.

It was narrated that Imām al-Bāqir ؑ said:

> As if I can see the companions of the Qā'im عجل الله تعالى فرجه الشريف that have filled the Earth from the East to the West. Everything, even the wild beasts and the jungle birds, will obey them, and everything will seek their satisfaction, so much so that a piece of land will pride

itself over others and say: Today a companion of the Imām passed over me.[84]

This depiction echoes the profound dialogue depicted in Sūrat al-Zalzalah, where the Earth itself narrates its news:

﴿إِذا زُلزِلَتِ الأَرضُ زِلزالَها﴾

﴿*idhā zulzilati l-'arḍu zilzālahā*﴾

﴿وَأَخرَجَتِ الأَرضُ أَثقالَها﴾

﴿*wa-'akhrajati l-'arḍu athqālahā*﴾

﴿وَقالَ الإِنسانُ ما لَها﴾

﴿*wa-qāla l-'insānu mā lahā*﴾

﴿يَومَئِذٍ تُحَدِّثُ أَخبارَها﴾

﴿*yawma'idhin tuḥaddithu akhbārahā*﴾

﴿بِأَنَّ رَبَّكَ أَوحىٰ لَها﴾

﴿*bi-'anna rabbaka awḥā lahā*﴾

---

[84] Ṣadūq, Shaykh Muḥammad b. ʿAlī, *Kamāl al-Dīn wa Tamām al-Niʿmah*, Vol. 2, p. 673.

﴿يَومَئِذٍ يَصدُرُ النّاسُ أَشتاتًا لِيُرَوا أَعمالَهُم﴾

﴿yawma'idhin yaṣduru n-nāsu ashtātan li-yuraw a'mālahum﴾

﴿فَمَن يَعمَل مِثقالَ ذَرَّةٍ خَيرًا يَرَهُ﴾

﴿fa-man ya'mal mithqāla dharratin khayran yarahū﴾

﴿وَمَن يَعمَل مِثقالَ ذَرَّةٍ شَرًّا يَرَهُ﴾

﴿wa-man ya'mal mithqāla dharratin sharran yarahū﴾

﴿When the earth is rocked with a terrible quake and the earth discharges her burdens, and man says, 'What is the matter with her?' On that day she will relate her chronicles for her Lord will have inspired her. On that day, mankind will issue forth in various groups to be shown their deeds. So whoever does an atom's weight of good will see it, and whoever does an atom's weight of evil will see it﴾*[85]

77. Knowing Their Right

In the narrations of Ahl al-Bayt ﷺ, the expression "knowing their right" was mentioned as a prerequisite for

---

[85] Sūrat al-Zalzalah, Verses 1–8.

* Or 'separate groups.'

the acceptance of visiting them. Thus, it becomes imperative for us to grasp the meaning of this term, as it serves as a pathway to drawing nearer to the Imām of our time ﷺ. Even though we are deprived of physical visits with him, understanding his rights is important for us to connect with him truly.

To comprehend what it means to know his rights, let us reflect on this narration from Imām aṣ-Ṣādiq ﷺ:

> And the lowest level of knowledge regarding the Imām is that he is like the Prophet, except for the degree of prophethood, and is his successor. His obedience is obedience to God and obedience to the Messenger of God, and surrendering to him in every matter, referring back to him, and adhering to his word.[86]

This narration underscores the theoretical and practical dimensions of the Imām's rights. It highlights the inseparable link between obedience to the Imām and obedience to God ﷻ. Moreover, it emphasizes the practical aspect of this knowledge—following the Imām's guidance in every aspect of life. Thus, deviating from the Imām's directives signifies a lack of understanding of his rights, regardless of any claims of closeness to him.

---

[86] Majlisī, ʿAllāmah Muḥammad Bāqir, *Biḥār al-Anwār*, Vol. 4, p. 55.

78. Characteristics of the Companions of the Imām

Those whom God ﷻ has prepared to support his representative, Imām al-Mahdī عج, are at the highest level of divine closeness. It was narrated that:

> They shall be men who do not sleep at night. They shall be busy all night in prayers. The sound of them reciting the Qur'ān will seem like the humming of bees. They shall spend the night standing and in the morning mount their horses. In the night, they will be like monks and ascetics, and in the day, they shall be like ferocious lions.[87]

Furthermore, their inner fortitude contributes to their resolute determination, as the narration depicts:

> their hearts will be like iron, each of them will be gifted the strength of forty men[88]

They are also known to exhibit the highest degree of obedience to their Imām عج, as they were described:

---

[87] Majlisī, ʿAllāmah Muḥammad Bāqir, *Biḥār al-Anwār*, Vol. 52, p. 308.

[88] Ibid., p. 386.

> Diligent in obeying him[89]

For those adorned with such noble traits, martyrdom in the path of God ﷻ is their ultimate aspiration, and the Imām's companions were described as:

> They are hopeful of martyrdom in the Way of God. Their slogan will be:
>
> > O Avenger of al-Ḥusayn![90]

What is truly remarkable is that they:

> shall all be young and none shall be old except a small number equivalent to the kuḥl applied to the eyes or the salt sprinkled in the food.[91]

79. Like a Sheep Separated From The Flock

Straying from the path of the Imām ﷺ during the occultation brings about a deep sense of confusion, akin to drowning in a vast sea of misguidance. This feeling is exacerbated by the sight of deceptive individuals who falsely claim to emulate the Imām's noble mission of

---

[89] Ṣadūq, Shaykh Muḥammad b. ʿAlī, *Kamāl al-Dīn wa Tamām al-Niʿmah*, Vol. 1, p. 268.

[90] Majlisī, ʿAllāmah Muḥammad Bāqir, *Biḥār al-Anwār*, Vol. 52, p. 308.

[91] Nuʿmānī, Muḥammad b. Ibrāhīm, *Kitāb al-Ghaybah*, p. 316.

delivering salvation from oppression and establishing justice.

Imām al-Bāqir ﷺ beautifully illustrated the consequence of straying from this righteous path, likening it to a sheep wandering away from its flock. He expressed:

> Anyone who worships God ﷻ with an effort that exhausts oneself and does not follow an Imām appointed by God, their striving is not accepted, and they are lost and confused. God dislikes their deeds; they are like a sheep that has strayed from its shepherd and flock, so it roams, vulnerable to predators, until nightfall when it finds itself among another flock with its shepherd. It leans towards them, deceived and comforted by their presence, spending the night with them in their pasture. But when the shepherd takes his flock away, she denies her shepherd and his flock, confused and lost, and runs away, seeking her shepherd and flock. Until she sees another flock with its shepherd, then she leans towards them, deceived and comforted by their presence. The shepherd shouts at her,
>
>> Return to your shepherd and flock, for you are lost, confused, and without a shepherd to guide you to your pasture or bring you back.

> While she is in this state, the wolf seizes the opportunity and devours her.[92]

80. A Miraculous Birth

The birth of Imām al-Mahdī stands as one of the most significant moments in history, rivaled only by the creation of Ādam and the advent of Prophet Muḥammad's message. It was a moment steeped in divine significance, marked by extraordinary occurrences.

Describing this extraordinary birth, Muḥammad b. ʿUthmān al-ʿAmrī recounted:

> When the successor, al-Mahdī, was born, a light radiated from his head to the outskirts of the sky. Then, he went down in prostration to his Lord, Exalted be His remembrance. He then raised his head and said,
>
>> I testify that there is no god but He, and so do the angels and the possessors of knowledge who stand with justice. There is no god but He, the Invincible, the Wise.[93]

Another remarkable moment occurred when white birds descended from the heavens, gently caressing the newborn

---

[92] Kulaynī, Shaykh Muḥammad b. Yaʿqūb, *al-Kāfī*, Vol. 1, p. 449.

[93] Majlisī, ʿAllāmah Muḥammad Bāqir, *Biḥār al-Anwār*, Vol. 51, p. 16.

with their wings before soaring back into the sky. Upon learning of this, Imām al-ʿAskarī ﷷ remarked:

> These were angels seeking blessings from this blessed child. They shall stand by him as helpers when he emerges.[94]

Indeed, God ﷻ distinguishes His beloved servants with remarkable events, reminiscent of the awe-inspiring occurrences surrounding the births of Prophet Muḥammad ﷺ and Imām ʿAlī ﷷ.

81. Two Similar Speeches

When Imām al-Mahdī ﷷ emerges, his words will echo the speech of his grandfather, Imām al-Ḥusayn ﷷ, as he stood before the enemies on the day of ʿĀshūrāʾ. Imām al-Ḥusayn ﷷ reaffirmed his lineage to the Messenger of God ﷺ, reminding them of the verse that speaks of the love and reverence owed to the Prophet's Household ﷷ. Despite his hope that this emotional reminder of his connection to the Prophet ﷺ would soften their hearts, his words fell on deaf ears.

Likewise, Imām al-Mahdī ﷷ is destined to remind humanity of this connection, as narrated by Imām al-Bāqir ﷷ:

[94] Ṣadūq, Shaykh Muḥammad b. ʿAlī, *Kamāl al-Dīn wa Tamām al-Niʿmah*, Vol. 2, p. 431.

The Qā'im will lean his back, when he appears, against the Ka'bah, seeking refuge in it. He will call out to the people until he says:

> I ask you by the right of God, and the right of His Messenger, and my right, for I have a right of kinship to the Messenger of God[95]

In the footsteps of his grandfather, Imām al-Ḥusayn ﷺ, Imām al-Mahdī ﷺ will rise and appeal for assistance, lamenting the injustices inflicted upon him. As Imām al-Bāqir ﷺ foretold, the speech of Imām al-Mahdī ﷺ will say:

> I ask you to support us and to protect us from those who have wronged us. We have been wronged, offended, expelled from our homes, separated from our families, deprived of our rights[96]

82. Avenging His Forefathers

The profound attachment of the Imāms ﷺ to their son, Imām al-Mahdī ﷺ, runs deep, rooted not only in his inherent virtues but also in his destined role as their avenger for the injustices inflicted upon them. The Commander of the Faithful, Imām 'Alī ﷺ, explained a part of their struggle when he said:

[95] Mufīd, Shaykh Muḥammad, *al-Ikhtiṣāṣ*, p. 257.

[96] Ibid.

> I remained patient with a thorn in the eye and a lump in the throat[97]

With his awaited emergence, Imām al-Mahdī ﷻ will bring forth the long-awaited justice for the trials and tribulations endured by his forefathers. Imām aṣ-Ṣādiq ﷺ said:

> When our Qā'im rises, he will take revenge for God, His Messenger, and for us[98]

Before that, the Prophet of God ﷺ, in his sermon on the day of Ghadīr, alluded to this duty, foreseeing the challenges that would befall the community. He said:

> O People! believe in God and His Messenger and the light that has been sent down. God sent down the light in me, then in 'Alī, then the descendants from him up to the Mahdī who shall re-establish the right of God as well as all our rights[99]

83. Prayers Against the Oppressors

In his watchful care over his followers during the veil of occultation, Imām al-Mahdī ﷻ shields them from the

---

[97] Sharīf Raḍī, Muḥammad b. al-Ḥusayn, *Nahj al-Balāghah*, The Shiqshiqiyyah Sermon.

[98] Majlisī, 'Allāmah Muḥammad Bāqir, *Biḥār al-Anwār*, Vol. 52, p. 376.

[99] Sayyid b. Ṭāwūs, *Iqbāl al-A'māl*, Vol. 1, p. 457.

harm inflicted by oppressors, those who unjustly claim power, and those who stray from the righteous path. He does so by revealing their falsehoods and then praying against them.

Whether he removes these adversaries through physical means or the power of his prayers, the outcome remains the same: the oppressor's reign is cut short. So, it is no wonder that when news suddenly emerges of an oppressor's demise, it brings relief and hope to the oppressed. An example of this intervention can be found in one of the Imām's letters:

> And regarding the fake Sufi (that is, Hilālī), which you mentioned, may God cut his life short.

After his death, a letter came,

> He targeted us and we were patient with him. And God cut short his life because of our Duʿāʾ.[100]

84. The Virtue of Living in the Time of the Occultation

Many of us often dream about living in the times of the earlier Imāms ﷺ. During this period, believers could approach their Imām directly for guidance on both

---

[100] Ṣadūq, Shaykh Muḥammad b. ʿAlī, *Kamāl al-Dīn wa Tamām al-Niʿmah*, Vol. 2, p. 489.

religious and daily matters. However, Imām aṣ-Ṣādiq sheds light on a significant truth, emphasizing the heightened importance of supporting Imām al-Mahdī. The achievements during his era surpass those of the preceding Imāms.

In response to a query about why we should yearn to be companions of al-Qā'im and witness establishing the just and true government, especially when our deeds today, under your Imāmate and obedience, surpass those living during the reign of the Government of Truth, Imām aṣ-Ṣādiq said:

> Glory be to God! Do you not wish that God, the blessed, the sublime, should make Truth and Justice appear in the lands? That God should cause people's speech to harmonize, and that God should unite the diverse hearts of people? That they should not rebel against God, to whom belong Might and Majesty, in His land? That His restriction should apply among His creatures, and that God should return the rights to His people so that it may become manifest, so that nothing of the Truth might be concealed through fear of any one of His creatures? By God, O Ammar, indeed no one among you will die in the condition you are in, but he will be more perfect before God than many of the martyrs of Badr and Uḥud. May you rejoice![101]

---

[101] Majlisī, 'Allāmah Muḥammad Bāqir, *Biḥār al-Anwār*, Vol. 52, p. 128.

85. Al-Khiḍr as a Companion

God ﷻ is the Most Wise in all His words and His actions. What transpired between al-Khiḍr and Mūsā ﵉ indicates that God, the Most High, has a will beyond His general legislative will. The divine decree and wisdom were attached to the notion that this righteous servant, al-Khiḍr ﵊, would be a companion to the Imāms ﵈ in general, and specifically to the Imām of the era ﵊ as he is the one who experiences solitude and loneliness during his occultation.

It was narrated that Imām ar-Riḍā ﵇ said:

> Khiḍr ﵇ drank from the spring of life. Thus, he is alive and will not die till the bugle is blown. Indeed, he comes to us and greets us with Salām. His voice is audible, but he remains unseen. And he is present wherever his name is mentioned. Thus, whoever of you mentions him, must say Salām to him. Every year, he participates in the Ḥajj ceremonies. He performs all the rituals and camps at ʿArafāt, saying *Amīn* to the prayers of believers. And God ﷻ changes the loneliness of our Qā'im ﵊ during his occultation into his companionship and removes his loneliness through him (Khiḍr).[102]

[102] Ibid, Vol. 13, p. 299.

86. Bad Outcome

Sometimes, we may feel a sense of pride and accomplishment in our worship and achievements, but what truly matters is whether these efforts find divine acceptance. True acceptance comes when our Imām عليه السلام approves of our actions, leading to favorable outcomes in our lives and a blessed end.

Consider the cautionary tale of those who seemed successful outwardly but lacked the Imām's approval, facing instead his condemnation. One such figure, Ibn Hilāl, was renowned for his scholarship and devoutness, having undertaken the pilgrimage an impressive fifty-four times, twenty of which were on foot. He was held in high esteem by many, with his teachings recorded and esteemed in ʿIrāq, and many rejected any criticism against him. However, everything changed when a letter from Imām al-Mahdī عجل الله تعالى فرجه الشريف arrived, bearing a damning verdict:

> May God not forgive his sin nor overlook his mistake

The Imām's disapproval of Ibn Hilāl was further clarified when he stated:

> He refused to carry out our commands unless they aligned with what he desired and wished. May God cast him into the Hellfire[103]

---

[103] Ibid., Vol. 50, p. 318.

This explanation illustrates a broader truth: anyone who opposes the directives of the Imām of the Time عجل الله تعالى فرجه الشريف faces expulsion and condemnation.

87. The Joy of the Departed at His Return

Imagine the indescribable joy and delight that will envelop those fortunate enough to witness the reappearance of the Imām عجل الله تعالى فرجه الشريف. As the Imām places his hand on the heads of the believers, every believer will have a heart that is stronger than steel, and each is given the strength of forty men.

Yet, this joy extends beyond the living to the realm of Barzakh (purgatory). Those who, during their earthly lives, eagerly awaited the Imām's عجل الله تعالى فرجه الشريف return but passed away before witnessing it will experience immense happiness. In a narration, it is beautifully expressed:

> Every dead believer will feel happy in his grave. The dead will begin to visit each other in their graves, and they bring the good news of the appearance of al-Qā'im to each other.[104]

These departed souls, however, differ from those who will rise in the minor resurrection, emerging from their graves to support the Imām عجل الله تعالى فرجه الشريف physically.

---

[104] Ṣadūq, Shaykh Muḥammad b. ʿAlī, *Kamāl al-Dīn wa Tamām al-Niʿmah*, Vol. 2, p. 653.

88. The Fateful Role

Imām ʿAlī ﷺ, with his profound knowledge and understanding of the challenges ahead during the occultation, and his foresight into his son Imām al-Mahdī's ﷺ mission to establish truth, spoke of the state of the nation before his reappearance:

> He will redirect desires towards the path of guidance, while people will have twisted guidance to suit their desires. He will realign their perspectives with the teachings of the Qurʾān, while the people will have twisted the Qurʾān to suit their views.[105]

In his words, we sense a hint of intentionality in what the misguided people will be doing in that era. One who swaps one thing for another understands both. Therefore, the people of falsehood differentiate within themselves between guidance and desires, just as they differentiate between the Qurʾān and personal opinion, and they are like those mentioned in the Qurʾān:

﴿وَجَحَدُوا بِهَا وَاسْتَيْقَنَتْهَا أَنفُسُهُمْ ظُلْمًا وَعُلُوًّا﴾

﴿*wa-jaḥadū bihā wa-stayqanathā anfusuhum ẓulman wa-ʿuluwwan*﴾

[105] Sharīf Raḍī, Muḥammad b. al-Ḥusayn, *Nahj al-Balāghah*, p. 195.

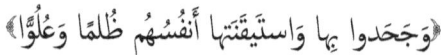

﴾*They impugned them —though they were convinced in their hearts— wrongfully and defiantly*﴿[106]

89. Addressing the Occultation

Throughout occultation, our scholars have undertaken the admirable task of unraveling its intricacies and addressing the queries surrounding it. One such query arose: What purpose does an invisible Imām serve? To this, Sayyid Murtaḍā ﵀ offered insight:

> The benefit to the believer becomes evident when he realizes that he has an absent Imām whose reappearance is anticipated at any moment. In such awareness, he might find solace, allowing his hand to rest assured in all circumstances. Yet, the fear of the Imām's potential reprimand persists, urging the believer to refrain from reprehensible actions and prompting him to fulfill many duties diligently. Thus, during the Imām's occultation, the believer's state resembles that of someone residing in another land. It might be argued that during concealment, the connection is even more profound. During the occultation, the Imām could still be present in his homeland, beside him, observing him without his knowledge. The believer, unaware of the Imām's whereabouts, maintains vigilance, performing duties and avoiding transgressions, making the state of

[106] Sūrat an-Naml, Verse 14.

occultation an opportunity for spiritual growth, as previously discussed.[107]

90. Addressing the Imām's Long Life

The question of Imām al-Mahdī's ﷺ prolonged lifespan has sparked various discussions, leaving no stone unturned in its exploration. Among the most compelling explanations offered on this matter is one articulated by Sayyid Murtaḍā ؒ, who said:

> The world is a creation and it has a Creator, who has set the ordinary norms of short and long lives, and He is capable of lengthening lives and taking lives. If this is clear, then the inquiry becomes easy. If our opponent accepts this but says this is out of the ordinary, we have already responded that it is not at all out of the ordinary. The frailty and feebleness of the body that comes with the passage of time and old age are not inevitable. God has set the ordinary pattern that this comes along as time goes by. This is not, however, necessary, and God can make the unordinary happen. If this is accepted, it will be proven that the phenomenon of long life is possible. We recorded narratives of people who remained unchanged by the passage of time and in their old age. How is it that

[107] Ṭūsī, Shaykh Muḥammad b. Ḥasan, *Kitāb al-Ghaybah*, p. 104.

someone who believes God will grant the believers eternal youthful life in Paradise can reject this?[108]

91. Offspring in Paradise

Many of us dream of having children who will cherish our memory long after we are gone, offering comfort and companionship in the eternal bliss of paradise. There, God ﷻ promises to bring together the believers, their spouses, and their offspring. However, for some, the inability to have children in this world brings a constant sense of longing and sadness. Yet, there is a letter from our Imām that can lift this burden. Imām al-Mahdī عجّل الله تعالى فرجه الشريف was asked about the people of paradise and whether they reproduce, and the Imām عجّل الله تعالى فرجه الشريف answered:

> In Paradise, there is no pregnancy for women, no childbirth, no menstruation, no postpartum bleeding, nor any suffering in childhood. It contains whatever the souls desire and delights the eyes, as mentioned by God ﷻ. So when a believer desires a child, God creates it without pregnancy or childbirth in the form that He wills, just as He created Ādam as a lesson.[109]

[108] Ibid., p. 303.

[109] Majlisī, ʿAllāmah Muḥammad Bāqir, *Biḥār al-Anwār*, Vol. 53, p. 125.

92. Etiquettes of Ziyārah and Servitude

The Imām taught us the etiquette of servitude to God, and the etiquette of being in the presence of the Infallible, because perfection lies in combining the light of guardianship and monotheism. When someone asked him about the manner of performing prayers and visits at the graves of the Imāms, he replied:

> As for prostrating on the grave, it is not permissible in voluntary prayers, obligatory prayers, or visits. What should be done is to place the right cheek on the grave. As for the prayer, it is performed behind the grave, with the grave in front of the worshiper. It is not permissible to pray in front of it, to its right, or its left, because the Imām should neither be preceded nor made equal.[110]

What is noteworthy here is that he did not say "preceding the grave" but "preceding the Imām," as if to teach us that the interaction with the Imām during the visit should be like interacting with a living person, for he is, as they all were, the best of martyrs.

---

[110] Majlisī, ʿAllāmah Muḥammad Bāqir, *Biḥār al-Anwār*, Vol. 53, p. 165.

93. Comprehensive Awareness of Events

In one of his letters, the Imām عجل الله تعالى فرجه الشريف reveals his profound understanding of the challenges faced by our community. He assures us that he is fully aware of our circumstances:

> We are perfectly aware of all your affairs and problems[111]

By emphasizing that nothing is hidden from him, he shows us his deep concern for every aspect of our lives:

> and nothing regarding you is hidden from us[112]

This also reveals the depth of sorrow in his heart, as he understands the pain of the challenging events occurring in our nation. His awareness goes beyond that of an outsider who lacks the paternal sense of compassion and empathy the Imām عجل الله تعالى فرجه الشريف feels for this nation.

He then discusses two reasons behind the troubles facing our community. Firstly, our departure from the righteous path followed by our predecessors, which represented the path of the previous Imāms عليهم السلام:

---

[111] Ibid., p. 175.

[112] Ibid.

> inclined towards what the righteous predecessors turned away from extensively[113]

Secondly, abandoning adherence to the divine covenant, as it represents the path of servitude to Him as a goal for mankind's creation:

> and they have abandoned the covenant taken from them[114]

94. Sayyidah Fāṭimah ؑ as an Example

The family of the Prophet ﷺ, starting with the Prophet himself and ending with Imām al-Mahdī عج, held Sayyidah Fāṭimah ؑ in the highest regard.

The Prophet ﷺ, whose words stem not from personal desire, often praised her, saying:

> May her father be sacrificed for her[115].

In another instance, he affectionately referred to her as:

113 Ibid.

114 Ibid.

115 Ṣadūq, Shaykh Muḥammad b. ʿAlī, *al-Amālī*, p. 434.

> Her father's beloved[116]

Imām ʿAlī ﷺ, grief-stricken after her passing, expressed his sorrow, saying:

> My grief knows no bounds, and my nights will remain sleepless[117]

Imām al-Jawād ﷺ, not yet four years old, hit the ground with his hand and raised his head to the sky, reflecting for a while. When asked by Imām ar-Riḍā ﷺ,

> May my soul be sacrificed for you, what makes you think for that long?

He replied:

> I am thinking of what was done to my mother, Fāṭimah ﷺ[118]

Imām al-ʿAskarī ﷺ emphasized her significance, stating:

---

116 Majlisī, ʿAllāmah Muḥammad Bāqir, *Biḥār al-Anwār*, Vol. 63, p. 487.

117 Kulaynī, Shaykh Muḥammad b. Yaʿqūb, *al-Kāfī*, Vol. 2, p. 492.

118 al-Ṭabarī, Muḥammad b. Jarīr, *Dalāʾil al-Imāmat*, p. 401.

> We are the Proof of God on His creation, and our grandmother Fāṭimah is the proof of God on us[119]

Imām al-Mahdī takes her as an example for himself, where he says:

> In the daughter of the Messenger of God, I have a perfect example.[120]

What can be understood from the Imām's words is that one aspect of emulating her relates to the consequences of matters, as indeed, despite God granting respite to her enemies, they will not be neglected. As Imām al-Mahdī said:

> And the ignorant will see the consequence of his actions, and the disbeliever will know to whom the final abode belongs.[121]

Undoubtedly, Imām al-Mahdī will seek justice for the injustices against her and Imām al-Ḥusayn. This aligns with the Prophet's promise to Sayyidah Fāṭimah:

---

[119] Iṣfahānī, Shaykh "Abdullāh Baḥrānī, *ʿAwālim al-ʿUlūm wal-Maʿārif wa al-Aḥwāl*, Vol. 11, p. 1030.

[120] Ṭūsī, Shaykh Muḥammad b. Ḥasan, *Kitāb al-Ghaybah*, p. 286.

[121] Ibid.

> Rejoice, O Fāṭimah! For the Mahdī is from you[122]

95. Known in the Heavens

Even before the Earth knew him, Imām al-Mahdī ﷺ was known in the Heavens. The Prophet ﷺ was given knowledge about him during his ascension to heaven. When he saw the lights, he asked: O Lord, who are these?, God ﷻ replied:

> They are the Imāms, and this is al-Qā'im who will uphold what I have deemed lawful and forbid what I have deemed forbidden, and through him I will seek revenge from My enemies, and he is the comfort of My allies.[123]

This narration, along with others of a similar nature, illuminates the exalted position of our Imām among the infallibles. Firstly, his pivotal role in establishing the Sharīʿah, distinguishing between the permissible and the forbidden. Secondly, his responsibility is in seeking retribution against those who oppose God's messages. Lastly, his mission was to inspire hope and solace in the hearts of devoted believers anticipating his return during the period of occultation.

---

[122] al-Qummī, ʿAlī b. Ibrāhīm, *Kifāyat al-Athar*, p. 124.

[123] Ṣadūq, Shaykh Muḥammad b. ʿAlī, *Kamāl al-Dīn wa Tamām al-Niʿmah*, Vol. 1, p. 253.

96. Guardians of Blood

The Imāms ﷺ often spoke of Imām al-Mahdī ﷺ, affirming that he is the rightful avenger for the injustices they endured. Among them is Imām aṣ-Ṣādiq ﷺ, who declared:

> We are the ones who seek retribution for our spilled blood; we are the ones who demand justice.[124]

The Master of the Martyrs, Imām al-Ḥusayn ﷺ, pointed out that the divine revenge against those who killed him would be carried out at the hands of his son al-Mahdī ﷺ. While addressing his son, Imām Zayn al-ʿĀbidīn ﷺ, exclaimed:

> O my son ʿAlī! By God, my blood will not be at peace until God sends the Mahdī, who will avenge my blood by killing seventy thousand hypocrites, disbelievers, and transgressors.[125]

Hence, one of the pivotal responsibilities awaiting Imām al-Mahdī ﷺ upon his emergence is to seek retribution for the blood of his grandfather, Imām al-Ḥusayn ﷺ. The tragedy on the day of ʿĀshūrāʾ was not merely an injustice against an oppressed individual. However, it marked the

---

[124] Majlisī, ʿAllāmah Muḥammad Bāqir, *Biḥār al-Anwār*, Vol. 24, p. 224.

[125] Ibid., Vol. 45, p. 299.

gravest violation against the dearest creation of God ﷻ in his era.

97. The Measure of Acceptance

During the occultation, some may witness various expressions of religious commitment and encounter symbols that resonate with those carrying deep concerns for the faith and its followers. However, it is crucial not to be swayed by these appearances. God ﷻ desires obedience based on His will, not the whims of His servants. Thus, anyone seeking to serve the religion outside the guidance of the Imām of their time risks wandering into confusion and misguidance, as mentioned by Imām aṣ-Ṣādiq ؑ:

> We, by God, are the path that God has commanded you to follow, and we, by God, are the straight path. We, by God, are those whom God has commanded His servants to obey. So whoever wishes, let them take from here, and whoever wishes, let them take from there. They will find no escape from us, by God.[126]

Imām ؑ mentioned that, knowing that many pretenders were among the people of misguidance and errors, whose deceitful tactics deceived the naive among the Muslims.

---

[126] al-Baḥrānī, Hāshim al-Tūbilī, *al-Burhān fī Tafsīr al-Qur'ān*, Vol. 3, p. 791.

98. The Signs and the Companions

The Imāms of Ahl al-Bayt ﷷ have been described as the signs and the companions. From this expression and similar ones, it is understood that the Imāms ﷷ are the clear signs that lead people to God ﷻ. This should not come as a surprise, considering that landmarks like aṣ-Ṣafā and al-Marwah, as well as the camels, are all considered among the signs of God ﷻ, serving as constant reminders of His presence. The author of *Mikyāl al-Makārim* further elaborates on this concept.

> Shaʿīrullāh (signs of God) denotes anything that has a special relationship to God ﷻ, directly or indirectly, as is evident from the verses of the Qurʾān and traditional reports. It is also an established matter that honoring the signs of God is honoring God ﷻ, and any disrespect to the signs of God is the same as disrespecting God ﷻ. Signs of God can be His names, His Books, prophets, angels, masjids, the believers, and occasions whose respect He has made obligatory, houses that He has ordered to be raised high, in whom His name is exalted. Therefore, the absent Imām is one of the signs of God that must be honored. As for the companions, it could be a reference to the tradition of the Holy Prophet ﷺ, in which he said,
>
> > My companions are like stars, whichever of them you follow, you will be guided.

That is the Holy Prophet ﷺ meant to imply these same purified and interceding Imāms of Judgment Day, and not anyone who accompanied the Prophet for some days and committed sins in his own life[127]

99. The Position of An Infallible in the Eyes of Another

No one understands the essence of an infallible better than another infallible who precedes him or succeeds him. Through various narrations, we find vivid descriptions of the Imām, often spoken by another Imām. This falls outside the realm of self-praise; it is a deep acknowledgment of the inherent qualities of the Imām. It is a form of praising the title that has become synonymous with the Imām.

An example of this is what Imām Zayn al-ʿĀbidīn ؑ said in the supplication of Arafah when defining the Imām of each era, praising him with attributes such as infallibility, the cave, the stronghold, and brilliance. He was quoted as saying:

> O God, surely Thou hast confirmed Thy religion in all times with an Imām whom Thou hast set up as a guidepost to Thy servants, and a lighthouse in Thy lands, after his cord has been joined to Thy cord! Thou

[127] Iṣfahānī, Sayyid Muḥammad Taqī Mūsawī, *Mikyāl al-Makārim*, Vol. 2, p. 295.

> hast appointed him the means to Thy good pleasure, made obeying him obligatory, cautioned against disobeying him, and commanded following his commands, abandoning his prohibitions, and that no one gets ahead of him or straggler should stay behind him! So he is the preservation of the shelter-seekers, the cave of the faithful, the stronghold of the adherents, and the brilliance of the worlds![128]

100.Building the Earth through Remembrance

The construction of the Earth during the era of reappearance does not solely refer to physical construction, although that is certainly facilitated by the blessings of the Imām's presence. Rather, it encompasses something far greater. It entails the establishment of a realm symbolized by the sovereignty of God ﷻ on Earth and the spread of His remembrance in the hearts. This is a phenomenon that has yet to happen throughout history. As mentioned in the ḥadīth of the Ascension, God ﷻ said:

> Through your Qā'im will I spread My glorification, slogan of unity, word of purification, word of greatness, and hymns of veneration on the earth. And through him will I cleanse the Earth from My enemies and make My friends inherit it. And through him will I disgrace the apostates and ensure that My word dominates. And through him will I revive My servants

[128] Sayyid b. Ṭāwūs, *Iqbāl al-A'māl*, Vol. 1, p. 353.

> and cities. And through him will I uncover My treasures and riches. And through him will I reveal the secrets and manifest the thoughts of people. To establish My command and proclaim My religion, I will assist him through My angels. He is My real friend and the genuine Mahdī for My Servants.[129]

101. The Wish of the Companions

The companions of the Imāms ﷺ enjoyed the blessings of their presence in their times. They saw their pure faces and listened to their blessed words. However, despite this, some expressed their longing to see our Imām ﷺ and wished to live in his era. Abū Baṣīr asked Imām aṣ-Ṣādiq ﷺ, saying:

> Do you think that I live until al-Qā'im appears?

Imām aṣ-Ṣādiq ﷺ said to him:

> O Abū Baṣīr, do you not know your imām?

Abū Baṣīr said,

> I know him. By God, it is you.

[129] Ṣadūq, Shaykh Muḥammad b. ʿAlī, *al-Amālī*, p. 632.

Imām aṣ-Ṣādiq ﷺ took Abū Baṣīr's hand and said:

> O Abū Baṣīr, by God, never mind if you are not under the shadow of al-Qā'im's tent with your sword![130]

What resonates profoundly in this exchange is Imām aṣ-Ṣādiq's ﷺ emphasis on genuine knowledge of the Imām being akin to wielding a sword in the noble army of Imām al-Mahdī ﷺ. This resonates with us as well. After true knowledge and recognition of our Imām ﷺ, it does not matter if we live to see his rule or not, for the same that applied to Abū Baṣīr applies to us.

102.Distinction Since Birth

From the moment Imām al-Mahdī ﷺ graced this world with his presence, his distinction was evident, much like the birth of ʿĪsā ﷺ. God ﷻ intended to show their distinction from the rest of creation from the moment of their birth, due to the great responsibilities that would be assigned to them. It is no wonder that a prophet like ʿĪsā ﷺ and a successor like Imām al-Mahdī ﷺ share the attribute of speaking in infancy. At the time of his birth, it was narrated that:

> Imām al-ʿAskarī ﷺ asked Lady Ḥakīmah to recite Sūrat al-Qadr to the mother of Imām al-Mahdī ﷺ upon his birth. Lady Narjis ﷺ remarked:

[130] Kulaynī, Shaykh Muḥammad b. Yaʿqūb, *al-Kāfī*, Vol. 2, p. 151.

> The matter my Master has informed you of has indeed come to pass.

Lady Ḥakīmah adds:

> I began reciting the verses, as the Imām ordered me. At this, the baby answered back to me from her abdomen; he was reciting like I was reciting, and he greeted me.

Lady Ḥakīmah said,

> I felt shocked when I heard that.

So Imām al-ʿAskarīi ﷺ called out to me:

> Do not wonder about the Command of God, the Mighty and Sublime; He gives us speech in infancy and makes us Ḥujjah on Earth at maturity.[131]

What Imām al-Mahdī ﷺ said at the time of his birth reinforces what we have discussed, that the permission for his speech in infancy was to dispel any doubts regarding him and his significant mission. Another narration from Lady Ḥakīmah, who was present at his birth, says:

> When Imām al-Mahdī ﷺ emerged from his mother's womb, he fell prostrating on his knees, raised his index finger towards the sky, and sneezed.

---

[131] Majlisī, ʿAllāmah Muḥammad Bāqir, *Biḥār al-Anwār*, Vol. 51, p. 13.

He said:

> Praise be to God, the Lord of the worlds, and may God bless Muḥammad and the Progeny of Muḥammad.

> The oppressors thought that the Divine Proof is invalid and destroyed. If we had been permitted to speak freely about him, all the doubts would be removed.[132]

103. Supplication for Various Groups

Among the eloquent prayers attributed to Imām al-Mahdī ﷺ is a renowned supplication where the Imām begins by seeking guidance from God ﷻ to lead us towards obedience and away from disobedience. He then proceeds to mention various groups within the community: the scholars, the learners, the listeners, the sick, the deceased, the elders, the youth, the women, the wealthy, the poor, the warriors, the prisoners, the leaders, the subjects, concluding with pilgrims and visitors.

Each word of this all-encompassing prayer assures us that the Imām ﷺ cares for every soul, tailoring his supplication to their unique needs. His attention encompasses all walks of life, inspiring us to follow his example. As believers who sincerely await the Imām ﷺ, we are expected to address

---

[132] Ṣadūq, Shaykh Muḥammad b. ʿAlī, *Kamāl al-Dīn wa Tamām al-Niʿmah*, Vol. 2, p. 430.

each of the mentioned groups and strive to fulfill our duties towards them. If the community responds to this call, as requested by the Imām in his heartfelt prayer, there would be no void in our community.

Lastly, let us reflect on how the Imām عجل الله تعالى فرجه الشريف initiates this prayer with a request crucial for every member of the community—indeed, it is at the top of the list of needs—which is the request for success in obedience and avoidance of disobedience. However, fulfilling this prayer does not imply predetermination; rather, it acknowledges God ﷻ's unique ability to touch hearts, as the One who turns hearts. He has the power to instill faith in some while guarding them against disbelief, immorality, and sin.

104. The Five Calls

The first sign of the Imām's عجل الله تعالى فرجه الشريف re-emergence is what is known as the five calls, as he stands next to the Kaʿbah, between Rukn and Maqām. He will call out:

> O people of the world, I am the uprising Imām. O people of the world, I am the avenger. O people of the world, my grandfather al-Ḥusayn was killed while he was thirsty. O people of the world, my grandfather al-Ḥusayn was left without clothing. O people of the

> world, they desecrated the body of my grandfather al-Ḥusayn[133]

What these initial calls reveal is the flood of emotions bursting from the Imām's heart after years of occultation, indicating the immense tribulations that befell his grandfather, Imām al-Ḥusayn عليه السلام, from killings, thirst, oppression, and plunder. He elaborated on these trials, among others, in the Ziyārat an-Nāḥiyah attributed to him.

The practical lesson in all of this is that the loving Awaiter must surely share in some of the tribulations that trouble the Imām's noble heart. Without a doubt, the possessor of such a compassionate heart during the occultation period forgives the faults of those who love and sympathize with him, as authentic love has the transformative power to purify any shortcomings in the beloved's character.

105. Description of the Companions

The words of the Commander of the Faithful عليه السلام carry profound insights into the character of his son's companions, Imām al-Mahdī عجل الله فرجه الشريف, when pondering their significance. Among these insights: they walk a unified path, both outwardly and inwardly. He says:

---

[133] al-Ḥā'irī, ʿAlī Yazdī, *Ilzām an-Nāṣib fī Ithbāt al-Ḥujjah al-Ghā'ib*, Vol. 2, p. 233.

> And it is as if I see them, all dressed alike, with the same stature, the same beauty, and the same attire.[134]

Another portrayal highlights their profound attachment to their Imām ﷻ. When they see him, it is as if they have found something they have been missing, underscoring the longing and heartfelt connection to what has been absent. Imām ʿAlī ﷺ said:

> It is as if they are seeking something that they have lost, feeling perplexed about their situation.[135]

Among these vivid portrayals is the striking resemblance of the Imām to the Messenger of God ﷺ, not just in appearance but also in character, virtue, and grace:

> Until there emerges among them, from behind the cover of the Kaʿbah, a man who resembles the Messenger of God in appearance, character, goodness, and beauty.[136]

Additionally, the Imām ﷻ will ask his companions to embody the attributes of perfection and servitude to God ﷻ, for whoever is summoned to respond to this great call must be at a high level of nearness to God. As mentioned by Imām ʿAlī ﷺ, when he said:

---

134 Sayyid b. Ṭāwūs, *at-Tashrīf bil-Minān fī at-Taʿrīf bil-Fitan*, p. 294.

135 Ibid.

136 Ibid.

They will question him:

> Are you Al-Mahdī?

He will reply:

> I am Al-Mahdī, urging them to pledge allegiance based on forty noble characteristics.[137]

Then he lists the virtues and qualities that one must embody if they desire to be in his noble company.

106. The Extension of Prophets

When Imām al-Mahdī ﷻ reappears, he will demonstrate his proximity and connection to all the prophets, showing that his mission is an extension of theirs. His purpose in appearing is to fulfill the aspirations of all prophets, as none of them were able to establish universal justice, even momentarily, in their lives. Moreover, it is natural for followers of previous religions, such as Judaism and Christianity, to be drawn to this discourse when they witness the remarkable signs of our Imām ؑ, combined with his profound understanding of all heavenly scriptures. He will call out:

> O People! whoever wishes to see Ādam and Shayth, here I am, Ādam and Shayth! And whoever wishes to

[137] Ibid.

see Nūḥ and his son Sām, here I am, Nūḥ and Sām! And whoever wishes to see Ibrāhīm and Ismāʿīl, here I am, Ibrāhīm and Ismāʿīl! And whoever wishes to see Mūsā and Yūshaʿ, here I am, Mūsā and Yūshaʿ! And whoever wishes to see ʿĪsā and Shimʿawn Ṣafā (Simon Peter), here I am, ʿĪsā and Simon Peter! And whoever wishes to see Muḥammad ﷺ and the Commander of the Faithful عليه السلام here I am, Muḥammad ﷺ, and the Commander of the Faithful عليه السلام! And whoever wishes to see al-Ḥasan and al-Ḥusayn عليهما السلام here I am, al-Ḥasan and al-Ḥusayn! And whoever wishes to see the Imāms from the descendants of al-Ḥusayn عليه السلام here I am, the Imāms عليهم السلام![138]

107.Revival of the Heavenly Scriptures

One of the blessings of the Imām's عجل الله فرجه emergence is his revival of the heavenly scriptures that have been distorted throughout history. Through this rectification, the wisdom and sublime meanings contained within these scriptures, which have been lost due to tampering, are restored. The revelations were always connected to the essence of divine wisdom in any era. Furthermore, the admiration of people of different faiths for these scriptures during his appearance, and the exposure of the falsehood they have been subjected to over centuries, causes them to disavow their scholars who have led them astray. Added to all of this

[138] Majlisī, ʿAllāmah Muḥammad Bāqir, *Biḥār al-Anwār*, Vol. 53, p. 9.

is the revival of the Qur'ān through its interpretation as revealed by God ﷻ.

These meanings are explained by the Imām عجل الله تعالى فرجه الشريف, as he leans his back against the Ka'bah. He begins by mentioning the scriptures that God ﷻ revealed to Ādam and Shayth عليهما السلام, and they will say:

> By God, these are truly the scriptures. He has shown us what we did not know about them, and what was hidden from us, and what was omitted from them, and altered, and distorted.[139]

Then he reads the scriptures of Nūḥ, Ibrāhīm, the Tawrāh (Torah), the Injīl (Gospel), and the Zabūr (Psalms), and the people of the Tawrāh, the Injīl, and the Zabūr will say:

> These are truly the scriptures of Nūḥ and Ibrāhīm and what was omitted, altered, and distorted from them. These are truly the complete Tawrāh, Zabūr, and Injīl. And are multitudes of what we have read from them.[140]

108. Correcting the Narrations

There is an indication in some of Imām al-Mahdī's عجل الله تعالى فرجه الشريف letters that he corrects some of the transmitted narrations

---

[139] al-Ḥillī, Ḥasan b. Sulaymān, *Mukhtaṣar al-Baṣā'ir*, p. 444.

[140] Ibid.

from his noble forefathers. This indicates that those who possess knowledge and wisdom regarding the House of Revelation are the ones whom God ﷻ has made trustees of His revelation.

They share equal knowledge and virtue, enabling the later Imāms ﷺ to rectify narrations transmitted on behalf of the earlier ones, as their knowledge originates from the same divine source. A clear instance of this is when the Imām ﷺ addressed a query regarding the qunūt supplication in the obligatory prayer:

> A man asked about the supplication (qunūt) in the obligatory prayer: When one finishes their supplication, is it permissible to return their hands to their face and chest due to the ḥadīth narrated:
>
> > Indeed, God ﷻ is too generous to let His servant's hands return empty; instead, He fills them with His mercy?
>
> Or is it not permissible? Because some of our companions mentioned that it is practiced in prayer.
>
> He ﷺ responded:
>
> > Returning the hands from the qunūt to the head and face is not permissible in the obligatory prayers, and what one should do is, after finishing the supplication, to return the palms of their hands

> to their chest and then towards their knees, calmly, and then perform the takbīr and bow in rukū'[141]

109.Confronting the Deviants

The Imām ﷺ, driven by his leadership of the community and his mission to correct its course and protect the religion of God ﷻ, faced the deviants of his time with all the strength at his disposal. This included exposing them in his addresses to his followers on occasion, and unequivocally cursing them during his prayers to God ﷻ on other occasions. One might wonder about the fate of those cursed by the Imām of his time with such intensity.

Three points are noteworthy here. One reason is that the Imām ﷺ explains the rationale behind the curse, as some might find it disconcerting unless they understand the underlying reason. Thus, the Imām ﷺ explains in one of his letters:

> Muḥammad b. 'Alī, known as ash-Shalmaghānī, is one of those upon whom God has hastened His judgment and to whom He has granted no respite. He has deviated from Islam and separated himself from it. He has become an apostate from the religion of God, making claims which indicate the denial of God, the Most Glorious and High, fabricating lies and

141 Majlisī, 'Allāmah Muḥammad Bāqir, *Biḥār al-Anwār*, Vol. 53, p. 9.

> falsehoods, and pronouncing untruths and great transgressions.[142]

Secondly, he explains the line of deviation within the Ummah, emphasizing that it is not confined to one individual. He adds another group to those who have been cursed, even though he had renounced them before, to emphasize the warning from them. In this regard, he writes:

> Inform them that we are in a state of caution and warning against them, just as we have done with their counterparts.[143]

Thirdly, the Imām ﷺ clarifies that the original avenger is God ﷻ, for He is the most deserving among all to defend His religion and to deflect the deviants from the path, and states that this is the tradition of God ﷻ:

> For the traditions of God are conformable to us. In Him we place our trust, and from Him we seek assistance. He is sufficient for us in all our affairs and is the best of Guardians.[144]

---

[142] Ṭabrisī, Shaykh Aḥmad b. ʿAlī Ṭabrisī, *al-Iḥtijāj ʿalā Ahl al-Lijāj*, Vol. 2, p. 475.

[143] Ṭūsī, Shaykh Muḥammad b. Ḥasan, *Kitāb al-Ghaybah*, p. 411.

[144] Ibid.

110.The Interpretation of the Qur'ān

The explanation of a verse differently from its apparent meaning, known as interpretation (*ta'wīl*), is exclusive to the infallible ones. This is because they have the utmost knowledge of the real intention of God ﷻ, and only they have the authority to interpret the Qur'ān in a way that diverges from its apparent meaning. This prohibition aims to prevent interpreting the Qur'ān based on personal opinions, thereby opening the door to arbitrary interpretations that align with the interpreter's inclinations.

An example of this is the verse the Imām ؑ interprets, mentioning the reason behind his explanation as a way to make it more convincing and to demonstrate that some verses can be interpreted in a manner different from their apparent meaning, with convincing evidence provided by the infallible interpreter.

Consider this narration from Sa'd b. 'Abdullāh, who asked Imām al-Mahdī ؑ about a verse in the Qur'ān:

> Inform me, O son of the Messenger of God, about God's saying to His Prophet Mūsā:

﴿فَاخلَع نَعلَيكَ ۖ إِنَّكَ بِالوادِ المُقَدَّسِ طُوًى﴾

﴿*fa-khla' na'layka innaka bi-l-wādi l-muqaddasi ṭuwa*ⁿ﴾

﴾*So take off your sandals. You are indeed in the sacred valley of Ṭuwā*﴿[145]

The scholars of the two groups claim that it is because the sandals were made from dead animal skin.

He ﷺ replied:

> Whoever says that has fabricated against Mūsā and displayed ignorance about his prophethood, because there are two possibilities: If Mūsā prayer while wearing was permissible, then it was permissible for Mūsā to wear them in that spot, even if it was sacred and pure. And if his prayer while wearing them was impermissible, then they are saying that Mūsā did not know what was permissible and impermissible, and he did not know what prayer was valid and what was not, which is disbelief.

I said,

> So, tell me, O my master, about the interpretation of it?

He said:

> Indeed, Mūsā ﷺ was in the sacred valley, so he said,

[145] Sūrat Ṭā Hā, Verse 12.

> O Lord, I have devoted my love to You and cleansed my heart from anyone besides You.

He had an intense love for his family. So God ﷻ said:

> ﴾*So take off your sandals*﴿[146]

> meaning, remove the love for your family from your heart if your love for Me is sincere, and your heart is washed from inclining towards anyone besides Me.[147]

111. Their Inseparability from the Truth

The Holy Prophet ﷺ summarized the status of Imām ʿAlī ؑ when he said:

> ʿAlī is with truth, and truth is with ʿAlī. Truth revolves around him wherever he is.[148]

This portrayal highlights Imām ʿAlī's ؑ embodiment of virtues and attributes essential for his role as the rightful successor to the Prophet ﷺ and the leader of the entire

---

[146] Sūrat Ṭā Hā, Verse 12.

[147] Ṭabrisī, Shaykh Aḥmad b. ʿAlī Ṭabrisī, *al-Iḥtijāj ʿalā Ahl al-Lijāj*, Vol. 2, p. 463.

[148] Majlisī, ʿAllāmah Muḥammad Bāqir, *Biḥār al-Anwār*, Vol. 10, p. 432.

Ummah. Similarly, this continuity extends to Imām al-Mahdī ﷻ, as he emphasized:

> They should know that the truth is by us and with us, and no one except us would claim thus, but that he or she would be a liar and fabricator. None except us can claim thus, except that he or she be deviated. Therefore, what we have stated here should suffice for them, rather than seeking further clarifications. Rather than desiring more explanation and details, they should rest content with this much, if God wills.[149]

Thus, when the Imām reveals a fundamental truth, one who reflects on the matter will not need much detail and explanation beyond that. It suffices for the believer to review the textual evidence of leadership on one side and the biography of the Imāms on the other side. This will make it clear that the major principles can apply to minor ones. By contemplating the entirety, one can understand the necessity of following the leadership of our Imām ﷻ as part of the chain of Imāms. The Messenger ﷺ conveyed this, beginning with Ḥadīth al-Kisā'[150] and culminating with the declaration of al-Ghadīr.

---

[149] Ṣadūq, Shaykh Muḥammad b. ʿAlī, *Kamāl al-Dīn wa Tamām al-Niʿmah*, Vol. 2, p. 511.

[150] *Ḥadīth al-Kisā'* (Tradition of the Cloak), also known as the Ḥadīth of the Household, is a narration in which the Prophet Muḥammad ﷺ gathered Imām ʿAlī, Sayyidah Fāṭimah, Imām al-Ḥasan, and Imām al-Ḥusayn ﵈ under his cloak and invoked the Verse of Purification (Sūrat al-Aḥzāb, Verse 33) regarding them.

112. Showing Displeasure

The Imām ﷺ expresses his strong disapproval when addressing theological deviations within the Ummah. This disapproval surpasses what is evident when such deviations occur at an individual level. He may even display a level of compassion toward those who have erred, seeking to guide them back to the path of obedience to God ﷻ.

Hence, some of his noble statements are severe towards those who falsely claim the position of Imāmate without rightful authority, even if to a minor degree, or assume religious authority without justification. He clearly expresses his severe displeasure with these types of people, exposing the harm caused by their actions and dissociating from them, supported by evidence and proof. In one of his letters, he writes:

> That false claimant has made a false claim on God ﷻ, and I do not know how he can prove the veracity of his claim. Can he prove it through the knowledge and jurisprudence of the religion of God? By God, he does not even know what is lawful and what is unlawful, what is right and what is wrong; what is clear and what is ambiguous. He does not even know the limits and times of prayers. Can he prove his Imāmate through piety? God ﷻ is a witness that he left obligatory prayers for forty days in order to learn black magic. You should be aware that he has wine cups and other items for illicit activities. Can he prove his claim with some

miracles? If it is so, let him bring some miracle or any other evidence of Imāmate.[151]

113. The Imām's عجل الله تعالى فرجه الشريف Affection for His Companions

The relationship of the Imāms with their companions was more tender than we might imagine. The Imāms عليهم السلام exhibit compassion and kindness surpassing even that of our parents. There is no doubt that our Awaited Imām عجل الله تعالى فرجه الشريف —despite his immense responsibilities—shares this distinctive bond with those close to his noble heart as well, especially with those who played a significant role during the period of occultation. We cannot discount the possibility of him shedding tears upon their death and even participating in their funeral processions.

An account regarding his father, Imām al-ʿAskarī عليه السلام, illustrates this beautifully. Aḥmad b. Isḥāq bid farewell to Imām al-ʿAskarī عليه السلام with heartfelt sorrow:

> O son of God's Messenger, departure is soon, and our grief is intense. We ask God to send Salawaat on you and your son. And we pray that your station be exalted and your enemies be disgraced. And may God not make this our last audience with you.[152]

---

[151] Ṭūsī, Shaykh Muḥammad b. Ḥasan, *Kitāb al-Ghaybah*, p. 289.

[152] Ṣadūq, Shaykh Muḥammad b. ʿAlī, *Kamāl al-Dīn wa Tamām al-Niʿmah*, Vol. 2, p. 464.

What is interesting here is that the man described his sadness at leaving the Imām as intense grief. In return, the Imām ﷺ also shed tears, revealing the mutual affection between them. As the Imām had foretold, Aḥmad b. Isḥāq passed away on his journey back, leaving his companions in suspense about his fate. One companion recounted that after Aḥmad b. Isḥāq's passing, Kāfūr, the servant of Imām al-ʿAskarī ﷺ, informed them:

> May God increase your reward in this calamity and may He compensate you for this tragedy. We have finished the funeral bath and shrouding of your friend. You may please get up for his burial, because his status, in the view of your master, is more exalted than that of you all.[153]

114. The Qualities of the Special Deputy

Each deputy among the four deputies of Imām al-Mahdī ﷺ had qualities that qualified them for this esteemed position. Just as the selection of the Prophet and his successor was from God ﷻ, so too was the one who deputized for them among the non-infallibles by special delegation.

Reflect on this text, which illustrates the vigilance and remembrance of the Hereafter that one of them had, in

[153] Ṣadūq, Shaykh Muḥammad b. ʿAlī, *Kamāl al-Dīn wa Tamām al-Niʿmah*, Vol. 2, p. 465.

addition to his knowledge of the date of his death, as the narrator says:

> I came to Abū Ja'far Muḥammad b. 'Uthmān on a certain day to offer him my greetings. He was there, and in front of him was a square frame of oak, with an inscriber writing verses from the Qur'ān and the names of the Holy Imāms on its sides. I asked him,
>
> > What is this tablet for, my master?
>
> He said:
>
> > This is for my grave; it will be in it, and I will be placed over it. Every day, I descend into it and recite a part of the Qur'ān and come back.
>
> Abū Ja'far b. 'Uthmān took my hand and showed me his tomb. He told me that on such and such day of such and such month of such and such year, I will go towards God ﷻ, and will be buried here, and this frame of oak will be with me.
>
> When I came out of his place, all his providential sayings came true. I was constantly watching his state. It was not long before he became ill and then died on the very day of the month and the year he had confided in me, and he was buried there.[154]

---

[154] Ṭūsī, Shaykh Muḥammad b. Ḥasan, *Kitāb al-Ghaybah*, p. 365.

115.Authentication of Deputies

The Imām ﷺ took great care in authenticating his representatives during the Minor Occultation, ensuring their legitimacy and counteracting those who falsely claimed authority during his occultation. Hence, the letter received by the followers in Ahvāz from the Imām vividly conveys this meaning, especially when he intended to appoint al-Ḥusayn b. Rūḥ to this position. In the letter, he wrote:

> We know him, may God grant him insight into all that is good, His pleasure, and bring him success. We have received his letter. He holds our trust in his current position, and he stands before us in a position and rank that brings him pleasure. May God continue to bestow His blessings upon him; He is the Mighty Guardian[155]

There is no doubt that the contents of the supplications mentioned in this letter—especially granting him knowledge of all that is good—reflect the greatness of the position entrusted to him by the Imām ﷺ.

116.Proof of Agency

Divine tradition dictates that major claims must be accompanied by evidence and proof at times, and by demonstrating miracles and divine interventions at others.

[155] Ṭūsī, Shaykh Muḥammad b. Ḥasan, *Kitāb al-Ghaybah*, p. 372.

This is what occurred with the prophets and their successors among their communities. It is well-known that what transpired during the period of Minor Occultation was a miniature form of guardianship. Although they may not have been designated as guardians in the technical sense, they were nonetheless appointed with specificity by the infallible one who does not act nor speak out of personal desire.

Hence, we see the necessity of the combination of the letter from the Imām عجل الله تعالى فرجه الشريف along with some of the magnificent miracles that manifested through the four deputies. These two aspects—textual authentication and miraculous signs —are evident in this transmission:

> When he (the first deputy) passed away, his son, Abū Jaʿfar Muḥammad b. ʿUthmān, assumed his position and took charge of all matters. Then, when he (Abū Jaʿfar Muḥammad) passed away, Abū al-Qāsim Ḥusayn b. Rūḥ from the Banū Nawbakht took his place. Subsequently, when he passed away, Abū al-Ḥasan ʿAlī b. Muḥammad al-Samarī took charge. None of them assumed this responsibility except by explicit appointment from the Imām of the Time عجل الله تعالى فرجه الشريف, and his appointment by his predecessor. The Shīʿah did not accept their statements until after the emergence of a miraculous sign, appearing at the hands of each one of them by the order of the Imām عجل الله تعالى فرجه الشريف. This sign indicated

the truth of their claims and the legitimacy of their positions.[156]

117. The Footsteps of Shayṭān

The Qur'ān warns against following the footsteps of Shayṭān, for the cursed one's strategy is to gradualy lead the servant from the realm of simple disobedience to the world of complex transgressions. This includes falsely claiming significant positions with lies and deception, then slipping into the depths of disbelief and apostasy, as attributed to some. This represents the abyss of human wretchedness. The community has been afflicted by some of these individuals during the lives of the Imāms, among them is Abū Muḥammad al-Shāriʿī, whom Shaykh al-Ṭūsī speaks about:

> He was from the companions of Abūl Ḥasan ʿAlī b. Muḥammad and then after him from the companions of al-Ḥasan b. ʿAlī ﷺ. He is the first to claim a position that God did not assign to him and for which he was not qualified. He blasphemed God and His Proofs (Ḥujjah) ﷺ and attributed to them what is not worthy of them, and they are disdainful thereof. The Shīʿah cursed him and turned away from him in dislike.

[156] Majlisī, ʿAllāmah Muḥammad Bāqir, *Biḥār al-Anwār*, Vol. 51, p. 362.

Hārūn says:

> Then he uttered words of disbelief and sacrilege. All such claimants, first, attribute lies to the Imām and claim that they are his representatives, calling the weak to believe in them through such perverted claims. Then they graduate to the claims of self-deification, as seen in the words of Ḥallāj, as expressed by Abū Jaʿfar ash-Shalmaghānī and his like. On all of them be the constant curse of God.[157]

What is interesting is that he mentioned the case of progression, from claiming authority falsely to attracting the weak-hearted to their allegiance, and there are many of them in every era. Hence, it is said,

> There is no false claim without its followers!

118.Exposure by the Deputies

In the era of Imām al-Hādī and al-Askari ﷺ, individuals like Abū Muḥammad al-Shāriʿī, who falsely claimed representation, were easily unmasked, thanks to the presence of the Imāms. However, challenges surfaced during and after the Minor Occultation, as direct communication with the Imām was cut off.

---

157 Ṭūsī, Shaykh Muḥammad b. Ḥasan, *Kitāb al-Ghaybah*, p. 397.

Despite this, the deputies spared no effort in exposing the lies of these individuals. For instance, Muḥammad b. Nāṣir al-Numayrī was among the companions of Imām al-ʿAskarī عليه السلام. When Imām al-ʿAskarī passed away, Muḥammad b. Nāṣir al-Numayrī claimed the position of Abū Jaʿfar Muḥammad b. ʿUthmān, asserting himself as the deputy of Imām al-Mahdī عجل الله فرجه الشريف and claiming to be the gateway to the Imām. God عز وجل exposed him for his apostasy and ignorance. Abū Jaʿfar Muḥammad b. ʿUthmān cursed him, disassociated from him, and denounced him.

There are reports that he cunningly tried to approach the deputy appointed by the Imām to gain his sympathy or extend an apology. However, his entry was denied, and he was turned away, left with disappointment.

119. The Depths of Lowliness

Astonishingly, some of the deviants and claimants of Babism (being gateways to the Imām) during the time of the Minor Occultation reached extreme levels of theological deviation. Take the case of al-Numayrī, who not only declared himself a messenger and a prophet but also insisted that Imām al-Hādī sent him. His beliefs included ideas like reincarnation, an exaggerated view of Imām al-ʿAskarī's عليه السلام position, and even the deification of him.

But it does not end there. He also reached the peak of moral deviation, as he also believed in the permissibility of marrying blood relations of prohibited degree (maḥram(s)) and same sex marriage. He believed that sodomy was an act of humility, meekness, and modesty on the part of the receiver and that it was an occasion of pleasure and delight for the active partner, and that God does not disallow any of such things!

What is even more perplexing is that such individuals had followers who disagreed among themselves about their successors. It was reported that when al-Numayrī fell ill before his death, he was asked about his successor. With a heavy, weak, and stuttering tongue, he muttered:

> Aḥmad.

No one knew which Aḥmad he referred to. His followers split into three groups, each asserting a different successor: one believed it was his son Aḥmad, another thought it was Aḥmad b. Muḥammad b. Mūsā b. Furāt, and a third group claimed it was Aḥmad b. Abī Ḥusayn b. Bushr b. Yazīd. They went their separate ways without reaching an agreement. [158]

120.Deception and Capturing the Hearts

One of the characteristics of false claimants in every era is deception, capturing the hearts of the masses with falsehood, and mesmerizing their minds with it, even in the

---

[158] Ṭūsī, Shaykh Muḥammad b. Ḥasan, *Kitāb al-Ghaybah*, p. 399.

presence of clear evidence. When Shayṭān seizes control of a person, he guides them as if driving a beast.

Among these deceivers was Ibn Abī al-Azāqir, who, upon his apostasy, narrated every lie, deception, and blasphemy to the Banū Basṭam. He attributed these falsehoods to Shaykh Abū al-Qāsim Ḥusayn b. Rūḥ, and they accepted and propagated them until Abū al-Qāsim (Imām al-Mahdī عجل الله تعالى فرجه الشريف) denounced and disassociated himself from Ibn Abī al-Azqar. He condemned him, warned the Banū Basṭam against associating with him, and ordered them to curse and disown him. However, they continued to support him.

When Ibn Abī al-Azāqir was shown the letter of condemnation, he wept profusely and said,

> This message has a very profound secret dimension. The curse is banishment. The meaning of his word, May God curse him, is May God banish him from punishment and Fire. Now you know my position.

He touched the ground with his cheeks and said:

> You must keep this matter a secret.[159]

What kind of distortion and deception is greater than turning curses into mercy? And how foolish is someone to support such a false claimant against the appointed deputy of their Imām of the Time?

---

[159] Ṭūsī, Shaykh Muḥammad b. Ḥasan, *Kitāb al-Ghaybah*, p. 404.

121. The Extent of Communication

The narrations describing the relationship between the Shīʿah and their Imām during the Minor Occultation indicate that the Imām's correspondences encompassed a wide range of Muslim lands. This implies a network of connections between the Imām ﷻ and his four deputies on one side, and the broader community of his followers on the other. Such connections showcase the Imām's compassion for his Shīʿah, a sentiment that persists even through the Major Occultation.

An additional testament to this is a personal account from someone residing with al-Qāsim b. ʿAlāʾ, who lived during the times of Imāms al-Hādī and al-Askari عليهما السلام. He recalls,

> I experienced this while staying with him in the town of Rān in Azerbaijan (Ādhirbāyjān). Continuous letters were arriving from our esteemed master, the Master of the Age, through Abū Jaʿfar Muḥammad b. ʿUthmān ʿĀmarī, and later through Abūl Qāsim Ḥusayn b. Rūḥ, may their souls be blessed. Then, for two months, the letters ceased to arrive. This caused him great concern[160].

This anecdote highlights their connection to the Imām ﷻ and his teachings, illustrating the concern he felt when

[160] Ṭūsī, Shaykh Muḥammad b. Ḥasan, *Kitāb al-Ghaybah*, p. 310.

communication ceased for two months while he was in a distant land.

122.His Prayers against the Oppressors

When the Imām ﷺ raises his heartfelt supplications against those who perpetrate injustice, he begins with two crucial points. Firstly, he emphasizes that God ﷻ does not tolerate oppression by saying:

> O God, I know with certainty that You do not command injustice, nor do You accept it, incline towards it, desire it, love it, or overlook it.[161]

He then acknowledges God's ﷻ control over Umm al-Kitāb (The Mother of the Book), suggesting the possibility of altering the decree concerning the delay of punishment for the oppressors. Even if a decision has been made, he humbly implores:

> If you have set for them a time that must be reached, or if you have written for them periods to attain, then You commanded, and Your speech is the truth, and Your promise is true:
>
> > God erases what He wills and confirms [what He wills], and with Him is the Mother of the Book.

---

[161] Majlisī, 'Allāmah Muḥammad Bāqir, *Biḥār al-Anwār*, Vol. 92, p. 275.

﴿يَمحُو اللّٰهُ ما يَشاءُ وَيُثبِتُ ۖ وَعِندَهُ أُمُّ الكِتابِ﴾

﴿yamḥū llāhu mā yashāʾu wa-yuthbitu wa-ʿindahū ummu l-kitābi﴾

﴿God effaces and confirms whatever He wishes and with Him is the Mother Book﴾*[162]

So, I ask You, with everything Your prophets and messengers have asked You, and I ask You with what Your righteous servants and near angels have asked You, to erase that from the Mother of the Book.[163]

The Imām ﷺ then outlines the consequences he wishes upon the oppressors:

So that their deadlines draw near, their durations are fulfilled, their days elapse, their lifespans are cut short, their wrongdoers are ruined, give some of them power over others until none of them remain, and none are spared, their groups disperse, their weapons are surrendered, and their unity is shattered.[164]

---

[162] Sūrat ar-Raʿd, Verse 39.

* Cf. 43:4.

[163] Ibid.

[164] Ibid.

123. Diverse Letters

The letters from Imām al-Mahdī ﷻ were diverse, encompassing matters of belief, jurisprudence, interpretation, ethics, and more. Each letter held a connection to the concerns of the Ummah, offering profound insights applicable to any era. Yet, the deep emotional bond between the Imām and his followers prompted some to share their troubles with him.

For instance, one individual secretly married a woman, and when the matter unfolded, she bore him a daughter. Overwhelmed with distress, he poured out his concerns, expressing his feelings in a letter to the Imām. The Imām's reply was for the man not to worry. His daughter lived for four years. Then a letter came to the man that stated,

> God has patience, while you were hasty.[165]

Noteworthy in this context is that the Imām's acknowledgement of the lack of patience among the servants—including the one to whom the letter was sent—came without their request. The Imām intended to increase their insight into their affairs. There is a lesson for all of us in that, to sense the Imām's care for his devotees in the era of the Major Occultation, even if meeting him or receiving a letter from him is not feasible.

---

165 Ṣadūq, Shaykh Muḥammad b. ʿAlī, *Kamāl al-Dīn wa Tamām al-Niʿmah*, Vol. 2, p. 489.

124.Forgetting him as a Punishment

Forgetting things now and then is a natural part of being human, but it turns into a heart-wrenching ordeal when it becomes a punishment from the divine. This happens when we fall short in remembering God ﷻ and His representative عجل الله تعالى فرجه الشريف. In such moments, forgetfulness becomes a form of divine discipline for our negligence. It is widely acknowledged that such forgetfulness often leads to other shortcomings.

In this light, let us reflect on the beautiful words found in *Mikyāl al-Makārim*:

> A sentence of Shaykh ʿAmrī is quoted in *Kamāl al-Dīn wa Tamām al-Niʿmah*:
>
> > Do not erase the remembrance of Ḥaḍrat from our hearts.

Ponder upon these words.

It is an important component of Duʿāʾ, and the Shīʿah are advised to include such words in their invocations. We should never ignore this important point. We must keep them in mind, especially when we have high hopes of having our invocations accepted. We must beseech God and request Him not to make us negligent of the Imām's remembrance.

We must not delay this so much that one is afflicted with the malady of unawareness before he starts praying. According to the traditions of the Holy Imāms ﷺ, the believer must pray before the descent of calamities. One should avoid all such sins that deprive one of the Imām's remembrance because it is a great misfortune, as mentioned in the supplications of the Imāms:

> O God! Forgive us those of our sins that cause the descent of misfortune (and wretchedness).

Indeed, the wretchedness of forgetting the remembrance of the Imām is such an unfortunate thing that it makes one liable for calamities and misfortune in this life as well as the Hereafter.[166]

---

[166] Iṣfahānī, Sayyid Muḥammad Taqī Mūsawī, *Mikyāl al-Makārim*, Vol. 2, p. 284.

During the Occultation

1. Following the Imām's Methodology

Merely yearning for the Imām ﷻ and wishing to meet him is not enough for a believer. It is essential to adopt his methodology by adhering to the rulings of a qualified jurist (marjaʿ al-taqlīd). Those who fail to follow a jurist cannot truly claim to love the Imām, as love for him entails obeying his representative in matters of what is permissible and forbidden. Similarly, even those who follow a jurist but fail to act according to his rulings cast doubt on their love for the Imām. Jurists serve as the appointed authorities by the Imām over us, diligently clarifying religious rulings for those seeking to adhere to Sharīʿah law.

This advice echoes that of Imām Jaʿfar aṣ-Ṣādiq ﷺ to his followers, after he clarified the prohibition of resorting to arbitration or adjudication by oppressors:

> They should look to those among you who have transmitted our traditions, understand our lawful and unlawful matters, and know our rules. Let them be satisfied with them as judges, for I have appointed them as arbiters among you.[167]

2. Provisions (rizq) through His Representative

Provisions, both material and spiritual, flow through the awaited representative ﷻ as decreed by God ﷻ on the Night of Destiny, where all matters are ordained.

---

167 Kulaynī, Shaykh Muḥammad b. Yaʿqūb, *al-Kāfī*, Vol. 1, p. 169.

Therefore, connecting with the Imām emotionally, ideologically, and behaviorally, amplifies these provisions and bestows abundant blessings. This is because the Imām is not merely a passive recipient of the decrees, but has the authority to intercede with God to alter the destinies of creation. We can say that God has given the Imām the position of a unified will, where his desires align with the Will of God, without the need for explicit supplication.

Therefore, it is inconceivable for Imām Muḥammad al-Mahdī to neglect those eager souls seeking perfection, whether they express it aloud or hold it silently in their hearts, without extending his guidance and support. Success in this domain, throughout the two periods of Occultation, was only achieved by those who sincerely knocked on his door and turned towards the Imām with unwavering commitment in seeking his help.

3. Overseeing the Deeds

It is no wonder believers are urged to reaffirm their allegiance of obedience to the Imām of their time, as he oversees their deeds, as God says:

﴿وَقُلِ اعْمَلُوا فَسَيَرَى اللَّهُ عَمَلَكُمْ وَرَسُولُهُ وَالْمُؤْمِنُونَ﴾

﴾*wa-quli 'malū fa-sa-yarā llāhu 'amalakum wa-rasūluhū wa-l-mu'minūna*﴿

﴿*And say, 'Go on working: God will see your conduct, and His Apostle and the faithful [as well]'*﴾[168]

Who are these believers who share in the oversight of deeds alongside God ﷻ and His Messenger ﷺ? They are God's ﷻ representatives who have been endowed with infallibility and guardianship, the only ones that can be rightfully included in the same category as God ﷻ and His Messenger. This is also reinforced in the following verse:

﴿إِنَّمَا وَلِيُّكُمُ اللَّهُ وَرَسُولُهُ وَالَّذِينَ آمَنُوا
الَّذِينَ يُقِيمُونَ الصَّلَاةَ وَيُؤْتُونَ الزَّكَاةَ وَهُمْ رَاكِعُونَ﴾

﴿*innamā waliyyukumu llāhu wa-rasūluhū wa-lladhīna āmanū lladhīna yuqīmūna ṣ-ṣalāta wa-yu'tūna z-zakāta wa-hum rāki'ūna*﴾

﴿*Your guardian is only God, His Apostle, and the faithful who maintain the prayer and give the zakāt while bowing down*﴾[169]

Moreover, when Imām aṣ-Ṣādiq ؑ was questioned about the believers referenced in the verse:

---

[168] Sūrat at-Tawbah, Verse 105.

[169] Sūrat al-Mā'idah, Verse 55.

﴾And say, 'Go on working: God will see your conduct, and His Apostle and the faithful [as well]'﴿[170]

He said:

> They are the Imāms.

4. The Continuity of the Line of Martyrdom

The revolution of Imām al-Ḥusayn ﷺ began and will only cease when this revolution bears its full fruits, and that will only be with the appearance of his son, Imām al-Mahdī ﷺ. The companions of Imām al-Ḥusayn ﷺ are not only those who were martyred with him on the day of ʿĀshūrā', but Imām al-Ḥusayn ﷺ has companions in every era, joining the ranks of the martyrs with him—in varying degrees—they are those who follow in the footsteps of his descendants in every aspect of existence.

Therefore, none of us need to know their rank or their proximity to the Imām of their time, for the nature of the era of Occultation dictates the concealment of the ranks of the servants. It is sufficient for us to be among the followers of our Imām ﷺ, written in his records in the unseen world, and that alone suffices as a source of pride and success!

---

[170] Sūrat at-Tawbah, Verse 105.

5. Constant Remembrance

The rank of the infallible is greater than we can imagine; they are the perfect example of implementing the will of God ﷻ in every aspect of their lives. Even their sleep differs from that of others, as their eyes may rest, but their hearts remain vigilant. Why else would the awaiting believer greet Imām al-Mahdī ﷮ in Ziyārah Āl Yāsīn in all his states, whether standing, sitting, bowing, or prostrating, while reciting prayers and glorifications? It is because Imām al-Mahdī ﷮ is constantly turning towards God ﷻ, mindful of Him in every moment, which makes him deserving of our continuous salutations.

Hence, the believer, in proportion to their remembrance of God ﷻ, deserves peace and blessings from the angels. Conversely, if they become heedless or commit a sin, the angels withdraw their blessings, leaving them vulnerable to the whispers of Shayṭān. Thus, whoever seeks to emulate their Imām should strive to minimize heedlessness as much as possible. If a whisper from Shayṭān touches them, they should hasten to remembrance, restoring vigor to their soul.

6. Sincerity in Asking

Some may think that if they ask God ﷻ for a matter involving hastening the Imām's reappearance and express readiness to support their Imām, yet lack personal readiness for such support, they justify it to themselves by saying it is merely a gesture of goodwill and a means of seeking nearness. They often view it as a prelude to asking for other needs afterward. However, this should not be the case. It is not fitting for a servant to utter anything other than what is truly in their heart when addressing their Lord. Doing so resembles lying in the realm of worship, even if unintentional, as they request something they do not have the internal desire for or show no effort towards achieving.

That is why Sayyid b. Ṭāwūs warned against insincerity when reciting in Du'ā' al-Iftitāḥ:

> and grant us death in Your way

especially when one is not truly prepared for it. [171]

7. Changing the Hearts

One of the eloquent phrases of Du'ā' Zamān al-Ghaybah (the du'ā' of the time of the Occultation) is the part where we read:

وَاجْعَلْ قَلْبِي لَيِّنًا لِوَلِيِّكَ

> and make my heart lenient towards Your Representative[172]

---

[171] Sayyid b. Ṭāwūs, *Iqbāl al-A'māl*, Vol. 1, p. 61.

[172] Ṣadūq, Shaykh Muḥammad b. 'Alī, *Kamāl al-Dīn wa Tamām al-Ni'mah*, Vol. 2, p. 512.

Meaning that the believer is asking for their Imām ﷺ to shape their heart as he sees fit. God ﷻ has the power to influence the hearts of individuals, so why wouldn't He grant His representative the same authority, especially since the Imām's will aligns with God's ﷻ will?

The Noble Qur'ān mentions numerous examples of divine intervention in the hearts of believers, such as the events that occurred to the people of the Cave and the mother of Mūsā. The Noble Qur'ān also mentions God's ﷻ intervention in the hearts of disbelievers:

﴿وَقَذَفَ فِي قُلُوبِهِمُ الرُّعْبَ﴾

﴿*wa-qadhafa fī qulūbihimu r-ruʿba*﴾

﴿*and He cast terror into their hearts*﴾[173]

If the Imām ﷺ intervenes with the hearts of those who love him, there would be no room for the intervention of others. It has been reported from Imām aṣ-Ṣādiq ﷺ that God instills fear in the hearts of the enemies of religion when facing the supporters of the Imām. It is narrated that he said:

> But when our Qā'im rises and our Mahdī appears, God will remove fear from the hearts of our Shīʿah and place it on the hearts of our enemies. At that moment, each

[173] Sūrat al-Aḥzāb, Verse 26.

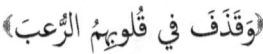

> of our Shīʿah would be sharper than a spear and braver than a lion.[174]

8. Benefitting from him during the Occultation

The believer can benefit from the blessings of their Imām عجل الله تعالى فرجه الشريف during his Occultation, even if this benefit is not as complete as it would be during his presence. It is similar to someone stepping out of their house and enjoying the warmth of the sun's rays above their head, even if clouds obscure it; they still feel its light and follow its guidance, even if they cannot see it with their own eyes. Likewise, some sincere believers among the awaiting ones experience this, where the time of Occultation does not feel much different from the time of appearance. It is similar to the experience of some individuals during the time of previous Imāms عليهم السلام, where they could not physically see the Imām due to being in distant lands, making communication difficult in that era.

The Holy Prophet ﷺ was asked about benefiting from the Imām during his Occultation. He said:

> By the One Who sent me with Prophethood! Surely they will benefit from his light and gain from his

[174] Majlisī, ʿAllāmah Muḥammad Bāqir, *Biḥār al-Anwār*, Vol. 36, p. 369.

> mastership in his occultation like the people derive benefit from the sun when the clouds hide it.[175]

It was also narrated that Imām al-Mahdī ﷻ himself said:

> As for how people will benefit from me during my Occultation, it is like getting benefits from the sun, which is concealed by the clouds. And I am the security for the people on the face of the earth, just as stars are security for the inhabitants of the heavens.[176]

9. Not Following other than the Imām

Imagine if we were to believe the sincerity of anyone who claims that what they say has been revealed to them, or the sincerity of what they see in a dream, what would set them apart from the prophets?

It is imperative for the believer to be cautious and discerning, and not to allow anyone between them and the Imām ﷻ except for the qualified jurists who have a deep understanding of the objectives of Sharīʿah. Otherwise, straying from the right path will lead one into the valley of misguidance, a path that many unfortunately find themselves on in today's world.

---

175 Ṣadūq, Shaykh Muḥammad b. ʿAlī, *Kamāl al-Dīn wa Tamām al-Niʿmah*, Vol. 1, p. 253.

176 Majlisī, ʿAllāmah Muḥammad Bāqir, *Biḥār al-Anwār*, Vol. 52, p. 92.

This is confirmed by the warning from Imām aṣ-Ṣādiq ﷺ against blindly following someone without examining their qualifications. Imām aṣ-Ṣādiq warned:

> Beware of following a person other than the Imām, and believing everything they say.[177]

Here, we add that those who initially follow the path of falsehood with intent, even if it is just at the beginning, cannot be excused if they end up lost at the end of the road, even if that was not their intention.

10. Reviving the Religion

One of the characteristics of the blessed Mahdī government is that the Imām will restore the religion to its essence. Over the years, the features of religion have changed, leading to a misunderstanding of the Qur'ān and Sunnah as they were revealed.

Therefore, one of the greatest blessings of the Imām's reappearance—aside from establishing justice—is the revival of neglected aspects of religion, and the elimination of innovations that have infiltrated it, particularly by those who strayed from the path of the Ahl al-Bayt.

177 Kulaynī, Shaykh Muḥammad b. Ya'qūb, *al-Kāfī*, Vol. 3, p. 729.

Imām ʿAlī ar-Riḍā ﷺ highlighted this aspect when he prayed for his son, Imām al-Mahdī ﷺ, when he asked God ﷻ to:

> Renew though him the signs of your religion that were erased and your judgments that were destroyed, until you rekindle your religion through him and at his hands as well-defined, pure and sound as it is, free from loopholes and heresies, and until you illumine the murk of unfairness using his justice, and extinguish the fires of atheism through him, and elucidate the positions of truth and concealed justice[178]

11. Continuous Justice

The reappearance and spread of justice by the Imām ﷺ throughout the earth was not just the wish of the prophets and their successors. As the accounts of the miraculous journey (Isrāʾ and Miʿrāj) show, this blessed end, the era of the Mahdī rule extending until Judgement Day, was decreed by God ﷻ. This divine decree has been ordained since the creation of the earth and all that dwells upon it. It is God ﷻ who holds the keys to the heavens and the earth, and He will ensure that everything submits to the Imām ﷺ, all for the fulfillment of the purpose for which the universe was created.

[178] Ṭūsī, Shaykh Muḥammad b. Ḥasan, *Miṣbāḥ al-Mutahajjid wa Silāḥ al-Mutaʿabbid*, Vol. 1, p. 410.

It has been narrated in Ḥadīth al-Miʿrāj:

> By My majesty and glory, I shall reveal My religion through them, and I shall exalt My words through them, and the last of them, I shall purify the earth from My enemies. And I shall make him the absolute master of the whole world. I shall make the wind subservient to his command, and I shall make the hard cloud proof for him so that he may ride upon it to go wherever he likes in the sky and the earth, and I shall assist him with My armies. And I shall strengthen him with My angels. So that My call is raised and all the creatures gather upon My Oneness. Thus, his rulership would endure and continue, and from My friends, I shall make one after the other the leaders of My faith till Qiyāmat.[179]

12. Preparing for his Reappearance

Praying for the reappearance of the Imām (ʿaj), the Master of the Command, is indeed a commendable act. However, in addition to that, the believer should earnestly prepare for his reappearance. This involves actively contributing to the development of a faithful community with the strengths and capabilities bestowed upon them by God (swt).

Indeed, one of the applications of God's (swt) words:

[179] Ṣadūq, Shaykh Muḥammad b. ʿAlī, *Kamāl al-Dīn wa Tamām al-Niʿmah*, Vol. 1, p. 256.

﴿وَمِمَّا رَزَقْنَاهُمْ يُنفِقُونَ﴾

(wa-mimmā razaqnāhum yunfiqūnᵃ)

(and spend˙ out of what We have provided for them)[180]

is directing energies and abilities towards building the society the Imām ﷺ desires.

Every believer should discover the latent potentials within themselves to serve their Imām ﷺ, whether in the era of his appearance or during his Occultation. It is essential to realize that the most significant position a person can reach before their death is one where their will aligns with the Will of their Lord. At that point, God ﷻ unleashes their hidden potentials to be used in the way The Wise chooses, including the path of preparing for the reappearance of His chosen representative ﷺ.

Here, a striking narration from Imām aṣ-Ṣādiq ﷺ highlights his aspiration to serve his awaited son, the Mahdī. He said:

---

180 Sūrat al-Baqarah, Verse 3.

* The expression 'to spend' is used in the Qur'ān elliptically to mean spending in the way of God and for the sake of His pleasure. Cf. 2:195, 261–262, 272; 8:60; 9:34; 47:38; 57:10.

> If I were alive during his time, I would spend my entire life serving him[181]

13. Praying for him Specifically on Fridays

Friday is the anticipated day of Imām al-Mahdī's reappearance, as inferred from some texts. Therefore, it is our duty as believers to increase supplications for his reappearance on this blessed day. We should perform some righteous deeds on his behalf or as a gift to him. Additionally, we should give charity on his behalf and behalf of those dear to him, saying when giving charity:

> O God, this is for You and from You. It is charity on behalf of our master, placed for his safety during his travels and his movements during the hours of night and day. And it is charity on behalf of those whose affairs concern him[182]

Sayyid b. Ṭāwūs summarized these etiquettes beautifully when he said:

> You must give preference to the needs of Imām over your own needs when you are reciting the Namāz-e-Ḥāja (prayer of having your need fulfilled). Before giving ṣadaqah on behalf of your family members, give ṣadaqah on behalf of Imām az-Zamān and pray for

---

[181] Nuʿmānī, Muḥammad b. Ibrāhīm, *Kitāb al-Ghaybah*, p. 245.

[182] Sayyid b. Ṭāwūs, *al-Amān min Akhṭār al-Asfār wal-Azmān*, p. 38.

> him. Additionally, give him preference in every good deed. All these things will invite the Imām's ﷺ attention and favors.[183]

And most importantly, we should strive to be among those who call for his obedience and lead others to his path, instead of being preoccupied with imaginary signs of his appearance or the like, which have no practical benefit. Let us invest our efforts in areas that yield tangible results, rather than pursuing endeavors that bear no fruit.

14. The Most Important Groups in the Ummah

Two key groups play an essential role in our community—the learners, whether in religious or worldly knowledge, and the leaders who guide us. Together, they shape the cultural and political landscape of our society. Imām al-Mahdī ﷺ outlined their roles in his well-known supplication during the period of Occultation. If individuals from these two classes fulfill their responsibilities, it will hasten the blessed reappearance of our Imām ﷺ.

For the first group, Imām al-Mahdī ﷺ seeks God's ﷻ guidance for them to exert effort and show willingness to learn:

---

183 Sayyid b. Ṭāwūs, *Kashf al-Muḥajjah li-Thamarat al-Muhjah*, p. 209.

> and those who are learning with diligence and desire to learn.[184]

The former pertains to physical efforts, while the latter relates to inclination. Those who combine these qualities successfully achieve their goals in both knowledge acquisition and practical application.

Turning to the second group, the leaders, the Imām ﷳ also asks God ﷻ to bestow upon them external and internal qualities:

> Let the rulers be just and compassionate.[185]

He asks God ﷻ to give them success in cultivating a sense of compassion towards the subjects, which is an internal matter, and success in establishing justice, an external matter. This highlights the importance of balancing internal growth with external action, a principle emphasized in the Imām's teachings. Success in any field requires attention to both aspects, a truth recognized by thinkers and researchers alike.

---

[184] al-Kafʿamī, Ibrāhīm b. ʿAlī, *Miṣbāḥ Kafʿamī*, p. 280.

[185] Ibid.

15. Enduring Roughness in Life

Believers need to learn to endure some difficulties in life. This is because life does not always follow a smooth path, and some acts of worship require strength and resilience.

If someone becomes accustomed to a life of ease and luxury, they may falter when faced with challenges in their responsibilities. Such a person will not be able to answer the call of our Imām ☙ at the time of his reappearance, because one who is sluggish during the period of Occultation will remain sluggish during the time of reappearance.

As Imām 'Alī ☙ said:

Indeed, the wild tree grows strongest and is slower in dying off[186]

Generally, individuals accustomed to extravagance and indulgence find it challenging to think beyond their comfort and interests. They are confined within the sphere of immediate pleasures, making it difficult to contemplate or care about matters outside their indulgence-oriented mindset. As God ☙ said in the Noble Qur'ān:

$$﴿ما جَعَلَ اللَّهُ لِرَجُلٍ مِن قَلْبَيْنِ في جَوفِهِ﴾$$

---

[186] Sharīf Raḍī, Muḥammad b. al-Ḥusayn, *Nahj al-Balāghah*, p. 418.

⟨mā jaʿala llāhu li-rajulin min qalbayni fī jawfihī⟩

⟨God has not put two hearts within any man⟩[187]

16. Repentance before the Reappearance

Turning towards repentance is the best way to bring happiness to the heart of our Imām ☝. It involves leaving behind all sins and transgressions and making a firm commitment not to repeat them in the future. Choosing righteousness and abandoning wrongdoing during the time of Occultation holds greater significance than doing so after the Imām ☝ reappears. It is like the early Muslims who believed and remained steadfast before the conquest of Makkah.

It is widely acknowledged that one who believes during times of obscurity, like black on white, is closer to God ☝ than one who believes after witnessing clear and manifest signs. This belief is supported by what is narrated from the Prophet ☝:

> Know that the faith of those who shall be there in the last period shall be astonishing and certainly great. There will be no prophet among them and Divine Proof (The Imām) will be hidden from them; despite

---

[187] Sūrat al-Aḥzāb, Verse 4.

> that, they will believe in black upon white (reference to written words only)[188]

True believers are embarrassed before three: from their Lord who observes their deeds, from their Imām of the Time who knows about them, and from the Angel who records their sins.

17. True Awaiting

Imagine if a farmer neglected his duty to plow the land, sow the seeds, and tend to his crops, and instead just sat idly by waiting for rain to fall. Would he ever reap a harvest? Conversely, the true farmer is the one who diligently plows, sows, and nurtures the land, and then looks up at the sky, eagerly awaiting rainfall. Their sincerity is evident in the anxiety and sorrow they feel when the rain fails to arrive.

Similarly, a sincere believer eagerly awaiting the reappearance dedicates themselves to duties during the Occultation, patiently awaiting the blessed arrival of their Imām عجل الله تعالى فرجه الشريف. As the period of Occultation lengthens, their sorrow deepens, much like a farmer yearning for rain. Consequently, the believer's sense of longing is renewed with the setting of each Friday, as it is the day he is expected to reappear.

---

[188] Ṣadūq, Shaykh Muḥammad b. ʿAlī, *Kamāl al-Dīn wa Tamām al-Niʿmah*, Vol. 1, p. 288.

18. Magnetic field of The Mahdī

Those who orbit the orbit of Imām al-Mahdī عجّل الله تعالى فرجه الشريف consistently with piety and steadfastness will find themselves drawn into its magnetic circle, following in the footsteps of his elite companions. Anyone who enters this sacred circle can never leave it, but rather grows increasingly attached to it day by day. Conversely, those who commit sins distance themselves from the orbit, let alone entering the circle.

Let us quote here the author of *Mikyāl al-Makārim*, where he says:

> The perfection of rewards and mentioned virtues hinges on the attainment of piety, as stated in His saying:
>
> ﴿إِنَّمَا يَتَقَبَّلُ اللَّهُ مِنَ الْمُتَّقِينَ﴾
>
> ﴾*innamā yataqabbalu llāhu mina l-muttaqīn*[a]﴿
>
> ﴾*God accepts only from the Godwary*﴿[189]
>
> Just as piety has degrees, so does acceptance. Those with stronger piety receive more complete and manifest rewards through their supplications. This principle

---

[189] Sūrat al-Mā'idah, Verse 27.

applies to all religious acts, whether obligatory or voluntary.

We emphasize that the perfection of rewards depends on this, because, based on numerous verses, such as:

﴿أَنِّي لا أُضيعُ عَمَلَ عامِلٍ مِنكُم﴾

﴾*annī lā uḍī'u 'amala āmilin minkum*﴿

﴾*I do not waste the work of any worker among you*﴿[190]

the reward for righteous deeds is inevitable. Even if the doer has committed sins, according to many narrations, the level of reward depends on the level of piety.[191]

19. Allocating Time for Supplication

The awaiting believer constantly remembers their Imām ﷻ whenever they perform an act done for seeking nearness to God ﷻ, whether it is giving charity, visiting a holy site, performing a recommended prayer, attending a mourning session for Ahl al-Bayt, or any other virtuous deed. We stress these sentiments based on the adage, "out of sight, out of mind." Therefore, those who do not renew

---

190 Sūrat Āl 'Imrān, Verse 195.

191 Iṣfahānī, Sayyid Muḥammad Taqī Mūsawī, *Mikyāl al-Makārim*, Vol. 2, p. 48.

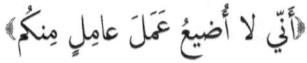

this connection to their Imām ﷻ risk forgetting his remembrance during the period of Occultation.

Hence, it is vital to carve out specific moments for supplication, such as during the Qunūt prayers, before sunset on Fridays, or upon encountering a holy site for the first time, or when bidding farewell to it.

Furthermore, Sayyid b. Ṭāwūs underscores this importance after discussing the recommended supplications following the ʿAṣr prayer on Fridays:

> If you have an excuse for not performing all that we have mentioned after the ʿAṣr prayer on Fridays, then beware of neglecting the supplication, for we know that from the grace of God ﷻ, who has favored us with it, so be consistent with it.[192]

20. Among the Characteristics of the Awaiters

One of the characteristics of the Awaiter is not delving deeply into worldly pursuits, meaning not becoming excessively engrossed in fleeting pleasures, especially if it stems from a desire for excess in living. Such indulgence can lead to hardness of the heart, reluctance to journey towards God ﷻ, and strengthening the influence of Shayṭān in whispering and tempting, as adorning the material world is among the traits of Shayṭān.

---

[192] Sayyid b. Ṭāwūs, *Jamāl al-Usbūʿ*, p. 521.

It is known that following desires aligns one with the party of Shayṭān and his followers. So, how can one be among the Awaiters who aspire to be among the supporters of the Imām عجل الله تعالى فرجه الشريف and the martyrs before him? Indeed, purity of character and aligning oneself with all his noble attributes is one of the most important conditions for being with the Imām عجل الله تعالى فرجه الشريف in this world and being resurrected with him in the Hereafter.

21. Praying for a Pure Heart

Anyone who desires to meet their Imām عجل الله تعالى فرجه الشريف should pray to God عز وجل to purify their heart and limbs. How can one look upon their Imām with eyes they always used to look at the forbidden? How can they address him with a tongue accustomed to sin? How can they greet him with a hand that has been used for wrongdoing? And how can they face their Imām with a heart consumed by worldly desires and limbs tainted by sin?

Therefore, one must strive to refine oneself to be worthy of the honor of meeting the Imām عجل الله تعالى فرجه الشريف, a meeting that is only granted to those with a pure heart. It is this purity of heart that will be the basis of judgment on the Day of Resurrection. If this inner purity is achieved, then we can say: even if a servant is deprived of meeting him in this world, he will not be deprived of meeting him in the Hereafter, a meeting of far greater significance.

22. Hand Tied

A significant source of distress for Imām al-Mahdī عجل الله تعالى فرجه الشريف is finding himself bound by his circumstances and unable to fulfill his duty or change what he finds unacceptable within his community. Witnessing his Shīʿah followers lagging and divided intensifies his anguish. The Imām needs supporters and helpers who understand the gravity of their responsibilities for this mission.

It is well-acknowledged that internal discord among his followers contributes to the delay in his honorable reappearance. If the Imām عجل الله تعالى فرجه الشريف were permitted to employ miraculous means, his reappearance would have occurred decades ago. However, he awaits the gathering of supporters and helpers who will assist him in his blessed movement. Additionally, he awaits the appropriate circumstances for humanity to accept his universal divine message. This will only occur when humanity reaches the peak of maturity and understanding.

As Imām aṣ-Ṣādiq عليه السلام once said:

> Indeed, the wisdom behind the occultation of the Imām will not be known except after his reappearance[193]

[193] Ṣadūq, Shaykh Muḥammad b. ʿAlī, *Kamāl al-Dīn wa Tamām al-Niʿmah*, Vol. 2, p. 482.

23. The Best Deeds of the Ummah

One of our duties during the Occultation is to eagerly await the reappearance of the Imām ﷺ. This obligation is emphasized in various traditions, including:

> The best deed of my Ummah is to await the relief.[194]

> Awaiting the relief is itself a form of relief.[195]

> Awaiting for the reappearance is one of the greatest forms of relief[196]

These narrations highlight the significance of anticipating the Imām's reappearance, while underscoring its true essence. True awaiting entails caring for the welfare of the community, rather than being preoccupied solely with individual concerns. It implies taking action, not just expressing desires and longing for it. This aligns with the teaching of Imām aṣ-Ṣādiq ﷺ, who said:

> Whoever wishes to be a companion and close associate of our Qā'im should await deliverance through him. Moreover, such a person should adopt piety and a virtuous life and continue to anticipate our Qā'im in

---

[194] Ibid., p. 644.

[195] Ṭūsī, Shaykh Muḥammad b. Ḥasan, *Kitāb al-Ghaybah*, p. 459.

[196] Ṣadūq, Shaykh Muḥammad b. ʿAlī, *Kamāl al-Dīn wa Tamām al-Niʿmah*, Vol. 1, p. 320.

> that state. If they live like that and if they die before the advent of the Qā'im, then they will reap the reward of someone who has been with the Qā'im. O my followers, be serious and work hard while awaiting the Qā'im's emergence. O you who are blessed with God's mercy, may you taste the sweetness of the final victory[197]

This is one of the eloquent narrations that explicitly connect the act of awaiting the reappearance with a sincere commitment to piety and righteousness, urging believers to act while striving to attain the best inner virtues. Thus, when the one who waits embodies these qualities, their concern shifts from whether they witness the reappearance of the time or not, as their reward is guaranteed regardless of the outcome.

24. Paying the Religious Dues

Fulfilling one's religious obligations by paying the prescribed dues brings about a profound sense of inner satisfaction. This feeling is particularly pronounced when witnessing the joy on the face of a needy descendant of the Prophet ﷺ or when they contribute to a charitable project that becomes an ongoing charity after their death. It is well known that God ﷻ blesses the wealth that is purified through fulfilling these obligations. It is reported from Imām aṣ-Ṣādiq ؑ that he said:

[197] Ṭūsī, Shaykh Muḥammad b. Ḥasan, *Kitāb al-Ghaybah*, p. 200.

> Nothing is dearer to God than allocating dirhams for the Imām [Khums]. God will elevate each dirham spent for this purpose in Paradise, making it as substantial as Mount Uḥud.[198]

This divine blessing manifests when God ﷻ opens unexpected sources of happiness for His servant, their family, and descendants. The act of spending is a means of purifying wealth, and it holds even greater significance when done in the path of pleasing God's ﷻ greatest authority عجل الله تعالى فرجه الشريف and by his command. Those who do so obey the Imām's commands, and he does not overlook those who follow his directives, especially when their spending goes against their desires.

25. Financial Accounting

It is the duty of a believer not to let the accounts of the Creator and the created accumulate without settling them by allowing more than a year to pass without paying this divine right. Shayṭān may interfere and create obstacles to deter them. It becomes challenging for one to fulfill these obligations when the cumulative amount becomes substantial.

It is well-known that fulfilling the obligatory amount from one's wealth, including the share of the Imām of the Khums, is not merely an act of generosity or kindness.

198 Kulaynī, Shaykh Muḥammad b. Yaʿqūb, *al-Kāfī*, Vol. 2, p. 712.

Rather, it is a right owed to God ﷻ and His Messenger ﷺ. A person is required to allocate this share from their wealth, similar to how each partner settles the share of their co-partner. Despite this, it is considered one of the means of obtaining forgiveness, divine satisfaction, blessings, and financial prosperity, as well as overcoming troubles and challenges.

26. Praying for Righteous Offspring

The required effort in being blessed with righteous offspring should not be delayed until the psychological and intellectual formation of the child begins. Rather, it should start even before the conception of the child, and then planning for it should begin.

It is widely recognized that supplication (duʿāʾ) plays a crucial role in achieving this goal. Therefore, it is recommended for spouses to recite the following verse consistently:

﴿رَبَّنا هَب لَنا مِن أَزواجِنا وَذُرِّيّاتِنا قُرَّةَ أَعيُنٍ وَاجعَلنا لِلمُتَّقينَ إِمامًا﴾

﴿rabbanā hab lanā min azwājinā wa-dhurriyyātinā qurrata aʿyunin wa-jʿalnā li-l-muttaqīna imāmaⁿ﴾

﴿Our Lord! Grant us comfort in our spouses and descendants, and make us imāms of the Godwary﴾[199]

[199] Sūrat al-Furqān, Verse 74.

Indeed, those who frequently repeat this supplication, whether during the day or night, in all their states, including moments of prostration and qunut, may hope to be blessed with exceptional offspring. This supplication is answered, as it is a weighty request, beseeching God ﷻ to grant His guided representative someone who will support and assist him. Some of our scholars were born through the blessings of their parents' prayers.

27. Resistance to Temptation

One of the characteristics of the followers of the Awaited Imām is their resistance to succumbing to worldly desires. They strive for perfection by resisting the temptations of their desires. Waiting for the reappearance of the Imām عجّل الله تعالى فرجه الشريف entails a constant commitment and steadfast struggle. It is not merely about expressing wishes, lamentations, and yearnings. The sincere Awaiter trains themselves to live a disciplined life that includes hardships. Those who strive under the Imām's banner are afflicted with hardships similar to those faced by their enemies, as was the case in the early days of Islam.

Therefore, those inclined towards lethargy and worldly indulgence are not candidates to be among his supporters. This is an ongoing principle in the life of nations, where the advocates of God ﷻ, including the prophets and righteous leaders, have historically been among the most resilient in enduring hardships.

28. Financial Obligation Towards the Imām

How can someone who neglects to give our Imām his rightful share, which God has ordained for him from their wealth, shed tears of longing for his meeting? Have you ever seen someone yearning to meet their debtor against whom they will stand in a legal dispute when they meet in court? Therefore, it is more appropriate for someone like this to reflect on their situation so they can rectify it and discipline themselves to go against their desires, rather than merely expressing emotions that require no effort.

Hence, we believe that many, when surprised by the time of reappearance, wish for its delay to avoid being implicated in the reproach or even punishment of their Imām due to their failure to fulfill what could have alleviated the burdens of the Shīʿah, especially in times of hardship and oppression on the weak and those awaiting his blessed rule.

29. Forty Days for the Imām

A believer should assign themselves forty days dedicated to praying for the Imām. It is fitting to utilize the blessed month of Ramaḍān for this purpose. For instance, one can stay awake during the predawn hours (*saḥar*) to recite Duʿāʾ al-ʿAhd, for example. Additionally, during the month of Ramaḍān, one can include the last ten days of Shaʿbān or the first ten days of Shawwāl.

How beautiful it is for the believer to commit to this supplication throughout the year, reciting it every morning to start the day by remembering the Imām of their time عجّل الله تعالى فرجه الشريف and pledging allegiance to him in support. In addition to the verbal commitment, there should also be a practical commitment to adhering to the Sharīʿah within its boundaries. This complete integration makes Forty Days a holistic journey in every sense of the word.

30. Rushing to Fulfill Needs

A believer cherishes the opportunity to hasten in fulfilling the needs of their Imām عجّل الله تعالى فرجه الشريف. They feel a deep sense of honor when they strive to meet the needs of others on behalf of their Imām عجّل الله تعالى فرجه الشريف, even though he is in Occultation from his followers. We ponder: How much joy does this action bring to the heart of our Imām عليه السلام, when done with such intention? How much closer does it draw us to our Imām?

Let them carefully select from among his followers those who are closest to him and possess the greatest piety. For the heart of the believer is the throne of the Most Merciful, and the purer the heart, the closer it is to the throne of God عزّ وجلّ. Therefore, the believer should seek out the most pious followers who are enduring trials in this world. Indeed, serving them is the red elixir!

31. Establishing Universal Justice

When a believer wishes to be among the martyrs in the path of Imām al-Mahdī عجل الله تعالى فرجه الشريف, as stated in Du'ā' al-'Ahd, they must be sincere in their supplication. This entails preparing themselves wholeheartedly for the task. Be no less supportive of the Imām of your time than those individuals who we see nowadays obeying the commands of corrupt leaders, sacrificing themselves for their misguided causes.

Just as the martyrs of Badr resisted the tyrants of Quraysh in their time, the martyrs of our Imām al-Mahdī عجل الله تعالى فرجه الشريف work towards establishing universal justice. If you find yourself called to be among them, know that you will be among those spreading justice across the world for as long as God عز وجل wills.

32. Bringing People to God عز وجل

One of the most important tasks of believers in the time of Occultation is to invite people to God عز وجل, encourage actions that draw them closer to Him, and instill love for Him in their hearts. It also involves guiding the lost souls back to Him. This noble endeavor not only brings us closer to God عز وجل, His Messenger ﷺ, and our Imām عليه السلام, but it also has far-reaching effects. By helping even one lost soul find its path, we prevent further misguidance and corruption from spreading among humanity.

Supporting this notion is what is reported that God ﷻ inspired Mūsā ﷺ:

> God ﷻ inspired Mūsā, saying:
>
> > Make Me beloved to My creatures, and make My creatures beloved to Me.
>
> Mūsā asked:
>
> > O Lord, how can I do that?
>
> God ﷻ replied:
>
> > Mention to them My blessings and favors so they may love Me. For to bring back someone who turned away from My gate or is misguided is better for you than worshiping for a hundred years, fasting during its days and standing in prayer through its nights.
>
> Mūsā asked:
>
> > And who is the one who turned away from Your gate?
>
> God ﷻ said:
>
> > It is the disobedient and the rebellious.

Mūsā inquired:

> Then who is the one who is misguided?

God ﷻ replied:

> It is those who are ignorant of the Imām of their time. Teach them the laws of their religion, what their Lord is worshiped with, and how to attain His pleasure. So help them know him, and one who knows the Imām and then becomes absent from him, those who are ignorant of the laws of their religion, teach it to them.[200]

It is worth noting: Whenever a servant brings sinners to the door of his Master, they increase in proximity and esteem before God ﷻ as well. This noble deed is among the best ways to get closer to the Imām of our time عجل الله تعالى فرجه الشريف as well.

33. The Mahdī-centered Family

One of the greatest concerns of a believer is to establish a Mahdī-centered family, which is achieved through purposeful upbringing guided by their outlook and words. As a believer reaches a certain level of faith, they influence others not only through their perspective but also through their speech and guidance. Moreover, duʿāʾ for their

---

200 al-Ḥurr al-ʿĀmilī, Shaykh Muḥammad, *al-Jawāhir al-Saniyyah fī al-Aḥādīth al-Qudsiyyah*, p. 156.

offspring in secret has a profound impact on their well-being, following the example of Prophet Ibrāhīm ﵇.

When God ﷻ appointed him as an Imām for the people, Ibrāhīm ﵇ also requested Imāmate for his descendants. God ﷻ said:

﴿وَإِذِ ابْتَلَىٰ إِبْرَاهِيمَ رَبُّهُ بِكَلِمَاتٍ فَأَتَمَّهُنَّ ۖ قَالَ إِنِّي جَاعِلُكَ لِلنَّاسِ إِمَامًا ۖ قَالَ وَمِن ذُرِّيَّتِي ۖ قَالَ لَا يَنَالُ عَهْدِي الظَّالِمِينَ﴾

﴿wa-'idhi btalā ibrāhīma rabbuhū bi-kalimātin fa-'atammahunna qāla innī jā'iluka li-n-nāsi imāman qāla wa-min dhurriyyatī qāla lā yanālu 'ahdī ẓ-ẓālimīn[a]﴾

﴿And when his Lord tested Ibrāhīm with certain words, and he fulfilled them, He said, 'I am making you the Imām of mankind.' Said he, 'And from among my descendants?' He said, 'My pledge does not extend to the unjust'﴾*[201]

Thus, the believer's concern is not only for their righteousness but also for their children to be among the righteous, so they can be supporters of the greatest reformer ﷺ during his Occultation and presence.

---

[201] Sūrat al-Baqarah, Verse 124.

* That is, the spiritual and temporal guide and leader of mankind. For other Qur'ānic occurrences of this term, see 17:71; 25:74; 28:5; 32:24; 36:12.

34. Praying Behind the Imām

As you stand in prayer before God ﷻ, imagine yourself standing behind your Imām عليه السلام, seeking his assistance to help you with your prayer. It is as if you are saying,

> O my beloved Imām! I face a daunting trial, as prayer can be heavy on hearts that lack humility.

After completing your prayer, if you notice any deficiencies in your prayer, ask God ﷻ to elevate your prayer alongside that of your Imām of the Time عجل الله تعالى فرجه الشريف. This means sending your flawed deed alongside his perfect ones! Therefore, let each of us be diligent in performing prayers at their earliest times. Just as someone with goods they intend to send to a land they fear for would place them with the merchandise of a trusted ruler to ensure their safe arrival, we too should entrust our prayers to the Imām of our time عجل الله تعالى فرجه الشريف.

35. Seizing the Night of Mid-Shaʿbān

After Laylat al-Qadr, the most auspicious night of the year is the Night of Mid-Shaʿbān. Let us all strive to stay awake during this special night and fill it with extra worship and remembrance of God ﷻ. As we recite in the supplication of this night:

> O God! On this night, the seekers have presented their requests before You, and the ambitious have resolved to seek Your guidance. The seekers are hoping for Your

> grace and bounties. And in this night, You bestow Your hidden bounties, the provisions, gifts and presents[202]

Let us try to reach for the blessings and spiritual rewards hidden within this night, for some destinies are written on the Night of Mid-Shaʿbān to be fulfilled on the grand Night of Qadr. If you find your heart lacking softness and your soul unchanged, beseech God ﷻ not to seal your heart on such a night. Then, pray for God ﷻ to shield you from the hellfire in honor of the one who was born on this night, as it is among the greatest rewards.

36. The Closest to His Noble Heart

When the Imām ؏ turns his attention to the people of the earth, who do you think is nearest to his noble heart? The Imām's gaze is upon the people who spend their nights in worship, as a sample of those distinguished. It has been narrated that when he encountered Ibn Mahziyār al-Ahvāzī, he said,

> Welcome. Do you know a man by the name of Jaʿfar b. Ḥamdān al-Khāṣībī from the city of Ahvāz?

Ibn Mahziyār replied:

> Yes,

[202] Sayyid b. Ṭāwūs, *Iqbāl al-Aʿmāl*, Vol. 2, p. 697.

So he ﷻ said:

> May God's mercy be on him. How long his nights were (in prayer), and how great his rewards.

The first attribute he praised him for was his commitment to night prayer, as the most noble among this nation are those who uphold the Qur'ān and those who spend their nights in worship.

It is not to suggest that those who sleep through the night from start to finish are excluded from mercy, but they may not hold as special a place in the Imām's heart. Therefore, those who aspire to distinction and closeness with the Imām ﷻ must embody these virtues, following his example. Imām Mūsā al-Kāẓim ﷺ described Imām al-Mahdī ﷻ as:

> Having a wheat complexion with yellowness due to staying awake at night for worship; may my father be sacrificed for him, the one who spends his nights bowing and prostrating[203]

The Imām ﷻ must get an ample share of the devoted follower's duʿā's if they are blessed with the opportunity to spend their nights in worship.

---

203 Majlisī, ʿAllāmah Muḥammad Bāqir, *Biḥār al-Anwār*, Vol. 83, p. 81.

37. The Neglected Duty

One of the best ways to join the ranks of the supporters of the Imām of the Time ﷻ is to fulfill the duty of enjoining good and forbidding evil. If this is not possible at the community level, then at least at the family level.

It is well known that neglecting the duty of enjoining good and forbidding evil results in serious consequences. It is understood here that if every individual were to fulfill their duty within their sphere of influence, whether it be their neighborhood or community, then evil would be eradicated or its scope greatly reduced. The philosophy behind the emergence of the Imām is the fulfillment of this obligation, which was the purpose of the Noble Prophet's ﷺ mission and his call to it.

38. Achieving Sincerity in Worship

Sincerity in worship does not necessitate pushing your soul to its limits or burdening it beyond what it can bear. To foster sincerity, consider dedicating two forty-day periods to cultivating discipline in your soul. The first forty-day period is preliminary, whereby you provide the soul with its lawful natural needs with the intention of strengthening it for worship. Alongside fulfilling your obligatory acts of worship and avoiding what is forbidden, try to incorporate some recommended practices. The second period is complementary, where some struggles are undertaken to discipline and strengthen the soul. Our souls naturally lean towards indulgence and play, but let us try to challenge ourselves and cultivate sincerity during this short period; with time, it will become a lasting trait within us.

39. Women's Role in the Occultation and Reappearance

Women have a role to play in both the era of Occultation and the era of appearance. Gender distinctions do not exist in the realm of souls; they belong to the transient physical world. The Noble Qur'ān presents us with remarkable women from the pre-Islamic era, such as Āsiyā, the wife of Firʿawn (Pharaoh), and Maryam, the mother of ʿĪsā عليه السلام. In Islam, too, we find esteemed women, notably Sayyidah Fāṭimah and her mother and daughter عليهنّ السلام.

These examples demonstrate that women possess the potential for spiritual growth and excellence when they dedicate themselves to serving God عزّ وجلّ and strive for spiritual perfection. While reaching the peak may be challenging for some, striving for higher levels of spirituality is both achievable and desirable.

40. Supplicating to Hasten the Reappearance

Some may wonder:

> Can the reappearance of Imām al-Mahdī عجّل الله تعالى فرجه الشريف truly be hastened by the supplication of an individual?

Considering the immense impact of his return, such as establishing universal justice until the End of Time, it might seem improbable. However, it is possible, and a similar scenario occurred in history, as narrated by Imām aṣ-Ṣādiq ﷺ.

> When the suffering became prolonged for the Children of Isrāʾīl, they clamored and cried to God ﷻ for forty mornings. So, God ﷻ revealed to Mūsā and Hārūn to deliver them from Firʿawn. He relieved them from a hundred and seventy years.

Imām aṣ-Ṣādiq ﷺ then said:

> If you had done the same, God ﷻ would have hastened our relief. But if you do not, then the matter will reach its destined end.[204]

41. Seeking Intercession

We have been instructed to seek intercession when we pray to God ﷻ. Our sins might stand in the way of our prayers being answered, so we turn to those close to God ﷻ, whose prayers are always heard. It is a common practice that when a believer faces challenges and feels like they have run out of options, they seek the help of their Imām, the Imām under whose banner they will be gathered on the Day of Judgment.

---

[204] Majlisī, ʿAllāmah Muḥammad Bāqir, *Biḥār al-Anwār*, Vol. 4, p. 118.

Mīrzā Ḥusayn Nūrī Ṭabrisī reported this du'ā' to be recited at the time of travel:

> In the name of God, the Beneficent, the Merciful. O God! I ask You by the right of Your Walī and Ḥujjat, the Master of the Age, that You make all my affairs easy for me. And suffice me against all oppressors, the unjust, and the traitors, and move them away from me. Bestow me with the companionship of Ḥaḍrat as I have reached the end of my efforts. And suffice me against all enemies and sorrows and griefs and in the religion and children and all of my people and my brothers and all the affairs related to him. Āmīn O, Lord of the worlds, Āmīn.[205]

It is worth noting that when a believer seeks the intercession of their hidden Imām for a need and another fulfills that need for them, it is as if they have fulfilled the need of their Imām ﷺ, because they have completed a task on his behalf. How fortunate is the one chosen to attain this great honor!

42. The Reason for the Setback

When reflecting on many of the narrations, we see a significant resemblance between our nation and the people of Mūsā ﷺ. This resemblance lies in the appointment of

[205] Ṭabrisī, Mīrzā Ḥusayn Nūrī, *Mustadrak al-Wasā'il wa-Mustanbaṭ al-Masā'il*, Vol. 8, p. 138.

Hārūn as a successor to Mūsā, the rejection of Hārūn by his people, and the unbearable harm inflicted upon Mūsā. Moreover, God ﷻ made the people's victory over their enemies contingent on their following Mūsā and Hārūn, when He said:

﴿بِآيَاتِنَا أَنتُمَا وَمَنِ اتَّبَعَكُمَا الْغَالِبُونَ﴾

﴾*bi-'āyātinā antumā wa-mani ttaba'akumā l-ghālibūna*[a]﴿

﴾*With the help of Our signs, you two, and those who follow the two of you, shall be the victors*﴿[206]

From this, we can say that just as the mere presence of Mūsā and his brother in their nation was not sufficient for victory, similarly, in our current era, victory is contingent upon following our Imām عج. Victory requires support and readiness to fight alongside him. This is the secret behind the delay in his reappearance – the lack of a sufficient number of followers who can achieve victory with him.

43. Unlocking our Hidden Potential

Some of us wish to spend in the cause of God ﷻ, hoping to leave behind a continuous charity after our death. However, financial constraints may prevent us from doing so. Nevertheless, there is a pathway open to everyone: utilizing the gifts bestowed upon us by God ﷻ, regardless

---

[206] Sūrat al-Qaṣaṣ, Verse 35.

of whether they are material wealth or not. For instance, those who possess the power of influence through their words can have a profound impact on others. In the era of Occultation, such individuals can achieve the highest levels of closeness to God ﷻ by utilizing this gift effectively. This can involve inviting others to goodness, spreading guidance to people, and alleviating the suffering of those in need, regardless of their financial situation. Through these efforts, one strives to support the awaited Imām عجل الله فرجه الشريف, utilizing the strengths they have been endowed with for his honorable cause.

44. The Traits of the Awaiting Believer

The awaiting believer does not invent a lifestyle for themselves, by taking shortcuts to achieve their goals or sticking to routines without balancing between the obligatory and recommended acts. There is a principle in Sharīʿah called *al-Tazāḥum*, which means there are important matters and more important ones. When Shayṭān cannot lure someone into doing what is forbidden, he tries to distract them with less important things, like focusing on the recommended acts instead of the obligatory ones, thus steering them away from what truly matters.

It is clear that the Imām does not just pick anyone to be among his closest circle; he selects those who possess inner purity and profound insight. They only do what pleases

God, and if faced with a choice, they opt for the harder path, even if it goes against their desires.

45. Group Worship Acts

Engaging in collective worship, such as Friday prayers and congregational prayers, reflects the essence of the Mahdī-centric community. It unites individuals around a shared focal point: the remembrance of God and discussions that deepen their connection to the awaited Imām during the period of Occultation. An awaiting believer should be vigilant in ensuring the success of these gatherings on every occasion by actively participating in them and encouraging others to join. Undoubtedly, these worship acts will carry even greater significance during the Imām's apparent presence.

46. Relieving the Distress of the Believers

It is essential to lend a hand to our Prophet and alleviate his concerns by assisting fellow believers and supporting those in need. You might wonder: Does the Imām focus on the smaller needs of the believers, given his weighty responsibilities?

The truth is: Yes, the Imām pays attention to both big and small matters because they are all linked to his community. A telling example is when Imām aṣ-Ṣādiq expressed happiness and pleasure with a believer who assisted his cousin.

Thus, every good deed we do brings happiness to the Imām, while every misstep brings him sadness. Some devout individuals have such a strong connection with the Imām that they feel sudden sorrow, realizing it is due to a tragedy somewhere, like the unjust killing of an innocent person, occurring in some part of the world.

47. Group Supplication

One of our duties during the Occultation is to demonstrate the glory of Islam and its adherents. We achieve this by maintaining religious rituals, such as Friday prayers and congregational prayers. Our Imām عجل الله تعالى فرجه الشريف likes to see the symbols of the religion apparent are kept alive, including the proper observance of Ḥajj, as he desires. However, the true essence of the Ibrāhīmic pilgrimage can only be experienced in his presence, as he is the true leader of the pilgrims. Unfortunately, he has been unable to fulfill this role during the Occultation.

Another crucial aspect of our responsibility is to engage in group prayers, especially when praying for the reappearance of our Imām. These prayers hold special significance when made sincerely by a gathering of believers. It has been narrated that Imām aṣ-Ṣādiq عليه السلام said:

> When a group of forty individuals gather and sincerely pray to God regarding a matter, God responds to their supplication. If they are not forty, even four people praying ten times each will have their prayers answered.

> And if they are not four, then even one person praying to God forty times will have their prayer answered by God ﷻ, the Powerful.[207]

Imām aṣ-Ṣādiq ﷺ said that when his father, Imām Muḥammad al-Bāqir ﷺ, was troubled by some matter, he would gather the women and children and supplicate to God ﷻ, and they would follow along with his supplication.

48. Self-Development

Many carry a sense of regret because they have not established a lasting charity for themselves, something that would endure after their death. However, they should know that the best kind of building one can achieve during the Occultation is the development and improvement of one's inner self, which is eternal. The impact of this is that the person becomes prepared to support their Imām ﷺ in every era.

God ﷻ describes Ibrāhīm as a nation by himself:

﴿إِنَّ إِبراهيمَ كانَ أُمَّةً قانِتًا لِلَّهِ﴾

﴾inna ʾibrāhīma kāna ʾummatan qānitan li-llāhi﴿

[207] Kulaynī, Shaykh Muḥammad b. Yaʿqūb, *al-Kāfī*, Vol. 4, p. 340.

﴾*Indeed Ibrāhīm was a nation [unto himself] obedient to God*﴿[208]

and without such inspiring figures throughout history, humanity would not have been inclined towards monotheism and virtuous actions. God ﷻ sends a renewer of faith at the dawn of every century, as narrated by our Messenger ﷺ, who said:

> God sends to this nation at the beginning of every hundred years someone who renews its religion.[209]

So why don't we pray to God ﷻ to make us among those who renew the faith after its decline?

49. Emulating Him in All Aspects

To truly love your Imām ﷺ means to follow his example in every aspect of life. Can we doubt that the Imām prays at the earliest times of prayer, for instance? So, aim to align your prayers with his, praying in congregation at the mosque with focus and humility. These are the key ingredients for a truly meaningful prayer: praying in congregation, at the beginning of prayers, in the house of God ﷻ, with genuine sincerity.

---

[208] Sūrat an-Naḥl, Verse 120.

[209] al-Qazwīnī, Mullā Khalīl b. Ghāzī, *al-Shāfī fī Sharḥ al-Kāfī*, Vol. 1, p. 80.

Similarly, take inspiration from the Imām ﷺ by offering the night prayers. Imām al-Kāẓim ﷺ described Imām al-Mahdī ﷺ as someone whose:

> wheat complexion is mixed with yellowness due to staying awake at night for worship[210]

Therefore, if you love your Imām, let your nights shine with the remembrance of God ﷻ, just as your days do. Believers are hopeful that God ﷻ will raise them to a praiseworthy station, and among the most praiseworthy stations is for the believer to be close to the Imām's heart.

50. Signs of the Reappearance

Some are fascinated by collecting narrations about the reappearance and interpreting signs. If they see fire, an earthquake, or a loud call in a certain place on earth, they rush to conclude that it is a sign of the coming relief, for example. Some attempt to deduce the time of reappearance through geomancy, sand divination, and the like. However, we are not asked to do such things. Instead, we were instructed to be fully prepared in knowledge and deeds. If the Imām ﷺ were to appear in our time, we would have the honor of joining his ranks. However, suppose his reappearance is delayed and his inevitable death precedes it. In that case, we will be rewarded for our efforts, and our names will be recorded among his supporters and helpers.

---

[210] Majlisī, ʿAllāmah Muḥammad Bāqir, *Biḥār al-Anwār*, Vol. 83, p. 81.

Therefore, we must consider what should be done rather than pondering future events and applying signs of reappearance to different events, which offers no certainty.

51. Superficial Love

Often, we claim to have divine love, but it is usually talk rather than a genuine feeling. Our real affections tend to be reserved for ourselves, our families, and those close to us. The same goes for our expressions of love for our Imām ﷺ. You can see it when people visit sacred sites, for instance. When they are moved by what they see, their first thoughts are usually to pray for themselves or their loved ones, often forgetting to pray for the return of their Imām ﷺ. And even if they do mention him, it is often in a passing manner, lacking genuine focus or sincerity.

Likewise, if someone withholds the Imām's rightful share and neglects to pay the obligatory Khums, they should not claim to love their Imām. True love inspires action, prompting one to eagerly meet their beloved's needs without being asked. Our Imām ﷺ has no needs other than those of his followers. So, when he hears of a distressed believer who has sought his aid, and you rush to help without hesitation, imagine the happiness it brings to him. You become the channel for meeting his needs by addressing the needs of your fellow believer.

52. Practical Closeness to Them

In one of his letters, Imām al-Mahdī ﷺ advised:

> So let each one of you act in a way that brings them closer to our affection, and let them avoid what draws them closer to our displeasure and anger.[211]

Our Imāms ﷺ are the advocates of monotheism and devotion to God ﷻ. A believer cannot expect their intercession without demonstrating eligibility for it, as Imām aṣ-Ṣādiq ﷺ said:

> Our intercession cannot be attained by one who takes their prayers lightly[212]

Therefore, earning the Imām's love ﷺ is not attained by just wishful thinking; it requires action. Sincerity is key here. The more earnestly a believer strives, the closer they get to earning his favor. The Qur'ān affirms this reality, where God ﷻ states:

﴿قُل إِن كُنتُم تُحِبّونَ اللَّهَ فَاتَّبِعوني يُحبِبكُمُ اللَّهُ وَيَغفِر لَكُم ذُنوبَكُم ۗ
وَاللَّهُ غَفورٌ رَحيمٌ﴾

---

211 Ṭabrisī, Shaykh Aḥmad b. ʿAlī Ṭabrisī, *al-Iḥtijāj ʿalā Ahl al-Lijāj*, Vol. 2, p. 498.

212 al-Barqī, Aḥmad b. Muḥammad b. Khālid, *al-Maḥāsin*, Vol. 1, p. 80.

﴿qul in kuntum tuḥibbūna llāha fa-ttabiʿūnī yuḥbibkumu llāhu wa-yaghfir lakum dhunūbakum wa-llāhu ghafūrun raḥīm[un]*﴾*

﴿Say, 'If you love God, then follow me; God will love you and forgive you your sins, and God is Forgiving, Merciful'﴾[213]

53. Responding to Spiritual Needs

Our Imāms عليهم السلام are quicker to respond to the fulfillment of spiritual needs when compared to fulfilling material needs. This is because they were tasked, like their grandfather Prophet Muḥammad ﷺ, with perfecting moral virtues among people.

Hence, believers are encouraged to seek the intercession of their Imām عجل الله تعالى فرجه الشريف to assist them in rectifying some of the spiritual afflictions they face and in bettering themselves. For instance, if one were to be blessed with the Imām's supplication in the depths of the night, their behavior could undergo a transformation for the better. This phenomenon is not uncommon, as even the greatest sinners have experienced profound changes in their lives, becoming among the pious in a single moment. Remarkably, we seldom witness such requests being made in sacred places, despite the profound impact they can have.

---

[213] Sūrat Āl ʿImrān, Verse 31.

54. Praying for the Strength of His Companions

The prayers of the past Imāms ﷺ were not just for Imām al-Mahdī ﷺ alone but also extended to his companions. The Imāms ﷺ sought from God ﷻ the strength and patience for these companions, hinting at the challenges ahead. Their roles demand resilience, patience, and divine support. It is understood that this applies both during the time of Occultation and eventual reappearance. The success of his companions in their service necessitates unwavering determination and patience. Imām aṣ-Ṣādiq ﷺ emphasized this in his prayer:

> ...execute for Your good friend from the descendants of Your Prophet, the caller to Your course with Your permission, Your trustee among Your creatures, Your eyes among Your servants, Your proof among Your creatures, may Your peace and blessings be upon him. O God, support him with Your assistance and assist Your servant, empower his companions, and grant them patience. Open for them a protected authority and hasten his relief, let him prevail over Yours and Your Prophet's enemies, O the Most Merciful of the merciful ones[214]

[214] Majlisī, ʿAllāmah Muḥammad Bāqir, *Biḥār al-Anwār*, Vol. 83, p. 62.

55. Praying for the Reappearance in the Middle of the Night

The middle of the night provides a time of solitude with God ﷻ, and prayers are often answered during such times. How beautiful it is for the devout believer, eagerly anticipating the Imām's return, to seize this opportunity by turning it into a station of prayers for the Imām عجل الله فرجه الشريف. It is known that the devout believer is among those who maintain the habit of performing the night prayer.

Therefore, committing to the supplication for the reappearance during these hours is crucial, as it represents a significant spiritual moment for believers and reinforces the presence of the Imām عجل الله فرجه الشريف in their hearts.

Furthermore, it is recommended to recite after the first two units of the night prayer:

> O God! Send your blessings on Muḥammad and his household, and hasten the relief of your guardian and the son of your guardian, and hasten the disgrace of his enemies[215]

[215] Ṭūsī, Shaykh Muḥammad b. Ḥasan, *Miṣbāḥ al-Mutahajjid wa Silāḥ al-Muta'abbid*, p. 139.

56. Ziyārah on his Behalf

Imagine how beautiful it would be for a believer when given the honor to visit one of the shrines of Ahl al-Bayt ﷺ to dedicate their Ziyārah or part of it to their Imām ﷺ during his Occultation. It has been reported that Imām 'Alī al-Hādī ﷺ once dispatched someone to perform Ziyārah at the shrine of Imām al-Ḥusayn ﷺ on his behalf, remarking:

> One of the places where God likes supplication and where He accepts supplication is the Hā'-i-re-Ḥusayn[216]

The author of *Mikyāl al-Makārim* also highlighted this practice, where he said:

> You should know that among those who have clarified and explained that it is recommended to perform ziyārah of tombs of the Holy Prophet ﷺ and the Holy Imāms ﷺ by proxy for the Ma'ṣūmīn and Mu'minīn, is Shaykh Muḥammad al-Ḥurr al-'Āmilī, who has devoted a chapter in *Wasā'il al-Shī'ah*: "chapter of recommendation of ziyārah on behalf of Mu'minīn and Ma'ṣūmīn". Then he [the author] mentioned the traditional report of Dāwūd Surmī, in which he said to His Eminence, Imām al-Ḥasan al-'Askarī ﷺ:

---

[216] Majlisī, 'Allāmah Muḥammad Bāqir, *Biḥār al-Anwār*, Vol. 99, p. 259.

> I performed the ziyārah of your father and dedicated it to you.

The Imām ﷺ replied:

> For that you shall get a great reward from God ﷻ, and we are thankful to you.[217]

57. Dispelling Adversity Through the Awaiters

Patience in enduring the consequences of the Imām's Occultation, steadfastness in following his command, and commitment to inviting people to him are among the prerequisites for the descent of special mercy upon his followers. One of the manifestations of this blessing is that God ﷻ makes these followers resemble their Imām ﷺ in some aspects. Through these sincere waters, God ﷻ bestows His blessings, dispels adversity, and showers His mercy. It has been narrated from Imām aṣ-Ṣādiq ﷺ that he said:

> Indeed, there will come a time upon people when their Imām will be hidden from them. So, blessed are those who remain steadfast in our command during that time. Even the least reward for them is that God ﷻ will call out to them, saying:

[217] Iṣfahānī, Sayyid Muḥammad Taqī Mūsawī, *Mikyāl al-Makārim*, Vol. 2, p. 243.

> O My servant, you believed in My unseen and affirmed My secret. So, rejoice in the excellence of the reward from Me. Truly, you are My servants in truth. From you I accept, and from you I pardon, and to you I forgive, and through you, I bestow rain upon My servants, and I avert calamities from them. Were it not for you, I would have sent down My punishment upon them.[218]

58. Prayers as a Gift

A simple yet profound way to connect with our Imām عجل الله تعالى فرجه الشريف is through prayer. Devoted believers can offer two humble units of prayer, with utmost sincerity, and dedicate the reward to the Imām عجل الله تعالى فرجه الشريف. By doing so, they seek to present to their Imām what befits his noble station, especially when done in moments when prayers are known to be answered. After completing the prayer, they say as narrated from Imām aṣ-Ṣādiq عليه السلام:

> O God, these two rakats are a gift from me to Your servant, Your Walī, cousin of Your Prophet, his successor, Amīr al-Mu'minīn, 'Alī b. Abī Talib. O God, so please accept them from me and convey them to him from me and reward me with the best that which I hope from You, Your Prophet, successor of Your Prophet, Fāṭimah az-Zahrā', daughter of Your Prophet,

---

[218] Ṣadūq, Shaykh Muḥammad b. 'Alī, *Kamāl al-Dīn wa Tamām al-Ni'mah*, Vol. 1, p. 330.

> al-Ḥasan and al-Ḥusayn, grandsons of Your Prophet and His Awliyā' from the progeny of al-Ḥusayn; O guardian of the believers, O guardian of the believers, O guardian of the believers.[219]

59. Gifting Good Deeds

It is a tradition among the generous to return gifts with even greater generosity, sometimes exceeding expectations, especially if the giver is exceptionally generous. With this in mind, we believe that one of the hallmarks of a true believer is to dedicate their good deeds, with prayers at the forefront, to the pure souls of Ahl al-Bayt, including our current Imām. It is as simple as intending to dedicate the deed before performing it, costing nothing more than a heartfelt intention. However, it is a powerful expression of love and longing for the recipient of the deed. It has been said that:

> Whoever dedicates the reward of their prayers to the Prophet of God, the Commander of the Faithful, and the Imāms who came after him, may God's blessings and peace be upon them all, God will multiply the reward of their prayers exponentially until their last breath. It will be said to them before their soul departs their body,

[219] Majlisī, 'Allāmah Muḥammad Bāqir, *Biḥār al-Anwār*, Vol. 88, p. 216.

> O so-and-so, your gift to us and your kindness towards us have been accepted. This is the day of your rewards and recompense. So, find tranquility and comfort in what God has prepared for you, and congratulations on what you have become.[220]

60. Gifting them the Qur'ān Recitation

One of the most important acts of worship during the blessed month of Ramaḍān is reciting the Qur'ān. How fitting it is for the faithful believer to dedicate a portion of their recitations to their awaited Imām ﷻ, as they recite the words of their Lord ﷻ. This can be done by dedicating some completions of the Qur'ān to him. Yet, some may question the significance of such gestures, saying that the Imām ﷻ does not need our deeds and recitations. However, there is evidence in the traditions indicating the significance of this act, as narrated when someone asked Imām ar-Riḍā ﷺ:

> My father would complete it [reciting the whole Qur'ān] forty times during the month of Ramaḍān, and I continued this after him. Sometimes I increased and sometimes I decreased, depending on my availability, engagement, activity, and laziness. Then, on the day of 'Īd, I would dedicate a completion to the Prophet Muḥammad ﷺ, another to 'Alī ﷺ, and

---

220 al-Ḥurr al-'Āmilī, Shaykh Muḥammad, *Wasā'il al-Shī'ah*, Vol. 8, p. 169.

another to Fāṭimah ؑ, and then to the Imāms ؑ until I reached you. So, I made one for you. What benefit do I get from that?

He said:

You will be with them on the Day of Judgment.

I said:

God is the Greatest! I get that?

He said:

Yes (three times).[221]

61. Spiritual Sponsorship of Orphans

There is a common belief that providing material support to an orphan, such as food and shelter, ranks among the highest acts of charity. However, upon deeper reflection, we realize that the spiritual orphan, one disconnected from their Imām of the Time عج, faces a more profound loss than one who has lost their father. Thus, supporting the spiritual well-being of such an orphan holds greater significance in the eyes of God ﷻ than simply meeting their material needs, as this sponsorship serves as a path to their eternal salvation.

221 Kulaynī, Shaykh Muḥammad b. Yaʿqūb, *al-Kāfī*, Vol. 4, p. 638.

This is emphasized in the saying of Imām al-ʿAskarī ﷺ:

> The worst orphan is one who has been separated from his Imām and cannot reach him; and when he needs guidance in a religious matter, he does not know what the Imām's opinion regarding it. Hence, one who is learned in our sciences, if he is near, should guide one who is ignorant of the law of the Sharīʿah. And know that, one who guides him and brings him to the right path, he would be our comrade and companion in elevated ranks of Paradise.[222]

62. Being with Them in Paradise

In various collections of ḥadīths and even in the Noble Qurʾān, we find many stories about rewards and blessings meant to inspire and motivate us. It is natural for humans to seek what brings us joy, whether it is in this life or the next. But there are those among us, especially in the time of the Occultation, who, by supporting the spiritual orphans of the family of Muḥammad ﷺ, reach a level where they are united with them in Paradise. This status surpasses the reward of luxurious palaces and heavenly companions. Imām al-ʿAskarī ﷺ once said:

> The worst orphan is one who has been separated from his Imām and cannot reach him; and when he needs

[222] Ṭabrisī, Shaykh Aḥmad b. ʿAlī Ṭabrisī, *al-Iḥtijāj ʿalā Ahl al-Lijāj*, Vol. 1, p. 16.

guidance in a religious matter, he does not know what the Imām's opinion regarding it. Hence, one who is learned in our sciences, if he is near, should guide one who is ignorant of the law of the Sharī'ah. And know that, one who guides him and brings him to the right path, he will be our comrade and companion in the elevated ranks of Paradise. This tradition is narrated to me by my father from his forefathers from the Holy Prophet[223]

63. Patience During the Occultation

Some individuals, especially those who call to God ﷻ during the period of Occultation, encounter some harm in their path of inviting others to the truth. This has been the norm since the time of Ādam. The journey to Him demands perseverance and hard work, yet some long for an easier path without obstacles.

This suffering has occurred frequently in the lives of the companions of the Imāms ؑ. For instance, during the time of Imām ar-Riḍā ؑ, a man wrote to him, complaining about the cruelty of the people of Wasit and their oppression towards him. The Imām ؑ, in response, wrote:

[223] Ibid.

> God, Glorified be His mention, took a covenant from our followers to endure in the state of falsehood. So, be patient with the decree of your Lord.[224]

64. The Greatest Patience

We understand that the tougher the challenge, the greater the reward, and the greatness of patience is measured by the magnitude of the calamity. The extended period of Occultation poses one of the most significant tests for believers. If our Imām ﷺ were among us, many of our struggles would likely feel less overwhelming. This was evident in the lives of the Prophet ﷺ and the imāms after him. Their presence among the people offered considerable solace during difficult times. In times of adversity, Muslims would turn to the Prophet ﷺ for guidance and comfort.

Hence, the narrations conveyed glad tidings that the reward for patient believers during their absence exceeds even the reward of those who fight in the way of God ﷻ. This sentiment is reflected in the following saying attributed to Prophet Muḥammad ﷺ:

> You are my companions. My brethren are a people in the latter days who believe in me without seeing me... Indeed, God ﷻ has acquainted me with them by their names and the names of their fathers before He

[224] Fayḍ Kāshānī, Mullā Muḥammad b. Murtaḍā, *al-Wāfī*, Vol. 5, p. 761.

> brought them out from the loins of their fathers and the wombs of their mothers. One of them holds steadfast to his faith like holding onto a burning coal in the night, or like holding onto a red-hot iron. They are the guiding lights amid darkness; God saves them from every dark and obscure trial.[225]

65. The Reason Behind the Community is Straying

The present condition of the Muslim community is far from enviable, and the root cause lies in its deviation from the divine path set by God ﷻ. Among these deviations is the neglect of the appointed Imām and Guide on Earth عجل الله تعالى فرجه الشريف. This dilemma we find ourselves in reflects the story of the Children of Isrā'īl when they wandered from the righteous path. Essentially, his command in governing the community and enacting laws is akin to the universal law governing all aspects of existence.

Imām 'Alī عليه السلام addressed this reality when he said:

> O people! If you had not evaded support of the truth and had not felt weakness from crushing wrong, then he who was not your match would not have aimed at you, and he who overpowered you would not have overpowered you. But you roamed about the deserts

225 Majlisī, 'Allāmah Muḥammad Bāqir, *Biḥār al-Anwār*, Vol. 52, p. 124.

> (of disobedience) like Banū Isrā'īl (Children of Isrā'īl). I swear by my life that after me, your tribulations will increase several times, because you will have abandoned the truth behind your backs.[226]

66. The One Despised by God ﷻ

Sometimes, we may feel content when reflecting on our faith, believing in the right things, acknowledging our Imām, and awaiting his reappearance. But if we examine our actions closely, we realize they do not match what our Imām عجل الله فرجه expects from us. This disconnect can lead to God's ﷻ displeasure, as Imām Zayn al-'Ābidīn عليه السلام warned:

> Be wary! Among those most disliked by God is someone who professes faith in their Imām but does not follow his teachings in their actions.[227]

Explaining this further, the author of *Mikyāl al-Makārim* states:

> It is mentioned in traditions that God may befriend a servant, but He does not like his deeds, and it is also possible that He does not like a servant but likes his actions. This is also accepted by reason because, in the view of God, love and hate depend on the legality or the illegality of that action according to Divine law. If

[226] Sharīf Raḍī, Muḥammad b. al-Ḥusayn, *Nahj al-Balāghah*, p. 241.

[227] Kulaynī, Shaykh Muḥammad b. Ya'qūb, *al-Kāfī*, Vol. 15, p. 535.

the person has faith in it, as a believer, but fails to act upon it, God will be displeased with his actions. After this introduction, it becomes evident that the aim of Imām's ﷺ statement is that the most hated person, from the aspect of their deeds, is one who accepts the way and religion of one's Imām ﷺ solely from the aspect of belief. That is, he believes in his Imāmate and Wilāyah, but opposes it through his actions and behavior. The consequence of this is that when a Muslim opposes his Imām by his deeds and behavior, the opponents get an opportunity to ridicule, and this is a greater sin.[228]

67. Spiritual Proximity to Them

There is a physical proximity to the Imāms ﷺ, which happens when one of us is in one of their holy shrines. But more important than that is the closeness in status and rank, meaning that a person should strive to be close to their souls by aligning with them as much as possible. This internal alignment is vital for achieving closeness to them in the Hereafter, which is the ultimate aspiration of every believer. This idea is reinforced by a saying of Imām aṣ-Ṣādiq ﷺ, who conveyed his father's message:

> O, my son! If you oppose me in deeds, you will not be gathered with me tomorrow.

---

[228] Iṣfahānī, Sayyid Muḥammad Taqī Mūsawī, *Mikyāl al-Makārim*, Vol. 2, p. 353.

Then he said:

> God ﷻ refuses to let a group who opposes another in deeds be gathered together on the Day of Judgement. By the Lord of the Kaʿbah that will not happen[229]

68. The Prayer of Imām al-Mahdī

The prayers narrated from the Imāms of the Ahl al-Bayt عليهم السلام are like a special path leading to that infallible figure. If one wishes to seek the attention of a particular Imām, they should offer prayers to God ﷻ using the prayer associated with that Imām, as it is linked to them. Thus, performing the prayer of Imām al-Mahdī عجل الله تعالى فرجه الشريف becomes a means of gaining his attention and care for those who offer it. It is said that Imām al-Mahdī عجل الله تعالى فرجه الشريف instructed:

> One who needs God ﷻ should rise after midnight on Friday eve, perform the bath; go to the place of his prayer, and perform two rakats of prayer. In the first rakat, recite Sūrat al-Fātiḥah, and when he reaches
>
> ﴿إِيَّاكَ نَعۡبُدُ وَإِيَّاكَ نَسۡتَعِينُ﴾
>
> ﴿*iyyāka naʿbudu wa-ʾiyyāka nastaʿīnu*﴾

[229] Kulaynī, Shaykh Muḥammad b. Yaʿqūb, *al-Kāfī*, Vol. 15, p. 573.

﴿*You [alone] do we worship,*
and to You [alone] do we turn for help﴾[230]

he should repeat it a hundred times. On the hundredth time, he should complete the Sūrat. Then recite Sūrat al-Ikhlāṣ once. After that, perform rukūʿ and sujūd, and in each of them, recite the zikr seventy times. Perform the second rakat also in the same manner. Recite the following duʿāʾ before the prayer. And if you do it, God ﷻ will fulfill any of your needs, whatever it may be, except that it be for cutting off relations.[231]

69. Fulfilling the Needs of Those Who Love the Imām

The general principle of love dictates that it extends from the beloved to everything associated with them. One way to earn the affection of Imām al-Mahdī ﷺ is by showing love and support to those associated with him and those eagerly awaiting his return, especially the devout believers among them. It has been narrated that Imām al-Kāẓim ﷺ said:

---

[230] Sūrat al-Fātiḥah, Verse 5.

[231] Ṭabrisī, Shaykh Faḍl b. Ḥasan, *Makārim al-Akhlāq*, p. 339.

> One who fulfills the needs of our righteous Shīʿah and friends, shall get the reward of helping us all[232]

How great the reward is for believers who support the needs of all the Imāms of the Ahl al-Bayt ﷺ! It is an honor that transcends all others! Even a simple visit, without any specific need, can bring blessings. Just visiting a fellow believer out of love for the Imāms draws one closer to them. It has been narrated that Imām ar-Riḍā ﷺ said:

> One who is unable to visit us should pay a visit to a righteous follower of ours, as a reward, our ziyārah will be written for them[233]

70. Preparing, even with just an arrow

The diverse expressions found in the narrations of Ahl al-Bayt ﷺ regarding those awaiting the Imām ﷺ during the occultation suggest that they are in a state of continuous struggle (*jihād*) throughout the ages until he reappears. Sometimes, preparing for the reappearance is referred to as Murabata. Its meaning is to stand firm in his cause. Sometimes, it entails defending the Muslims' fronts. Imām Abū Jaʿfar Muḥammad b. ʿAlī ﷺ asked [the narrator of this conversation]:

---

[232] Majlisī, ʿAllāmah Muḥammad Bāqir, *Biḥār al-Anwār*, Vol. 97, p. 122.

[233] al-Qummī, Ibn Qūlawayh, *Kāmil al-Zīyārāt*, p. 319.

> What is the duration of Murābaṭah in your view, in the last period?

I [the narrator] said:

> Forty days.

The Imām عليه السلام said:

> But, Murābaṭah for us is Murābaṭah forever[234]

At other times, the Imām advises those awaiting the Imām to prepare, even if it is just with a single arrow, whether in a literal or metaphorical sense. It is reported from Imām aṣ-Ṣādiq عليه السلام that he said

> If one of you prepares for the Ẓuhūr of al-Qā'im عجل الله تعالى فرجه الشريف even with a weapon as little as an arrow, when God sees the intention, I am sure, He will prolong your life.[235]

71. Perfection of Intellect and Morals

In the era of reappearance, there is a significant improvement in various aspects of life. Among them is the perfection of intellect, which necessitates the removal of conflicting ignorant ideologies and desires. Another aspect is the perfection of morals, thereby fulfilling the ultimate

---

[234] Kulaynī, Shaykh Muḥammad b. Ya'qūb, *al-Kāfī*, Vol. 15, p. 835.

[235] Nu'mānī, Muḥammad b. Ibrāhīm, *Kitāb al-Ghaybah*, p. 320.

purpose of the Prophet's ﷺ mission, which was to perfect morals. These blessings are realized when the Imām عجل الله فرجه places his hand on the heads of the believers, symbolizing his blessed attention and the implementation of his divine guardianship.

The goal of uniting intellects is to unify diverse minds toward a common objective, fostering harmony among them and preventing discord. This is beautifully expressed in Imām al-Bāqir's عليه السلام statement:

> When our Qā'im rises, God ﷻ will place his hands over the heads of the people, so their intellects will come together and their forbearance and patience will become perfect.[236]

72. Character like the Prophet's

The best way to describe the character of Imām al-Mahdī عجل الله فرجه is that his character mirrors that of his noble grandfather, the Prophet ﷺ. It has been narrated that the Prophet ﷺ said:

> Even if only one day remains of this world, God ﷻ will send a man with my name and character, he will be known as Abū 'Abdullāh.[237]

---

[236] Kulaynī, Shaykh Muḥammad b. Ya'qūb, *al-Kāfī*, Vol. 1, p. 56.

[237] Majlisī, 'Allāmah Muḥammad Bāqir, *Biḥār al-Anwār*, Vol. 51, p. 94.

When we say his character resembles that of the Prophet ﷺ, we mean his overall qualities and traits, including his demeanor. This should inspire sincere believers eagerly awaiting his arrival to emulate his conduct, thereby following in the footsteps of his grandfather. By doing so, they will strive to adopt his noble attributes to the best of their ability.

73. Steadfastness on the Path of the Imāms

Remaining firm in allegiance to the Imām, and seeking success in supporting him—whether he is present or absent—requires divine guidance and assistance. This can only be achieved through the individual's efforts to attain it, as demonstrated by remaining steadfast on the path and following the example of the supporters of the prophets and messengers throughout history.

Imām aṣ-Ṣādiq ؑ explains steadfastness in the verse as steadfastness on the path of the Imāms ؑ. The narrator says:

> I asked Abā ʿAbdillāh ؑ about the saying of God ﷻ:
>
> ﴿الَّذينَ قالوا رَبُّنَا اللَّهُ ثُمَّ استَقاموا﴾
>
> ﴿*lladhīna qālū rabbunā llāhu thumma staqāmū*﴾

﴾*those who say, 'Our Lord is God!'*
and then remain steadfast﴿[238]

So he ﷺ said:

> They remained steadfast the Imāms, one after another.[239]

Remaining steadfast on the path of the Imām ﷺ during his occultation entails remembering him, praying for him, and following his commands.

74. Circles of Companions Around the Imām

Narrations indicate that the leaders, alongside Imām al-Mahdī ﷺ, are among the companions of Badr; they are the elite of the believers in their time, forming the innermost circle closest to his noble presence. It is natural for anyone to aspire to be part of this inner circle with him. Additionally, it has also been narrated that the wider circle includes ten thousand men, and there is no harm in aspiring to be part of this broader community as well. It has been narrated from Imām Muḥammad al-Jawād ﷺ:

> The number of the people of Badr from his companions will gather together for him: three

[238] Sūrat Fuṣṣilat, Verse 30.

[239] Kulaynī, Shaykh Muḥammad b. Yaʿqūb, *al-Kāfī*, Vol. 1, p. 547.

hundred and thirteen from the remotest parts of the Earth. That is the statement of God:

﴿أَيْنَ مَا تَكُونُوا يَأْتِ بِكُمُ اللَّهُ جَمِيعًا ۚ إِنَّ اللَّهَ عَلَىٰ كُلِّ شَيْءٍ قَدِيرٌ﴾

﴿*ayna mā takūnū ya'ti bikumu llāhu jamī'an inna llāha 'alā kulli shay'in qadīr*un﴾

﴿*Wherever you may be, God will bring you all together. Indeed God has power over all things*﴾[240]

When these people have gathered for him, from the people of al-Ikhlāṣ (pure monotheism), God will make his affair apparent. When the allegiance for him is completed, and that will be ten thousand men, he will rise with the Permission of God.[241]

'Allāmah Majlisī ﷺ said:

His companions are not limited to three hundred and thirteen; rather, this number refers to those gathered around him at the onset of his emergence.[242]

---

[240] Sūrat al-Baqarah, Verse 148.

[241] Majlisī, 'Allāmah Muḥammad Bāqir, *Biḥār al-Anwār*, Vol. 52, p. 283.

[242] Ibid., p. 323.

75. Praying for his Protection

The Imām ☽ is the closest of creatures to God ✿ in his time, surrounded by His care in every aspect of his existence. Yet, this does not mean we should not pray for his protection. Just like his predecessors, the Imām may face human vulnerabilities; for example, Ibrāhīm ☽ endured illness, and Ayyūb ☽ suffered bodily afflictions.

Hence, there is every reason to pray for the safety of the Imām of our time, as he may also face such challenges. Imām ar-Riḍā ☽ prayed for the protection of Imām al-Mahdī ☽ and said:

> And protect him from the evil of all that You have created, originated, formed, and fashioned, and protect him from before him, behind him, to his right, to his left, above him, and beneath him, with Your protection which does not fail to protect him. And safeguard within him Your Messenger, his forefathers, your Imāms, the pillars of your religion, and place him in Your safekeeping which is not lost, and in Your proximity which is never violated, and in Your protection and might which cannot be overcome.[243]

Moreover, our prayers might extend as a form of seeking safety for those who are with him, his supporters and aides,

---

[243] Ṭūsī, Shaykh Muḥammad b. Ḥasan, *Miṣbāḥ al-Mutahajjid wa Silāḥ al-Muta'abbid*, p. 409.

if we were to say that our supplication has no impact on the Imām himself.

76. The Importance of Ziyārah Āl Yāsīn

One of the profound ziyārah that connects the believer with their Imām is Ziyārah Āl Yāsīn. It has been narrated that Imām al-Mahdī said:

> When you intend to turn your faces towards God and us by means of us, you should say just as God has said: Peace be upon (the) progeny of Yāsīn.[244]

This ziyārah holds special significance as it involves sending blessings to the Imām during his various acts of worship, such as standing and sitting in prayer and reciting supplications. Additionally, it reinforces correct beliefs about monotheism, affirms the leadership of the Twelve Imāms, and discusses beliefs about the Day of Judgment.

After the ziyārah, the reciter offers a comprehensive prayer, the fulfillment of which will lead to success. This prayer encompasses aspects related to wisdom and knowledge, determination in action, and matters of the heart, such as love and loyalty towards the Imām. From this visit, we understand that true believers awaiting the Imām are characterized by these virtues, rather than mere wishes and claims of waiting.

---

[244] Ṭabrisī, Shaykh Aḥmad b. ʿAlī Ṭabrisī, *al-Iḥtijāj ʿalā Ahl al-Lijāj*, Vol. 2, p. 493.

All these insights are reflected in the prayer recited after the ziyārah:

> O God! I ask you to fill my heart with the light of certainty, my chest with the light of faith, my mind with the light of sincere intentions, my resolve with the light of knowledge, my actions with the light of dedication, my speech with the light of honesty, and my religion with the light of clear evidence from You. Illuminate my sight with brightness, my hearing with wisdom, and my love with sincere loyalty to Muḥammad ﷺ and his Household ‎عليهم السلام.[245]

77. Physical Strength

Imām al-Mahdī ‎عجل الله تعالى فرجه الشريف embodies the aspect of divine strength in all dimensions of his existence, including his physical strength, as indicated by the narration of Imām ar-Riḍā ‎عليه السلام when he was asked:

> Are you the Ṣāḥibul Amr (Master of Affairs)? He replied: I am also Ṣāḥibul Amr, but not the Ṣāḥibul Amr who would fill the Earth with justice, as it would have been fraught with tyranny and oppression. How can I be that person? While you can see that I am physically weak. At the same time, the Qā'im is the one who, at the time of his reappearance, will be senior in age but appear as a youth. His body shall be so strong

[245] Ibid., p. 494.

> that if he catches hold of the biggest tree of the Earth, he shall be able to uproot it, and if he shouts between the mountains, their stones will roll down.[246]

From this, we understand that those who await the Imām ﷿ must also cultivate strength in all aspects of their being, including physical strength, because what they aim to achieve with him is not an easy task. From this narration and similar ones, it is understood that the Imām, in addition to his natural abilities, will receive divine assistance to fulfill his mission.

78. Seeking His Intercession

There are various narrations indicating that one of the best ways to ensure that our prayers are answered is through seeking the intercession of the Household of the Prophet ﷺ. It has been narrated that Imām ar-Riḍā ؑ said:

> If you encounter hardship, seek our assistance with God, which is the meaning of what God says:
>
> ﴿وَلِلَّهِ الأَسماءُ الحُسنىٰ فادعوهُ بِها﴾
>
> ﴿*wa-li-llāhi l-'asmā'u l-ḥusnā fa-d'ūhu bihā*﴾

---

[246] Ṣadūq, Shaykh Muḥammad b. ʿAlī, *Kamāl al-Dīn wa Tamām al-Niʿmah*, Vol. 2, p. 376.

﴾*To God belong the Best Names, so supplicate Him by them*﴿[247] [248]

Similarly, we are encouraged to seek intercession through the awaited Imām ﷺ, which Imām aṣ-Ṣādiq ﷺ advised when one needed to ask God ﷻ for something, as he said:

> If one of you faces a need, let them fast on Wednesday, Thursday, and Friday. When it is Friday, let them bathe, wear clean clothes, then ascend to the highest point in their home, pray two units of prayer, then raise their hands to the sky and say:
>
> > O God, I draw near to You through Your Prophet...
>
> until he ﷺ said:
>
> > And I draw near to You through the remainder, the remaining one established among the chosen ones, whom You are pleased with for Yourself, the good, the pure, the virtuous, the light of the earth and its support, the hope of this nation and its leader, enjoining what is good and forbidding what is evil, the sincere advisor, the trustworthy, fulfilling the

---

[247] Sūrat al-Aʿrāf, Verse 180.

[248] Mufīd, Shaykh Muḥammad, *al-Ikhtiṣāṣ*, p. 252.

trusts of the prophets, and the seal of the noble, pure successors ﷺ.[249]

79. The Example of the Lovers of the Imām

Looking back at the lives of devout believers and those who hold a deep affection for Imām al-Mahdī ﷺ, we find a beautiful tradition of performing good deeds on his behalf, such as pilgrimage and other acts of devotion. It is undeniable that such acts catch the Imām's attention, and he generously reciprocates beyond measure. An example of this cherished practice among the faithful is the story of Abū Muḥammad al-Daʿlajī, recounted by Quṭb ad-Dīn ar-Rāwandī in *al-Kharāʾij*. He was paid by another believer the price for a pilgrimage to perform it on behalf of the awaited Imām, and it was mentioned that this was a custom of the Shīʿah at that time. When he went for pilgrimage, he met the Imām ﷺ there and described him as a handsome young man, with a tanned complexion, engrossed in supplication and acts of worship.

80. Signs of the End of Time

During the period of the occultation, believers face a profound sadness as they witness what once embodied goodness and righteousness in the early days of Islam now

[249] al-Ḥurr al-ʿĀmilī, Shaykh Muḥammad, *Wasāʾil al-Shīʿah*, Vol. 8, p. 135.

being flaunted like mere worldly possessions. The Prophet ﷺ said about this time:

> The time will come upon my Ummah when nothing will remain of the Qur'ān except its inscription, and nothing of Islam except its name. They will be called Muslims while they will be the furthest from it. Their mosques will be full of people, but devoid of guidance.[250]

Regrettably, those who were once beacons of guidance have now become sources of misguidance, as expressed by the Prophet ﷺ, referring to the scholars of that time:

> Their 'ulamā' (religious scholars) will be the worst of creatures under the canopy of the heavens. Evil plots will originate from them and to them will they return.[251]

In essence, the Prophet ﷺ described the situation succinctly:

> Islam began as something strange, and it will return to being strange, so blessed are the strangers.[252]

---

[250] Majlisī, 'Allāmah Muḥammad Bāqir, *Biḥār al-Anwār*, Vol. 52, p. 190.

[251] Ibid., p. 191.

[252] Ṣadūq, Shaykh Muḥammad b. 'Alī, *Kamāl al-Dīn wa Tamām al-Ni'mah*, Vol. 1, p. 66.

Reflecting on this, we ponder: What honor lies in being instrumental in reviving Islam from its state of strangeness? This lofty goal can only be achieved through the efforts of Imām al-Mahdī ﷻ and his supporters in that critical time.

81. Swift Gathering

Imām al-Mahdī's ﷻ companions are spread far and wide, from the east to the west, representing diverse backgrounds, including both men and women. They are described in narrations as scattered autumn clouds that swiftly gather into one cohesive formation. It is narrated from Imām aṣ-Ṣādiq ﷷ that he said:

> They gather around him in one hour, swiftly, like the scattered autumn clouds[253]

This narration indicates their readiness to support the Imām wherever they may be. They are like soldiers in a camp, responding promptly to their leader's call. It also reflects the wide dispersion of his companions across the lands. Imām ar-Riḍā ﷷ stated:

> By God, if our Qā'im were to rise, God would gather our Shī'ah to him from all countries.[254]

---

[253] Majlisī, 'Allāmah Muḥammad Bāqir, *Biḥār al-Anwār*, Vol. 51, p. 55.

[254] Ibid., Vol. 52, p. 291.

Therefore, no one should underestimate anyone, as perhaps among them are the supporters hidden by God عزّ وجلّ, numbering as many as the companions of Badr.

82. Striving while Awaiting

The narrations, in various wordings, emphasize the necessity of combining waiting for the Imām with striving and diligence during the period of occultation. This serves as preparation for that noble government. Given the weight of responsibility placed upon the Imām عجّل الله تعالى فرجه الشريف, it requires individuals from this community who are capable of bearing it. For instance, Imām aṣ-Ṣādiq عليه السلام outlined conditions for deeds to be accepted. He عليه السلام stated:

> The testimony that there is no god but God, and that Muḥammad is His servant and messenger, and the acceptance of what God has commanded, and allegiance to us, and dissociation from our enemies (meaning the Imāms in particular), and piety, diligence, and tranquility, and waiting for the Qā'im.

Then he عليه السلام said,

> We have a state that God will bring about when He wills.

Then he ﷺ said:

> Whoever is pleased to be among the companions of the Qā'im, let him wait and let him act with piety and good manners while waiting, for if he dies and the Qā'im rises after him, he will have the reward similar to the reward of those who accompanied him. So be diligent and wait. Congratulations to you, O blessed group.[255]

The slogan for the era of occultation can be summed up in his words:

> Be diligent and wait.

83. Gloomy Signs

Some of the signs mentioned in various narrations about the end times can evoke strong feelings of sadness and concern. Imām aṣ-Ṣādiq ﷺ painted a vivid picture of this when he said:

> Do you not know that those who are in anticipation of our affair and patiently endure what they see of harm and fear, tomorrow they shall be in our army?[256]

In detailing the adversity and turmoil of that period, Imām aṣ-Ṣādiq ﷺ said:

---

[255] Nuʿmānī, Muḥammad b. Ibrāhīm, *Kitāb al-Ghaybah*, p. 200.

[256] Kulaynī, Shaykh Muḥammad b. Yaʿqūb, *al-Kāfī*, Vol. 15, p. 119.

When you see that immorality becomes prevalent. And men shall satisfy their lust with men, and women shall satisfy theirs with women. You will see that boys will be given to those whom they give women. You will see women marrying women. And you will see that wine is openly imbibed, and people who are gathered around tables do not care about God, the Mighty and the Sublime. Men derive their livelihood from their backsides, and women from their private parts. You will see women organizing assemblies for themselves, just as men do. Usury would be openly practiced, and none shall be chastised for it. You will see a woman praised for her adulterous exploits. You will see that no one is committing sins in the darkness of the night. Rather, you will see them committing sins in broad daylight. You will see wives dominating and suppressing their husbands. They act contrary to their desires and spend money on them. You will see that people are intoxicated in the morning and late afternoon without any care for anyone or anything. You will see them having sexual intercourse with animals. You will see women dominating rulership, and they will have power over everything that fulfills their sensual desires.[257]

[257] Majlisī, ʿAllāmah Muḥammad Bāqir, *Biḥār al-Anwār*, Vol. 52, p. 256.

84. Waiting is the Relief

One of the remarkable narrations about waiting for relief (the reappearance of Imām al-Mahdī) is the question posed by Abū Baṣīr to Imām aṣ-Ṣādiq ﷺ:

> I said to Imām aṣ-Ṣādiq ﷺ:
>
> > May I be your sacrifice! When does deliverance (Reappearance of the 12th Imām) come?
>
> He ﷺ said:
>
> > O Abū Baṣīr, are you among those who love this world? Whoever believes in this matter has indeed received deliverance already[258]

This narration suggests that those who sincerely await the Imām's reappearance find solace as if they are already living in that era, even if they have not yet witnessed his appearance. Moreover, it implies that they do not long for any worldly benefits associated with his return. Thus, the Imām's surprise at the questioner, asking if they are awaiting the reappearance of the Imām ﷺ because they seek worldly gains. Does not sincere awaiting the reappearance in itself bring deliverance?

---

[258] Nuʿmānī, Muḥammad b. Ibrāhīm, *Kitāb al-Ghaybah*, p. 330.

85. The Honor of Correspondence

In the correspondence of the Imām ﷺ to Shaykh Mufīd, we find avenues for reflection. Among them is that he prays for him at the beginning of the letter:

> May He always give you divine opportunity to help the truth[259]

It is noteworthy that such prayers extend beyond letters, as he prays for his followers, especially during times of answered prayers. This is evident from what is mentioned in his letter:

> May God ﷻ help you as He helped our righteous followers in the past.[260]

indicating a continued tradition of prayer and support for the righteous believers who came before Shaykh Mufīd.

Additionally, the Imām ﷺ explained why Shaykh aMufīd was honored with this correspondence, stating that it is due to him

> Speaking up truthfully in our favor.[261]

---

[259] Mufīd, Shaykh Muḥammad, *al-Muqni'ah*, p. 7.

[260] Ṭabrisī, Shaykh Aḥmad b. 'Alī Ṭabrisī, *al-Iḥtijāj 'alā Ahl al-Lijāj*, Vol. 2, p. 499.

[261] Ibid., p. 497.

Moreover, it is noteworthy that this correspondence occurred with the permission of God ﷻ, as the Imām's actions and words align with the Divine Will, just as those of his great-grandfather, the Prophet ﷺ.

Another important point is how the Imām links piety with protection from hardships, as he assured:

> I promise that if any of your brothers in faith acquires the fear of God ﷻ, he will be safe from sorrow and calamities.[262]

This underscores that this matter is not merely about gaining immunity through knowledge; practical commitment is essential alongside it.

86. Changing the Course of Events

Shifting the course of human society and dismantling established civilizations before the Imām's عجل الله تعالى فرجه الشريف reappearance is not a simple task unless it aligns with the divine will. It has been said by the Commander of the Faithful عليه السلام:

> Moving mountains is easier than replacing the reign of a government before its deadline. Seek help from God and exercise patience. Verily, the Earth belongs to God;

[262] Majlisī, 'Allāmah Muḥammad Bāqir, *Biḥār al-Anwār*, Vol. 53, p. 177.

> He inherits it to whomever He wills of His servants. The final victory is for the pious ones.[263]

Hence, we assert that dismantling existing powers across the globe requires preparation from awaiting believers and continuous prayers for divine intervention to overthrow oppressors. Let us recall, in this context, the years of hardship that the Prophet ﷺ spent in Makkah, followed by the years of patience and steadfastness in Madīnah, culminating in the eventual triumph with the conquest of Makkah.

87. The Ultimate Victory

It can be understood from some narrations that the ultimate victory and perfect relief will come only with the Imām's عجل الله تعالى فرجه الشريف reappearance, even though certain forms of victory and success can occur during certain phases of the occultation. Without this ultimate victory, there would not be a distinction between the time of reappearance and the period of occultation. This reinforces the idea that challenges and difficulties persist within the community until his reappearance. Imām al-ʿAskarī عليه السلام said:

> Our Shīʿah will remain in sadness until my son appears, whom the Prophet foretold would fill the earth with

[263] al-Ḥarrānī, Ibn Shuʿba, *Tuḥaf al-ʿUqūl*, p. 112.

> justice and equity as it has been filled with injustice and oppression.[264]

As inferred from this text, a state of sadness envelops the awaiting believers throughout occultation, as they witness injustice and the delay of relief. It is understood that this sadness, if embraced by the believer, prevents them from becoming too attached to worldly pleasures, unlike the common practice of many. This enduring sense of sorrow is considered a characteristic of believers and is a sacred matter, as it is related to sacred principles and concerns.

88. The Best People of the Time

It is logical to conclude that one who believes in the Imām ﷻ during the period of occultation is superior to one who believes in him after his reappearance. After the reappearance and the manifestation of signs, their belief is no longer considered belief in the unseen. This also applies to the belief in Judgment Day, as believing in when it occurs is not a belief in the unseen. A narration that confirms what we have just said, in addition to the good news that these individuals are considered akin to the companions of the Prophet ﷺ, is what was narrated by Imām Zayn al-ʿĀbidīn ؑ:

> During this period of occultation, those who believe in his Imāmate and who await his reappearance shall be

---

[264] Ṣadūq, Shaykh Muḥammad b. ʿAlī, *al-Khiṣāl*, p. 29.

> better than the people of all times because God, the Mighty and Sublime, would bestow them with intelligence, understanding, and recognition, and for them, occultation would be the same as presence. Their status shall be like that of the holy warriors who fought under the command of the Messenger of God ﷺ. It is they who are sincere and our true Shīʿah. They shall call the people to the religion of God openly and secretly.[265]

89. Fulfillment of Rights

During the period of occultation, the Imām عجل الله تعالى فرجه الشريف expects his followers to refrain from any unjust behavior towards others, especially in matters concerning finances and other matters. It is crucial for a sincere believer, perceived as associated with the Imām, to maintain a positive reputation that reflects well on the Imām, rather than being a source of shame to them. That is why it is said that one of Imām al-Mahdī's عجل الله تعالى فرجه الشريف initial actions upon his reappearance is to settle the debts owed by his followers and clear them of any financial obligations to others. This insight comes from a narration by Imām aṣ-Ṣādiq عليه السلام:

> The first thing the Mahdī will do is to call out throughout the world:

[265] Majlisī, ʿAllāmah Muḥammad Bāqir, *Biḥār al-Anwār*, Vol. 52, p. 122.

Anyone owed a debt by one of our followers should come forward.

He will then settle these debts, whether they are as small as a piece of garlic or a mustard seed, or as large as heaps of gold, silver, or property.[266]

However, sincere followers should settle their financial and other obligations to others before the Imām عجل الله does so on their behalf, as it could potentially place an obligation upon the Imām.

90. Ignorance of Some Shīʿah

Ignorance among those claiming to be followers of the Imām عجل الله is one of the factors that causes him harm during the occultation period. Some of those affiliated with him, under the pretext of exaggeration in proving their allegiance to him, end up deviating from the truth on one hand, and leading others to turn away from the path of guardianship and Imāmate on the other hand. Here is a stern reprimand to them in one of his letters, when he mentions some of them:

O Muḥammad b. ʿAlī! The uneducated and the ignorant among the Shīʿah, and (people like) the one whose religion is outweighed by a mosquito's wing, have hurt us.

---

[266] Majlisī, ʿAllāmah Muḥammad Bāqir, Biḥār al-Anwār, Vol. 53, p. 34.

> So I make God ﷻ, the one apart from whom there is no one worthy of worship, a witness, and it is a sufficient testimony, and (I make witness) Prophet Muḥammad ﷺ, His angels, His prophets, and His beloved people. Peace be upon them all. And I make you a witness and all those who hear this message, I declare my dissociation to God ﷻ and His messenger ﷺ from anyone who says that we know ghaib, share His kingdom or attributes to us a position other than the one chosen by God ﷻ for us and which we were created for, or transgresses with regards to us in what has been explained to you and laid out at the beginning of this message.
>
> And I make you all witness that whoever we dissociate from, then indeed God ﷻ, His angels, His messengers, and His beloved people also dissociate from him.

Then the Imām ﷺ issues a threat by saying:

> And I declare this message, which is in this letter, a trust (responsibility/duty) on your neck and the neck of everyone who hears it, not to conceal it from anyone among my devotees and Shīʿah, so that this message reaches all the devotees [of Ahl al-Bayt ﷺ. Thus, everyone who this message reaches and does not follow what I have ordered and reject what I have ordered to be rejected, then the curse of God has befallen them, as well as the curse of the righteous worshippers whom I have mentioned.

> So anyone who comprehends this message but does not conform to what it has ordered and forbidden, then upon him is damnation of God and those pious people that have been mentioned.[267]

Here, it is necessary to mention an explanation by the scholar ʿAllāmah Majlisī ﵀ regarding this ḥadīth, where he says:

> What is meant by denying their knowledge of the unseen is that they do not know it except through revelation and inspiration from God ﷻ. As for what comes from that realm, it cannot be denied since it constitutes the cornerstone of the miracles of the prophets and the successors ﷺ which include information about the unseen. God, the Most High, exempted them from this limitation in His saying:
>
> ﴿إِلَّا مَنِ ارْتَضَىٰ مِن رَّسُولٍ﴾
>
> ﴿*illā mani rtaḍā min rasūlin*﴾
>
> ﴿*except to an apostle He approves of*﴾[268] [269]

---

[267] Ṭabrisī, Shaykh Aḥmad b. ʿAlī Ṭabrisī, *al-Iḥtijāj ʿalā Ahl al-Lijāj*, Vol. 4, p. 300.

[268] Sūrat al-Jinn, Verse 27.

[269] Majlisī, ʿAllāmah Muḥammad Bāqir, *Biḥār al-Anwār*, Vol. 25, p. 268.

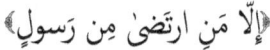

91. Guiding Those Who Stray

The Imām عجل الله تعالى فرجه الشريف always sought to guide those who had strayed or expressed doubts back to the path of righteousness. He did this by reaching out to them to address their concerns before confronting them, hoping that this approach would lead to genuine reflection and inner transformation.

When Mahziyāri arrived in ʿIrāq with doubt and confusion about the Imām, Imām al-Mahdī عجل الله تعالى فرجه الشريف wrote the following to his representative:

> Tell Mahziyāri that we have heard the things that you mentioned about your Imām.

Then he عجل الله تعالى فرجه الشريف presented convincing proof from the Noble Qurʾān:

> Ask him:
>
> > Have you not heard God's saying:

﴿يا أَيُّهَا الَّذِينَ آمَنوا أَطيعُوا اللَّهَ وَأَطيعُوا الرَّسولَ وَأُولِي الأَمرِ مِنكُم﴾

﴿yā-ʾayyuhā lladhīna āmanū aṭīʿū llāha wa-ʾaṭīʿū r-rasūla wa-ʾulī l-ʾamri minkum﴾

﴾*O you who have faith! Obey God and obey the Apostle and those vested with authority among you*﴿[270]

> Is this authority till the Judgment Day for anyone else other than him, who is concealed from your view? [271]

Then Imām al-Mahdī ﷺ points to the practical reality, where the Prophet ﷺ foretold the twelve Imāms, concluding this blessed series with himself, so that the proof of divine succession remains unbroken. When one star sets, another rises, as he said in his letter:

> God, the Mighty and Sublime, has endowed you with intellect so that you may contemplate, and He has appointed signs so that you may obtain guidance from them, from Ādam ﷺ to Imām al-ʿAskarī ﷺ. When one sign disappeared, another appeared, like one star sets and another rises. Do you think that after Imām al-ʿAskarī ﷺ God, the Mighty and Sublime, has not maintained any connection between Himself and the people? It is not so. The command of God shall continue to be effective till the Judgment Day, and they shall continue to guide.[272]

---

[270] Sūrat an-Nisāʾ, Verse 54.

[271] Ṣadūq, Shaykh Muḥammad b. ʿAlī, *Kamāl al-Dīn wa Tamām al-Niʿmah*, Vol. 2, p. 487.

[272] Ibid.

Finally, the Imām عجّل الله تعالى فرجه الشريف showed his eagerness to guide Mahziyāri, especially since he had followers in Ahvāz, by sharing something of the secret between the Imām and Mahziyāri's father before his passing, to increase his certainty and reassurance.

In all of this, there is a practical lesson for all of us in following the path of our Imām عليه السلام during the occultation period, which is to rescue those who are astray and misguided by employing all possible means, while adhering to wisdom and good counsel in our guiding efforts.

92. The Basis of Actions

Our inner faculties and qualities form the foundation for our actions and behavior in daily life, whether they are positive or negative. If we act contrary to the nature of those faculties, our actions become insincere and artificial. That is why ethicists caution against negative inner tendencies, like envy, which can drive us to harmful behavior and lead us to sin against others we envy.

These negative inner faculties, as mentioned, led ash-Shalmaghānī to be cursed by Imām al-Mahdī عجّل الله تعالى فرجه الشريف. Shaykh an-Najāshī recounted about ash-Shalmaghānī:

> He was among our advanced companions, but envy towards Abū al-Qāsim al-Ḥusayn b. Rūḥ led him to

> abandon our school of thought and adopt inferior doctrines until epistles came out about him[273]

93. The Imām's Representatives

The four deputies were chosen directly by the Imām ﷺ and acted as his specific agents. However, the general concept of agency, as it applies to issuing legal opinions, also applies to jurists to some extent. They are the authorities in religious matters during the period of occultation. Whatever a jurist does during the major occultation, he does on behalf of his Imām, just as it was during the minor occultation. Imām al-'Askarī ﷺ mentioned this regarding his agent Abū 'Amr 'Uthmān b. Sa'īd al-'Amrī, when he said:

> This man Abū Amr (Ḥaḍrat 'Uthmān b. Sa'īd) is a reliable and trustworthy person. He was dependable for the previous Imām and is dependable for me in my lifetime and even after my death. Whatever he conveys to you is from our side, and everything he gives to you is from us.[274]

This representation also includes handling religious dues. It is interesting to note that the Imām's followers were widespread, and they ensured that they delivered their religious dues directly to him. An example of this is the

---

[273] al-Najāshī, Aḥmad b. 'Alī, *Rijāl al-Najāshī*, p. 378.

[274] Ṭūsī, Shaykh Muḥammad b. Ḥasan, *Kitāb al-Ghaybah*, p. 355.

delegation from al-Yaman when they came to see Imām al-'Askarī ؑ. They said:

> O, our master! By God, 'Uthmān is truly one of the best of your Shī'ah. You have indeed increased our knowledge by assigning him to your service. He is your deputy and is trusted with the wealth of God ﷻ.

Imām al-'Askarī ؑ replied:

> Yes, indeed, and bear witness that 'Uthmān b. Sa'īd al-'Amrī is my deputy, and his son Muḥammad is the deputy of my son, your Mahdī.[275]

94. The Money Test

Dealing with money can be a major test, even for those who claim to be close to God ﷻ. One of the key qualities expected of the Imām's representatives during the occultation is their integrity in matters of wealth and finances. Many have stumbled in this regard, despite their claims of allegiance and adherence to the guidance of the Imāms. Were some who were hesitant to hand over what was rightfully the Imām's share, wanting to ensure that what was entrusted to them reached him properly. This conscientiousness regarding wealth was a characteristic of the ambassadors during the minor occultation.

[275] Ṭūsī, Shaykh Muḥammad b. Ḥasan, *Kitāb al-Ghaybah*, p. 356.

The following narration serves as an example of this:

> It was my habit that when I submitted the money in my possession to Shaykh Abū Jaʿfar Muḥammad b. ʿUthmān al-ʿAmrī, the last encounter I had with him, he commanded me:
>
>> Take to al-Ḥusayn b. Rūḥ.
>
> So I paused (in hesitation) and said:
>
>> Take it from me as usual.
>
> He replied to me as if he was surprised by my statement:
>
>> Rise, may God protect you and give it to al-Ḥusayn b. Rūḥ.
>
> When I saw displeasure on his face, I left while exclaiming:
>
>> At the command of the Imām عليه السلام?
>
> He said:
>
>> Rise, and give to al-Ḥusayn b. Rūḥ as I commanded you.

> I was then left with no other choice but to do as commanded.[276]

95. Absolute Submission

To be close to the Imām of our time ﷺ, one must embody absolute submission to him in every aspect. This was a defining characteristic of the Imām's chosen companions, particularly during the Minor Occultation. Initially, it was presumed that one among them might assume the deputyship due to his close ties with the appointed deputy. However, circumstances unfolded differently. Yet, this loyal companion remained steadfast in submitting to the Imām's decision. This is evident in the following account:

> We did not have any doubt that if something should happen to Abū Jaʿfar, no one would take his place, but Jaʿfar b. Aḥmad b. Maṭīl or his father, for he was Abū Jaʿfar's confidant and was frequently present at his house. It was known that towards the end of his life, Abū Jaʿfar did not eat any food that was not prepared at the house of Jaʿfar b. Aḥmad b. Maṭīl and his father, due to an incident that had occurred. His food was at Jaʿfar's house and his father's. Our scholars did not doubt that if something happened, the position would be handed to him. When he passed away and Abūl Qāsim was selected, they submitted to him and did not reject him. They were all with him and at his service

[276] Ṭūsī, Shaykh Muḥammad b. Ḥasan, *Kitāb al-Ghaybah*, p. 367.

> just as they were with Abū Jaʿfar. Jaʿfar b. Aḥmad b. Maṭīl continued to serve Abūl Qāsim as his deputy until his death, as he had also served Abū Jaʿfar ʿĀmarī. Anyone who criticizes Abūl Qāsim criticizes Abū Jaʿfar and finally criticizes the Divine Proof (Ḥujjah).[277]

It is fitting to reflect on the last paragraph, where criticizing the representative of the Imām is likened to criticizing the Imām himself. Similarly, this principle also applies to his general representatives during the major occultation.

96. Loyalty

The appointment of the four deputies was not haphazard; they had to embody another crucial quality: unwavering loyalty to the Imām عجل الله تعالى فرجه الشريف. This is exemplified by Abū Sahl an-Nawbakhtī, who, when asked why Shaykh Abū al-Qāsim al-Ḥusayn b. Rūḥ was chosen as the deputy instead of him, responded:

> They are more knowledgeable about who they have chosen. I am a man who meets adversaries and engages in debates with them. Should I have known his whereabouts, as Abūl Qāsim does, and been pressed in my debates for proof, perhaps I would have led them to his place. As for Abūl Qāsim, even if the Divine Proof (Ḥujjah) were to be entrusted to him, even if scissors

[277] Ṭūsī, Shaykh Muḥammad b. Ḥasan, *Kitāb al-Ghaybah*, p. 369.

> cut him, he would not give up his secret nor reveal the Imām's place.[278]

What is intriguing is how al-Nawbakhti draws a line between possessing scholarly expertise and debating skillfully with opponents and the willingness to sacrifice oneself to protect and defend the Imām from harm. It is important to note that possessing one of these traits does not necessarily imply possessing the other. From this expression, we understand the status of Imām al-Ḥusayn's عليه السلام companions. While some may not have been renowned for their scholarly prowess, their readiness to sacrifice themselves earned them the reputation of being among the most devoted and sincere companions.

97. The Money Test

One of the challenges that truly demonstrates the devotion of a sincere believer awaiting the Imām's return is the trial concerning money, as discussed in the Qur'ānic verses that address the allure of material desires, including the riches of gold and silver. During the period of minor occultation, individuals made great sacrifices and endured hardships to ensure that funds reached the Imām عجل الله تعالى فرجه الشريف or his appointed representative. Among them was Ibrāhīm b. Mahziyār, as narrated by his son:

[278] Ibid., p. 391.

When Abū Muḥammad ﷺ passed away, doubts clouded my mind. My father had amassed funds intended for the Imām. Determined to deliver it, he boarded the ship, and I accompanied him. Then he fell ill, and he said to me,

> Return me, for it is death. Fear God regarding this money.

He entrusted me with it, and then he passed away. I thought,

> My father would not leave any incorrect instructions.

So, I carried this wealth to ʻIrāq without informing anyone. If anything became clear to me, I would act accordingly and pay it; otherwise, I would spend it. I bought a house by the shore and stayed there for days. Suddenly, a messenger brought a letter, saying,

> O Muḥammad, you have this and that with you,

until he detailed all that was with me. I handed over the wealth to the messenger and stayed for days without lifting my head. I felt reassured when I received another letter saying,

> We have established you in the position of your father, so praise God ﷻ.[279]

98. Positive Endings

There is a remarkable story showcasing how people can undergo incredible changes, to the point where they transition from a life of drinking to serving as deputies of the Imām during the minor occultation. This story revolves around al-Ḥasan b. al-Qāsim b. Alā'. He received prayers from both the Imām ﷺ and his father, who was concerned about him. This highlights the immense power of prayer in profoundly shaping someone's journey. Here is how it unfolded between father and son:

Qāsim said to his son Ḥasan,

> God will grant you a great position, so accept it with gratitude.

Ḥasan said,

> Father, I accept it.

Qāsim said,

> How?

> As you order me, father.

---

[279] Sa'īd al-Kāshānī, *al-Kharā'ij wal-Jarā'iḥ*, Vol. 1, p. 361.

He said,

> Give up drinking.

Ḥasan said,

> You are right, father. I will give it up and many other things you do not know about.

Qāsim raised his hands to the sky and said,

> God, cast Your obedience into Ḥasan's heart and prevent him from sins.

He said this three times. Then he asked for a piece of paper and wrote his final will by hand. Ḥasan accepted his father's will.

A short while after that, a letter of consolation came to his son from our Imām, at the end of which was a Duʿāʾ for him,

> May God cast His obedience into your heart and may He prevent you from sins,

the Duʿāʾ his father had prayed for him. At the end, it stated,

> We made your father an Imām for you and his actions an example for you.[280]

This story highlights the profound impact of a parent's character and actions on their child's upbringing. This principle remains relevant even in times of great concealment.

99. The Criteria for Acceptance

Some may feel a sense of accomplishment when they contribute to the wealth of their time's Imām. However, the acceptance of such contributions, like any other good deed, hinges on the sincerity of the giver and their adherence to righteous principles, as emphasized in the Qur'ān:

﴿إِنَّمَا يَتَقَبَّلُ اللَّهُ مِنَ الْمُتَّقِينَ﴾

﴿*innamā yataqabbalu llāhu mina l-muttaqīn*[a]﴾

﴿*God accepts only from the Godwary*﴾[281]

Furthermore, the giver should be one that the Imām عجل الله فرجه الشريف is pleased with and those without doubts in their beliefs regarding khums, as mentioned in one of his letters:

---

[280] Ṭūsī, Shaykh Muḥammad b. Ḥasan, *Kitāb al-Ghaybah*, p. 314.

[281] Sūrat al-Mā'idah, Verse 27.

> As for the funds that are sent to us, and after which they fell into doubts and became regretful of having paid it to us, then anyone who wants, we would return to him, and we do not need the money of those who harbor doubt about God.[282]

The wealth must come from lawful sources. How can the giver expect to draw closer to God with wealth earned unlawfully? This principle is reiterated in the Imām's letter:

> As for the money that you send to me, it is not acceptable to me, except that money which is pure[283]

100. The Blessings of the Soil of Karbalā'

The soil of Karbalā' holds a special significance, known for its potential to heal (a testament to the sacrifices made upon it). This unique blessing was emphasized by our Imām ﷺ in a letter where he addressed the use of a rosary (tasbīḥ) made from Karbalā''s soil:

> It is permissible to use it for tasbīḥ, as there is nothing better for tasbīḥ than it. One of its virtues is that the

[282] Ṣadūq, Shaykh Muḥammad b. 'Alī, *Kamāl al-Dīn wa Tamām al-Ni'mah*, Vol. 2, p. 485.

[283] Ibid.

> one who uses it for tasbīḥ forgets the count and turns the beads, and for him, the tasbīḥ is accepted.[284]

Numerous narrations from previous Imāms ﷺ also speak of the rewards bestowed upon believers using such a rosary, even if their minds wander during its use. Imām al-Kāẓim ﷺ stated:

> Our Shīʿah should not be without four things: the first is khumrah (turbah) on which they offer prayers, a ring that they wear, a miswak with which they clean their teeth, and a tasbīḥ made from the clay of the grave of Imām al-Ḥusayn ﷺ, containing thirty-three beads. Whenever one turns to them, remembering God, God writes forty good deeds for each bead. And when one turns them idly, playing with them, God writes for them twenty good deeds.[285]

101.A Profound Supplication in the Holy Month

Among the eloquent supplications during the blessed month of Ramaḍān is one attributed to our present Imām ﷺ, where he asks God ﷻ to make this noble month the best of all the months that have passed. In the supplication, he says:

---

[284] Ṭūsī, Shaykh Muḥammad b. Ḥasan, *Tahdhīb al-Ahkām fī Sharḥ al-Muqniʿah*, Vol. 6, p. 76.

[285] Ibid., p. 75.

> O God, I ask You by Your sanctity to make this day of mine the best day of worship in Your sight since You placed me on this Earth. Grant it the greatest reward, the most abundant blessings and well-being, the widest sustenance, and make it a day of salvation from the Fire, and a day of utmost forgiveness. Perfect Your pleasure upon me, and bring me closer to what You love and are pleased with.[286]

This supplication, if answered, promises to renew and multiply blessings in every fasting month, given the specific blessings sought by the Imām towards the end of his prayer. This sentiment is also reflected in the words of his grandfather, Imām aṣ-Ṣādiq ﷺ, who prayed:

> And make this month of ours the greatest month of Ramaḍān in blessings that has passed upon us since we descended to this world[287]

102.Piety as a Prerequisite for Service

Anyone who desires to serve their Imām ﷺ, at any level or capacity, must possess a certain degree of piety. Being in the service of the Imām is akin to treading on sacred ground, which the impure are not allowed to step on. During the

---

[286] Ṭūsī, Shaykh Muḥammad b. Ḥasan, *Tahdhīb al-Aḥkām fī Sharḥ al-Muqni'ah*, Vol. 3, p. 141.

[287] Kulaynī, Shaykh Muḥammad b. Ya'qūb, *al-Kāfī*, Vol. 7, p. 644.

Imām's occultation, he does not accept anyone tainted with a grave sin to serve him.

An example of this occurred during the minor occultation when someone was sent with servants to the city of the Prophet ﷺ, and one of the servants drank alcohol when they reached Kūfah. As soon as they left Kūfah, a letter arrived from the military ordering the dismissal of the servant who drank, and he was removed from service.

This incident teaches us that those who commit wrongdoing in secret leave no room for goodness to flow through them during the occultation. This explains the sudden withdrawal of success in serving the faith, which some may attribute to coincidence or chance. Instead, it may be attributed to the Imām's directive to remove those unsuitable for service, exemplified in the incident of alcohol consumption.

103.Supplication Near Imām al-Ḥusayn's Grave

The Imāms عليهم السلام encouraged people to visit the shrine of Imām al-Ḥusayn عليه السلام when facing challenges. They even sent individuals to pray near his grave on their behalf, which left many puzzled. An example from the life of Imām al-Hādī عليه السلام illustrates this:

Abū Hāshim al-Ja'farī said,

> Muḥammad b. Abū Ḥamzah and I visited Imām al-Hādī ﷺ when he was ill.

He ﷺ said to us,

> Send some men to al-Ḥā'ir (Karbalā', where Imām al-Ḥusayn ﷺ was buried) at my expense!

When we left him, Muḥammad b. Ḥamzah said to me,

> Does he send us to al-Ḥā'ir while he has the same position as the one (Imām al-Ḥusayn) who is in a-Ḥā'ir?!

The words of Muḥammad b. Ḥamzah influenced Abū Hashim, and so he went to Imām al-Hādī ﷺ and told him. Imām al-Hādī ﷺ said to him,

> It is not so. God has some places that He likes to be worshipped, and al-Ḥā'ir of al-Ḥusayn is one of those places.[288]

Similarly, such recommendations were repeated during the minor occultation, where the Imām ﷺ advised someone to visit the shrine of Imām al-Ḥusayn ﷺ to have their needs fulfilled. The details of this are narrated as follows:

---

[288] al-Qummī, Ibn Qūlawayh, *Kāmil al-Zīyārāt*, p. 273.

He [the narrator] said:

I was dumb and unable to speak a single word. When I was thirteen or fourteen, my father and uncle took me to Shaykh Abūl Qāsim b. Rūḥ and requested that he beseech the Imām to ask God ﷻ to open my tongue through his blessings. Shaykh Abūl Qāsim Ḥusayn b. Rūḥ said:

> You have been commanded to go to the tomb of Imām al-Ḥusayn.

We came back from there and decided to travel to Karbalā'. We performed the ritual bath for Ziyārah.

Meanwhile, my father and uncle called out,

> Sarwar.

I replied to them in a clear tone:

> Here I am.[289]

---

[289] Ṭūsī, Shaykh Muḥammad b. Ḥasan, *Kitāb al-Ghaybah*, p. 309.

Emotional Connection

1. Reflecting on the Imām's Difficulties

Just the mere thought of the hardships endured by the Imām عجّل الله تعالى فرجه الشريف is enough to stir deep emotions within us, especially when thinking about the intense sorrow and grief he endured throughout the ages. As the vigilant overseer of God's creation, he witnesses firsthand the ongoing trials and tribulations of his community. Additionally, he bears the weight of the sorrows experienced by his predecessors and is tasked with seeking justice and retribution on their behalf.

Turning the pain of being separate from him and his sadness into a personal matter, as if losing him is akin to losing our dearest, draws us closer to his exclusive sphere of attraction, reserved for his devoted followers. This sentiment is hinted at in the sujūd of Ziyārat ʿĀshūrāʾ, where the visitor says:

> All praise be to God for my great misfortune,

attributing the misfortune to themselves, as if they were the afflicted in the tragedy of Imām al-Ḥusayn عليه السلام.

2. The Concern for the Ummah

Our Imām عجّل الله تعالى فرجه الشريف is not worried about himself; he is always under the watchful care of God عزّ وجلّ. No enemy can harm him, but any distress he feels is for the sake of his grandfather's nation, the believers. Thus, believers need to follow his example in looking after the Ummah's welfare, both in worldly matters and in the Hereafter. Blessed is the one who shoulders the responsibility, using their wealth to aid the needy and their words to guide the lost.

In this way, believers become guardians of the orphans of the Prophet Muḥammad's family ﷺ, those separated from their Imām during his occultation. Sometimes, they address outward shortcomings, and other times, they mend inner deficiencies. If the guardian of an orphan can achieve such a lofty status, as mentioned by the Noble Prophet ﷺ, then imagine the status of one who cares for eternal souls!

Imām al-Ḥasan al-ʿAskarī said:

> The reward for supporting an orphan from the family of Muḥammad, someone disconnected from the Imām and lost in the darkness of ignorance, by rescuing them from ignorance and enlightening them about what was once unclear to them, when compared to the virtue of sponsoring an orphan who has lost their parents and providing them with food and drink, is like the superiority of the sun over the Alcor star.[290]

3. The Works of God and the Imāms

It has been narrated that Imām Muḥammad al-Mahdī said:

---

[290] Ṭabrisī, Shaykh Aḥmad b. ʿAlī Ṭabrisī, *al-Iḥtijāj ʿalā Ahl al-Lijāj*, Vol. 1, p. 16.

> We are the devising of God, and the rest of creation is our devising[291]

When someone is described as the work of another person, it suggests that immense care and attention have been invested in shaping that individual, making them a product of nurturing and upbringing. The Imāms serve as conduits for divine blessings, as echoed in supplication:

> Where is the means of access that continuously connects the earth with the heavens[292]

These blessings include being in the thoughts of one's Imām, guiding them towards fulfillment and spiritual growth. If God ﷻ manages the universe through angels, including those who regulate the affairs of the universe and take souls, then surely the Imām of creation plays an even more vital role in its guidance.

This text also illustrates the nature of the relationship between all the infallibles and their righteous followers, as Imām Muḥammad al-Bāqir ﵇ says:

---

[291] Ṭūsī, Shaykh Muḥammad b. Ḥasan, *Kitāb al-Ghaybah*, p. 285.

[292] Mufīd, Shaykh Muḥammad, *Kitāb al-Mazār*, p. 579.

> Our Shīʿah would be attaching themselves to us, and we would be attaching ourselves to the Prophet, and our Prophet would be attaching himself to God ﷻ[293]

4. Love for their Followers

Even though the Imāms ﷺ live in their sacred realm, the depth of which cannot be fully comprehended except by those close to their rank, when they look upon their followers, they sense a profound connection with them. These followers are the product of their guidance and care in this world, and they will be their companions in the Hereafter. However, they have consistently emphasized the importance of assisting them through piety and diligence, laying the foundation for their intercession.

Imagine how great it is that your Imām ﷺ yearns for your soul and fragrance, just as his noble predecessors did. It has been narrated that Imām Jaʿfar aṣ-Ṣādiq ﷺ said:

> Abū Jaʿfar ﷺ and I passed by the Shīʿah between the grave and the pulpit. I said to Abū Jaʿfar ﷺ:
>
> > There are your Shīʿah and followers, may I be sacrificed for you.
>
> He asked,

---

293 al-Barqī, Aḥmad b. Muḥammad b. Khālid, *al-Maḥāsin*, Vol. 1, p. 182.

> Where are they?

I replied,

> I see them between the grave and the pulpit.

He said,

> Take me to them.

So, I took him to them, and he greeted them. Then he said,

> By God, I love your scent and your souls. So, assist me with piety and diligence. Verily, one does not attain what is with God except through piety and diligence.[294]

5. The Works of God ﷻ

It is gleaned from some narrations that the Imāms, despite their preoccupation with the higher realms and their immersion therein, also feel sadness over what befalls the nation of their grandfather. They worry about people's doubts in their faith and uncertainties about the reappearance. This shows how their hearts encompass the struggles and concerns of the nation, even though they need anything besides God ﷻ.

---

[294] Kulaynī, Shaykh Muḥammad b. Yaʿqūb, *al-Kāfī*, Vol. 15, p. 547.

It has been reported that Imām al-Mahdī عجل الله تعالى فرجه الشريف said:

> Information regarding the doubt and denial of a group of you in religion and the matter of guardianship (*wilāyah*) has reached us. Our sorrow and anger are for you and not for ourselves, as God ﷻ is with us; therefore, except for Him, we are not needful of anyone, and the truth is with us. Therefore, I am not afraid of someone turning away from us. And we are the first creations of our Lord, and other creatures and people were created afterwards.[295]

It is also necessary to reflect on the last paragraph. Just as the Imām is honored to be under the watchful eye and upbringing of God ﷻ, the same applies to the creation, which is honored by the Imām's care, making each individual a product of his upbringing.

6. Not Harming the Imām

When a believer awaiting the Imām عجل الله تعالى فرجه الشريف reaches a level of inner purity, they steer clear of anything that could harm them. They strive so that they do not fall under the condemnation described in this verse:

﴿إِنَّ الَّذِينَ يُؤْذُونَ اللَّهَ وَرَسُولَهُ لَعَنَهُمُ اللَّهُ فِي الدُّنْيَا وَالْآخِرَةِ
وَأَعَدَّ لَهُمْ عَذَابًا مُهِينًا﴾

---

[295] Ṭūsī, Shaykh Muḥammad b. Ḥasan, *Kitāb al-Ghaybah*, p. 285.

*ʿinna lladhīna yuʾdhūna llāha wa-rasūlahū laʿanahumu
llāhu fī d-dunyā wa-l-ʾākhirati wa-ʾaʿadda lahum
ʿadhāban muhīnaⁿ*

*《Indeed those who torment God and His Apostle are cursed
by God in the world and the Hereafter, and He has prepared
a humiliating punishment for them》*[296]

It is understood that harming him comes from disobeying
the Sharīʿah, as he is the guardian solely focused on matters
of faith and pleasing God ﷻ. Narrations from the Ahl al-
Bayt ﵊ have consistently stressed this, such as what Imām
al-Bāqir ﵇ conveyed to Jābir al-Jaʿfī:

> Nothing draws one closer to God ﷻ, except through
> obedience. We have no immunity from the fire for
> anyone, nor does anyone argue against God. Whoever
> is obedient to God is our friend, and whoever disobeys
> God is our enemy. Our guardianship (*wilāyah*) is only
> attained through righteous action and piety.[297]

7. No Fear or Sorrow

In a world filled with turmoil and worries, finding solace
becomes crucial. One way to do so is by connecting with
the source of security and stability in existence. This source
is embodied in the Imām appointed by God ﷻ, who

---

[296] Sūrat al-Aḥzāb, Verse 57.

[297] *al-Amālī*, p. 530.

receives what has been destined for creation on the Night of Decree. He has the power, if he desires, to ask God ﷻ to change a believer's fate from one of misery to one of happiness. Recognizing and understanding this truth is essential.

Moreover, for those eagerly anticipating his return, they find reassurance in being part of the Imām's affairs, both in theory and in reality. There is hope that he will embrace his followers and lead them from the darkness of hardships into the light of relief. Imām aṣ-Ṣādiq عليه السلام alluded to this reality when he said:

> Fortunate are the Shīʿah of our Qāʾim who, during the period of his occultation, await his reappearance and obey him upon his reappearance. They are Awliyāʾ of God for whom there shall be neither fear nor grief.[298]

8. The Tragedy of al-Ḥusayn عليه السلام

The heartbreaking event of al-Ḥusayn's عليه السلام martyrdom stands as one of the most significant tragedies in history. Its impact echoed through the heavens and stirred the angels to seek justice for his unjust killing. Although the angels pleaded with God ﷻ for permission to avenge al-Ḥusayn's عليه السلام murder, they were informed that the task would be carried out by the Mahdī, from the progeny of Prophet

[298] Ṣadūq, Shaykh Muḥammad b. ʿAlī, *Kamāl al-Dīn wa Tamām al-Niʿmah*, Vol. 2, p. 357.

Muḥammad ﷺ. This understanding comes from the words of Imām aṣ-Ṣādiq ؑ:

> When al-Ḥusayn ؑ was killed, the heavens, the Earth, and all that is upon them, including the angels, trembled. They said,
>
>> O our Lord, permit us to destroy the creatures until we eliminate them from the face of the earth for violating Your sanctity and killing Your chosen one.
>
> Then, He revealed to them,
>
>> O my angels, O my heavens, and O my earth, stay calm.
>
> Then God unveiled a veil, and behind it was Muḥammad ﷺ, along with twelve of his successors. God pointed at al-Qāʾim amongst them and said:
>
>> O my angels, O my heavens, and O my earth, with this one, victory shall be achieved.
>
> He repeated this statement three times.[299]

---

[299] Kulaynī, Shaykh Muḥammad b. Yaʿqūb, *al-Kāfī*, Vol. 2, p. 704.

9. Submission and Devotion

Many of us long to live during the time of the Commander of the Faithful عليه السلام, standing proudly among his supporters in his battles against the treacherous, the unjust, and the apostates. Even today, those who wish they were by his side and genuinely aspire to be counted among his allies, adhering to what Imām ʿAlī عليه السلام advocated, are indeed considered among his companions. An illustrative account of this is when the Commander of the Faithful عليه السلام battled the Khawārij on the Day of Nahrawān. A man approached him, saying:

> O Commander of the Faithful! How blessed are we to witness this moment with you, to fight alongside you against these Khawārij,

The Commander of the Faithful عليه السلام replied,

> By the One who splits the seed and brings forth life! Indeed, in this moment, we were joined by people whose fathers and grandfathers had not yet been born.

The man questioned,

> How can people join us if they have not been born?

To which he responded,

> Yes, there are people who will emerge in the end times, who will stand with us and submit to our cause. They are truly our partners in our mission.[300]

Thus, Imām 'Alī ﷺ emphasized the connection between submission to them and becoming their partners, as evident from this narration.

10. The Imām's Complaint to his Grandfather

Indeed, the Noble Prophet ﷺ was the refuge for complaints of all the infallibles. Starting right after his passing, as witnessed with Imām 'Alī and Sayyidah Fāṭimah az-Zahrā' ﷺ. When Imām 'Alī ﷺ laid Sayyidah Fāṭimah ﷺ to rest, he turned to the Prophet, saying:

> the trust has been (thus) returned (to you) and the deposit (with me) has been redeemed; and az-Zahrā' has been snatched away (from me)[301]

Sayyidah Fāṭimah ﷺ herself complained to her father about the injustices she faced after his passing, and said:

[300] al-Barqī, Aḥmad b. Muḥammad b. Khālid, *al-Maḥāsin*, Vol. 1, p. 262.

[301] Ṭūsī, Shaykh Muḥammad b. Ḥasan, *al-Amālī*, p. 282.

> This is how they treat your beloved daughter[302]

Even Lady Zaynab عليها السلام turned to her grandfather ﷺ in anguish after the tragedy of Imām al-Ḥusayn عليه السلام, crying out:

> O grandfather, this is your al-Ḥusayn lying in the wilderness[303]

This tradition of seeking refuge in the Prophet ﷺ continues in his pure lineage until the time of reappearance of Imām al-Mahdī عجل الله فرجه الشريف. He, too, will voice his grievances to his grandfather, saying:

> O, my grandfather, you spoke of me, you clarified my lineage and name to the people, yet this nation, steeped in disbelief, denied me, casting doubts upon my existence. They said,
>
> > He was not born, nor did he exist. Where is he, when was he, and where will he be?
>
> He perished, his father passed without a successor, and they hastened what God had deferred until this known time. I endured with patience, hopeful, God has now

---

302 Majlisī, ʿAllāmah Muḥammad Bāqir, *Biḥār al-Anwār*, Vol. 30, p. 294.

303 al-Kūfī, Lūṭ b. Yaḥyā Abū Mikhnaf, *Wāqiʿat aṭ-Ṭaff*, p. 259.

> granted me, O my grandfather, the permission to fulfill His decree.[304]

11. The Agony of Imām al-Ḥusayn's Martyrdom

The mention of Imām al-Ḥusayn held a special place in the hearts of the early prophets, including the Arch-Prophets (Ulū al-ʿAzm). For them, his remembrance sparked profound emotions, as they understood his significance as one of the five noble individuals, the proofs of God upon creation, whose light shone even before the creation of Ādam. They also foresaw the magnitude of the tragedies that would befall him.

Imām al-Mahdī mentioned a sample of this in one of his letters. In it, he recounted:

> Prophet Zakariyyā beseeched God to teach him the names of these five individuals. Gabriel descended and imparted this knowledge to him. Whenever Zakariyyā mentioned the names of Muḥammad, ʿAlī, Fāṭimah, and al-Ḥasan, his distress eased. However, the mention of al-Ḥusayn brought tears to his eyes, and grief overwhelmed him. He said one day:
>
> > My Lord! Why is it that when I mention four of them, I find solace in their names amidst my

304 Ṭūsī, Shaykh Muḥammad b. Ḥasan, *al-Amālī*, p. 282.

worries, but when I mention al-Ḥusayn, my eyes well up with tears and my heart feels heavy?

God ﷻ then informed him about the story of al-Ḥusayn. Upon hearing this, Zakariyyā ؑ did not leave his place of worship for three days. He prevented people from entering and spent his time in weeping and lamentation, mourning the tragedy of al-Ḥusayn ؑ,

> My God, will they make the best of Your creature sit in mourning for his son? O Lord, would this tremendous tragedy befall him? Would they make the shock of this calamity reach their abode?

Then he said:

> Bestow a son upon me so that I may be pleased in my old age and that his love may warm my heart. After that, make me sit in his mourning as You would make Muḥammad, Your beloved, sit.

So, God ﷻ gave him Yaḥyā, and later, his martyrdom made him aggrieved. And the period of Yaḥyā's pregnancy was six months, like in the case of al-Ḥusayn.[305]

Considering Prophet Zakariyyā's ؑ anguish before Imām al-Ḥusayn's ؑ birth, imagine the depth of sorrow of his

---

305 Ṭūsī, Shaykh Muḥammad b. Ḥasan, al-Amālī, Vol. 2, p. 461.

son, Imām al-Mahdī عجل الله تعالى فرجه الشريف, who knows the details of the fate of his grandfather. It moved him to shed tears of blood, not just tears of sorrow.

12. A Prayer Filled with Anguish

The prayer attributed to our Imām of the Time عجل الله تعالى فرجه الشريف speaks volumes about the depth of his emotional turmoil and the constriction he feels due to what he and his followers endure during the period of occultation. He bears a burden so heavy that many of us would wish to ease even a fraction of it. What is remarkable about this prayer attributed to him, as mentioned by scholars, is that its length stems from the tightness in his chest. Otherwise, God would respond to His servant even if he prayed once, sincerely and humbly saying,

> O Lord.

These sentiments are evident in the supplication, where he says:

> My Lord, I lengthened my prayer and increased my words, because the tightness of my chest compelled me and drove me to do it, even though I know that even a small amount like a pinch of salt in the dough would be enough for You. Rather, it suffices for You the determination of will, and for the servant to say with sincere intention and truthful tongue,

O my Lord,

so that You are as Your servant's faith in You (Meet the expectations of your servant of You). And my heart has implored You with a firm determination. [306]

Indeed, this prayer and others like it, attributed to Imām al-Mahdī ﷺ, reveal the intensity of his suffering during the period of occultation. Conversely, a heart would not pour out such a prayer filled with anguish and sorrow. Here, he declares that the tightness of his chest compels him to elaborate in prayer and persist in urgency, making this supplication among the longest attributed to him!

13. Wishing to Meet Him

Meeting with our Imām ﷺ is the wish of every awaiting believer. However, what is more important is for the believers to strive to make a fundamental change in their lives. Our Imām ﷺ desires nothing from us except to be righteous servants of God ﷻ, followers of the noble teachings of his grandfather, Prophet Muḥammad ﷺ, and to be vigilant and accountable for our actions.

As one draws nearer to God ﷻ, they also draw closer to His appointed leader. It is important to realize that the path to closeness with the Ahl al-Bayt ﷺ is no different from the path to closeness with God ﷻ. The Sharīʿah makes it clear

[306] Majlisī, ʿAllāmah Muḥammad Bāqir, *Biḥār al-Anwār*, Vol. 92, p. 278.

that there is no separation between the Qur'ān and the progeny, as they are inseparable equals.

The Imāms of the Ahl al-Bayt ﷺ deliberately attribute blessings to God ﷻ as the ultimate source, and designators of His chosen leaders as the conduits for the dissemination of these blessings to the rest of creation. This underscores a truth that may elude some. It is narrated that Imām Zayn al-ʿĀbidīn ؑ said:

> O Abū Ḥamzah, do not sleep before the sunrise, for I detest it for you. Indeed, God apportions the sustenance of His servants at that time, and through our hands, it is distributed.[307]

14. Awaiting is a Branch of Longing

Awaiting is a branch of longing and love. It requires action and commitment; otherwise, one's love is considered false and pretentious, as God ﷻ says:

﴿قُل إِن كُنتُم تُحِبّونَ اللَّهَ فَاتَّبِعوني يُحبِبكُمُ اللَّهُ﴾

﴾qul in kuntum tuḥibbūna llāha fa-ttabiʿūnī yuḥbibkumu llāhu﴿

307 al-Ḥurr al-ʿĀmilī, Shaykh Muḥammad, *Wasāʾil al-Shīʿah*, Vol. 6, p. 49.

﴾*Say, 'If you love God, then follow me; God will love you'*﴿[308]

Those who claim to love without following are characterized by two traits: dishonesty in love and a lack of genuine love for God ﷻ. This does not negate the possibility of a person pretending and claiming to love God ﷻ, perhaps out of ignorance or false pride. In such cases, Shayṭān delights in keeping them trapped in a false sense of love, rather than genuine devotion.

The significance of awaiting the Imām goes beyond mere longing, as evidenced by a narration from Imām aṣ-Ṣādiq ﵇, quoting his grandfather, Imām 'Alī ﵇:

> One who awaits the reappearance of our Qā'im is like one who rolls in his blood in the path of God.[309]

Thus, the use of the metaphor "rolling in blood," commonly associated with jihād, underscores the profound importance of awaiting the Imām.

15. Feeling the Weight of his Occultation

One of the most effective ways to connect with our Imām ﵇ during his absence, beyond prayers and visits, is to feel the weight of his absence genuinely. Those who shoulder this noble concern do not cease their growth journey; they

---

[308] Sūrat Āl 'Imrān, Verse 31.

[309] Ṣadūq, Shaykh Muḥammad b. 'Alī, *al-Khiṣāl*, Vol. 2, p. 625.

strive to better themselves and improve their worship. They also aim to extend kindness to others and actively seek ways to bring joy to the Imām ﷽ and ease his burdens.

When someone's heart is filled with concern for the Imām ﷽ during his occultation, they establish a closeness to him and might even receive his special attention. Examining the stories of devoted followers throughout history underscores this reality: those who have been touched by his care, in any form, are the ones whose hearts burn with longing for him, craving his presence and closeness.

16. Gathered Under his Banner

Indeed, God ﷻ has appointed an Imām for every era, and the Imām of our time is Imām al-Mahdī ﷽, under whose banner we will be gathered on the Day of Judgment. Our actions in this world are believed to be presented to him regularly, particularly on Mondays and Thursdays, as mentioned in certain texts.

Therefore, those seeking success and blessings in their deeds should strive to connect with his blessed presence, or at least ensure that no harm reaches his noble heart, as true devotees cannot bear to witness their beloved in distress.

After experiencing his love in our hearts, linking our deeds to their impact on his heart can help ensure vigilance and accountability in our lives. It is common for people in this world to willingly sacrifice their desires for the sake of those they love, as countless stories of love and devotion attest, and who better to do this for than our Imām?

17. Showing Genuine Longing

Awaiting a guest requires showing genuine interest, extending a sincere invitation, and preparing oneself fully for their arrival. Otherwise, if the guest comes and finds indifference, they will understand that their visit is unwelcome and burdensome. Therefore, we say: whoever claims to await the Imām must meet the standard of awaiting in its truest sense.

It is easy to claim longing without any real commitment. However, genuine waiting means being ready to support the Imām in all arenas, especially in these challenging times. As we recite in the ziyārah:

> My support for you is prepared[310]

Further evidence of the connection between sincere awaiting and action comes from Imām aṣ-Ṣādiq, who outlined the conditions for acceptance of deeds:

> The testimony that there is no god but God, and that Muḥammad is His servant and messenger, and the acceptance of what God has commanded, and allegiance to us (the Imāms), and dissociation from

---

[310] al-Qummī, Ibn Qūlawayh, *Kāmil al-Zīyārāt*, p. 218.

> our enemies, and piety, diligence, and tranquility, and waiting for the Qā'im.

Then he said:

> We have a state that God will bring about when He wills.[311]

18. The Imāms' Grief

One of our duties during the Imām's ﷺ occultation is to carry the concern for his absence. His absence is a cause for deep concern and sorrow, especially when considering the suffering, injustice, and bloodshed on Earth, all of which could be linked to his absence. His reappearance, as promised, will bring justice and equity to a world currently filled with oppression and injustice.

Contributing to hastening his reappearance is crucial for the reformation of humanity, not just for Muslims. Therefore, anyone who carries this concern should play a part in hastening his reappearance, which will bring about global justice, even if it is only for a day. Thus, no one should underestimate the power of their prayers, as the answer lies within the supplications of the righteous.

---

[311] Nuʿmānī, Muḥammad b. Ibrāhīm, *Kitāb al-Ghaybah*, p. 200.

19. The Sign of Closeness

To truly understand the depth of your connection with the Imām of your time عجّل الله تعالى فرجه الشريف, reflect on the direction of your heart during moments when prayers are known to be answered. Did you visit Imām al-Ḥusayn's shrine عليه السلام and find yourself moved to tears? What desires naturally surfaced in your prayers, without any prompting? Similarly, if you journeyed to the sacred House of God and stood before the Holy Kaʿbah and Ḥajar al-Aswad, what prayers arose effortlessly from your heart?

A true lover of the Imām of their time, who shares in his pains, feels embarrassed to prioritize personal needs—such as paying off debts or seeking healing for the sick—over the Imām's needs. After all, the benefit of hastening the relief of the reappearance extends to the entire world, as the Imām's mission is not limited to any particular region or country.

20. Practices for Deepening the Love

Regularly remembering the Imām of the Time عجّل الله تعالى فرجه الشريف is essential for cultivating a deeper love for him in our hearts. This can be practiced by consistently praying for his reappearance during our prayers, giving charity in his name each morning and evening, naming a child after him, adhering to the supplications dedicated to him, reciting Duʿāʾ al-Nudbah on major Islamic holidays, and reciting the supplication for the time of occultation every Friday afternoon.

For those who make a habit of praying for him on Fridays using the supplication for the time of occultation, it is important to note that there is a section in this supplication that acts as a remedy for all ailments:

> And make my heart lenient towards Your representative[312]

If this prayer is answered, and one's heart is entrusted to our Imām 🕊, all their affairs will find a favorable outcome. When the Imām takes charge of a heart, he ensures it receives the best care.

21. Expressing Grief

The Imāms' mention of Imām al-Mahdī 🕊 often evokes wonder, given the profound sorrow they display for his situation and the condition of his Shīʿah during the occultation. The concealment of the Imām, the prevalence of trials, the divergence of opinions, and the hostility of enemies contribute to their profound sorrow as the present Imām brings relief to his followers through his presence. Moreover, unlike the other Imāms 🕊 who lived relatively short lives, Imām al-Mahdī 🕊 has endured prolonged hardships.

---

[312] Ṣadūq, Shaykh Muḥammad b. ʿAlī, *Kamāl al-Dīn wa Tamām al-Niʿmah*, Vol. 2, p. 512.

This account only scratches the surface of the Imām's emotions when discussing him. Ṣadīr aṣ-Ṣayrafī narrated that when he, along with a group of his companions, entered upon Imām aṣ-Ṣādiq 🕮, they found him sitting on the ground, covered with a Khaybarī sheet made of hair, his neck was open, and his sleeves were folded up. He was weeping intensely, like a mother mourning the loss of her only child. When they asked the Imām 🕮 the reason for his weeping, he took a deep sigh that expanded his chest and said:

> I looked at the Book of al-Jafr this morning, and that is the book that encompasses the knowledge of deaths, trials and tribulations and the knowledge of all that has been and all that will be until the Day of Judgment, which God, glory to His name, has exclusively imparted to Muḥammad and the Imāms after him, peace unto him and them.

> I viewed therein the birth of our Qā'im and his disappearance and its protraction and the length of his lifespan and the trials of the believers through him and after him in that period and the generation with doubts in their hearts from the length of his disappearance and the apostasy of most of them from their religion... [until he said]: So emotions overpowered me and grief overwhelmed me.[313]

---

313 Ṣadūq, Shaykh Muḥammad b. 'Alī, *Kamāl al-Dīn wa Tamām al-Ni'mah*, Vol. 2, p. 352.

22. The Prayer of the Desperate

It is essential for a believer to pray to their Imām عجل الله تعالى فرجه الشريف with the supplication of the desperate and distressed, just as they pray for their own needs, if not more intensely. Our needs hold no comparison to the Imām's, especially considering the Prophetic tradition that states that a believer is not truly a believer until they hold the Messenger of God صلى الله عليه وآله dearer than themselves, his family dearer than their own, and consider what is important to him more significant than what is important to themselves.

Our concerns primarily revolve around ourselves, then our immediate family and circle. However, the Imām عجل الله تعالى فرجه الشريف carries the concerns of his followers worldwide and hears the cries of those who call upon him. Yet, he is unable to assist them due to the constraints of his occultation. One can only imagine the magnitude of suffering the Imām endures, unable to relieve the distress of his beloved followers. Similarly, one can imagine his happiness with those who help him in addressing the needs of those who seek his help.

23. The Essence of Hosting and Hospitality

Every Friday, believers recite the Ziyārah for Imām al-Mahdī عجل الله تعالى فرجه الشريف, saying:

> O my master, O the Present Imām of our time! Blessings of God be upon you and your family (Ahl al-

> Bayt). This is the day of Jumuʿah (Friday), and it is the day on which your advent is expected and the coming of relief for the believers (from their difficulties) by your hands, and (in which will be the) execution of the disbelievers with your sword.
>
> And I am, O my master, in it (this day), your guest and neighbor, and you O my master are generous, from the sons of the generous ones. And you have been commanded to receive guests and welcome neighbors. So then receive me and welcome me, blessings of God be upon you and your family (the Ahl al-Bayt), the purified ones.[314]

A believer truly understands the spirit of hospitality and care by beginning their day with this prayer. It stems from sincere acknowledgment of the Imām's sacred presence as the guardian of our community. This acknowledgment does not negate the sense of his care on all other days of the week, even if each day is attributed to a different Imām from the Prophet's family, because every era's blessings flow through the Imām under whose banner we will gather on the Day of Judgment.

24. Commitment to Duʿāʾ al-ʿAhd

It is narrated that whoever commits to reciting Duʿāʾ al-ʿAhd for forty mornings will be counted among the

---

[314] Qummī, Shaykh ʿAbbās, *Mafātīḥ al-Jinān*.

supporters of Imām al-Mahdī عجّل الله تعالى فرجه الشريف. But earning this honor is not just about saying the words; it is about praying with sincerity. There is a big difference between simply reciting a prayer and understanding its meaning. It is like the difference between saying the word water and drinking it to quench your thirst. The real quenching of thirst comes from the substance of water itself, not just the repetition of its name.

Therefore, the blessings promised with prayers from the Ahl al-Bayt عليهم السلام are only truly received by those who deeply understand the essence of supplication, not just by those who recite it without thought. This also clarifies why prayers sometimes seem unanswered – it often boils down to a lack of true understanding and sincerity in our prayers.

25. Sensing the Loss

A believer should strive to sense the absence of their Imām through dedication and heartfelt effort, allowing this sentiment to take root deeply within themselves. It starts with a struggle, gradualy evolving into a constant state of sadness over his loss. Think of it like the stages of grief for Imām al-Ḥusayn عليه السلام: it might start with forced tears, then progress to genuine tears and sadness, eventually leading to a heartfelt reflection on his profound sacrifice and the tragedy he endured.

Experiences have shown that significant changes often start with deliberate effort, eventually becoming deeply embedded in the heart. For some, their love for the Imām عجّل الله تعالى فرجه الشريف does not happen overnight; it grows with repetition and reflection until mourning his absence becomes a genuine reflection of their emotions and state. This sentiment echoes the words of Imām aṣ-Ṣādiq عليه السلام:

> And the eyes of the believers will shed tears for him[315]

We also sense this emotional depth in parts of Duʿāʾ al-Nudbah, which beautifully captures the feelings of those who love the Imām عجّل الله تعالى فرجه الشريف.

26. The Barrier of Worldly Pleasures

Often, those deeply immersed in the pleasures of the world miss the gravity of loss. Their hearts find contentment in fleeting joys, making it hard for them to fathom the void left by the absence of their Imām. Their focus remains on themselves and their immediate wants, leaving them unable to grasp the emptiness caused by their Imām's absence. How can they experience distress and sorrow when they do not perceive any loss in their lives?

In contrast, those who ponder the void left by their Imām's absence find no comfort in temporary pleasures. Imagine a parent receiving a gift on the day they lost their child, would they feel any joy for the gift?

---

[315] Kulaynī, Shaykh Muḥammad b. Yaʿqūb, *al-Kāfī*, Vol. 2, p. 146.

Hence, when we reflect on the stories of those who experienced the care of Imām al-Mahdī عجّل الله تعالى فرجه الشريف throughout occultation, we notice that they carried a constant sense of sorrow in their hearts, drawing them closer to God عزّ وجلّ.

27. Sincerity in Supplication

A believer needs to be sincere when praying for the reappearance of their Imām عجّل الله تعالى فرجه الشريف. Through the blessing of their supplication, God عزّ وجلّ may hasten his reappearance, alleviating the sufferings of the Ummah across the globe when the divine rule is established.

Even if one argues that our supplication does not affect the timing of the reappearance, isn't it enough that the Imām عجّل الله تعالى فرجه الشريف sees this care from his followers during the period of the occultation? Moreover, such devotion is among the factors that contribute to receiving special care from him. When we pray for our Imām, we can be certain that, out of his generosity, he also prays for us. There is a profound contrast between our imperfect prayers and his flawless ones. His supplications are answered, with no barrier between him and God عزّ وجلّ.

Here is a beautiful statement from the esteemed Sayyid b. Ṭāwūs al-Ḥasanī, regarding this matter:

> Beware of thinking that I said this because he needs my supplication. Far from it! If you believe this, you are mistaken and suffering from a misconception in your

allegiance and belief. Rather, I said this because I showed you his immense right upon you and his significant benevolence towards you. When you supplicate for him before yourself and those dear to you, it is more likely that God ﷻ will open the doors of acceptance for you.[316]

28. Intermediaries in Supplication

A ḥadīth narrates that God ﷻ said:

> O Mūsā, pray to Me using a tongue that you have not disobeyed Me with.

Mūsā asked,

> My Lord, how can I pray with a tongue that has not disobeyed You?

God ﷻ replied,

> Pray to Me using someone else's tongue.[317]

So, why not seek forgiveness for our sins and ask those esteemed by God ﷻ to intercede on our behalf? Why not turn to the one who acts as a paternal figure for our

---

[316] Sayyid b. Ṭāwūs, *Falāḥ al-Sā'il wa Najāḥ al-Masā'il*, p. 45.

[317] al-Ḥurr al-ʿĀmilī, Shaykh Muḥammad, *al-Jawāhir al-Saniyyah fī al-Aḥādīth al-Qudsiyyah*, p. 146.

community today, following the footsteps of his noble forefathers, the Messenger of God ﷺ and Amīr al-Mu'minīn ؑ? The Messenger of God ﷺ said:

> ʿAlī and I are the fathers of this Ummah[318]

Therefore, let us start by seeking forgiveness from God ﷻ, then turn to our Imām ؑ with this heartfelt plea:

﴿يا أَبانَا استَغفِر لَنا ذُنوبَنا إِنّا كُنّا خاطِئينَ﴾

﴿*yā-'abānā staghfir lanā dhunūbanā innā kunnā khāṭi'īna*﴾

﴿*Father! Plead [with God] for forgiveness of our sins! We have indeed been erring*﴾[319]

If this practice were not acceptable, the Noble Qur'ān would not have conveyed it through the speech of Yūsuf's ؑ brothers, addressing their father Yaʿqūb ؑ. However, all of this is contingent upon not returning to deliberate disobedience and negligence.

29. Traits of the Sincere Lover

A true lover of the Imām can never neglect to read the Duʿā' Zamān al-Ghaybah, whether it be on a Friday or any

---

[318] Ṣadūq, Shaykh Muḥammad b. ʿAlī, *Kamāl al-Dīn wa Tamām al-Niʿmah*, Vol. 1, p. 261.

[319] Sūrat Yūsuf, Verse 97.

other day. If they find themselves unable to do so due to limited time, they should at least take a moment alone before God ﷻ, asking Him to hasten the reappearance of their Imām عجل الله فرجه. There is an hour on Friday night, and another during daylight, when God ﷻ answers prayers. How could one miss such an opportunity, knowing that this is the anticipated day of his reappearance and relief for the believers?

Neglecting to pray during these times may signify a sense of distance from the Imām, as a genuine admirer seizes every opportunity to connect with their beloved, regardless of time and place.

30. The Manifestation of Mercy

The Imām عجل الله فرجه is the manifestation of divine mercy, which encompasses everything. Hence, he feels the deepest pain for the sufferings and injustices endured by this Ummah. If the Commander of the Faithful عليه السلام was distressed by the hardships faced by Muslims and even non-Muslim women under Islamic protection across distant lands, as he expressed:

> I have come to know that every one of them violated muslim women, and other women under the protection of Islam, and took away their ornaments... If any Muslim dies of grief after all this, he is not to be

blamed but rather there is justification for him before me.[320]

How then could our present Imām ﷺ not be moved by the trials of his Shīʿah and those who love him? It is our duty to reciprocate this affection, to mention him frequently, and to pray for the hastening of his reappearance. By doing so, we can alleviate his concerns and sorrows. When he witnesses his righteous rule spreading across the globe, it will bring him solace after years of waiting.

31. Recharging the Ummah's Spirits

Believing in the existence of the awaited Imām al-Mahdī ﷺ has a profound effect on energizing the Ummah and fostering hope within it. There is a distinction between aimless wandering and being driven by the powerful hope that beyond this long tunnel of injustice lies light and triumph. Therefore, the significance of anticipating the reappearance becomes evident, as it stands among the best of deeds. It is clear that awaiting his reappearance involves laying the groundwork for his arrival. Mere yearning or mere supplication does not fully capture the essence of genuine awaiting for his reappearance. After intense yearning, action is necessary to ensure the realization of meeting the one we eagerly await.

---

[320] Kulaynī, Shaykh Muḥammad b. Yaʿqūb, *al-Kāfī*, Vol. 9, p. 362.

Narrations from Ahl al-Bayt ﷺ are a testament to the fact that the infallible ones are among the most eager for Imām al-Mahdī's coming, as narrated when Imām Muḥammad al-Jawād ﷺ was asked:

> O son of the Messenger of God, who is the Imām after al-Ḥasan? Imām al-Jawād ﷺ cried intensely and said:
>
> > After al-Ḥasan, the Imām is his son al-Qā'im, the Awaited one[321]

This intense crying merely at the mention of the awaited Imām reflects the deepest longing imaginable.

32. Prioritizing the Interests of the Ummah

A genuine believer, deeply committed to their faith and the establishment of a divine government on Earth, places the community's welfare above personal gain. Even on days of personal celebration, like a child's wedding or a financial windfall, if they hear troubling news about the community, their joy dims in comparison to the worry and concern they feel. Their happiness is tied to personal matters, while their concern extends to the well-being of the Ummah.

Upon reflection, one would observe that the hardships of the Ummah often outweigh its joys. This often leads to a lasting sense of sadness in the believer's heart. What is

[321] Ṣadūq, Shaykh Muḥammad b. 'Alī, *Kamāl al-Dīn wa Tamām al-Ni'mah*, Vol. 2, p. 287.

remarkable is how this sacred sorrow does not cloud their judgment but rather strengthens their inner resolve, because this concern serves as a link to the divine realm, contrasting sharply with the worries of this fleeting life.

33. Praying for His Release

When you pray for a prisoner to enjoy life on Earth, you are essentially asking for their release from their hardships and constraints so that they can experience life freely. Similarly, our Imām ﷺ is a captive in the realm of occultation, because he witnesses the various afflictions faced by his followers. Yet, he is unable to alleviate them due to the constraints of his occultation, which in turn causes him intense sadness. Thus, when we pray for his release, we are not only seeking his liberation through his awaited appearance but also longing for relief for the entire community and humanity at large.

If we deeply contemplate this, we would feel a profound sorrow, coupled with a strong bond to our Imām ﷺ, as we understand the immense challenges he faces and realize that the redemption of humanity hinges on his return.

34. Defending the Imām

If a stranger claims to have a familial and inheritance connection to your father without evidence, and demands their share of the inheritance, what would you do? If you rebuke them and they persist, you would seek legal recourse against this false claimant. Similarly, in the time of occultation, if you see someone falsely claiming special proximity and representation of the hidden Imām, it is your duty to expose them. Be a defender of your Imām against any slander or falsehood, using all means possible to act as his advocate, dismantle the claims of the false accuser, and expose their deceit.

It is a heavy burden for him to see those who claim to represent him spreading lies that he cannot refute due to the constraints of the occultation. This burden adds to the challenges he already faces due to his concealed status, as described by Imām Mūsā al-Kāẓim ﷺ:

> He is that one who is wandering, lonely, remote, and hidden from his family who would be the avenger for his father.[322]

35. Prayers of the Believers for their Imām

We were instructed to pray for the hastening of the reappearance, as Imām al-Mahdī ﷺ said:

> Pray a lot for the hastening of my reappearance, as in it will be your relief.[323]

322 Ṣadūq, Shaykh Muḥammad b. ʿAlī, *Kamāl al-Dīn wa Tamām al-Niʿmah*, Vol. 2, p. 361.

323 Ibid., p. 458.

If our prayers did not have an impact on expediting his reappearance, we would not have been urged to pray. Hence, we should count on the supplications of every believer, whether during the quiet of night or in the middle of day, in obligatory or voluntary prayers, for those prayers have the power to hasten his return.

Though the reappearance is predetermined, we cannot overlook the fact that certain matters are subject to change, as in our saying:

> O God, do not withhold victory from us.

The withholding of victory means that a definitive victory is indeed achieved, but it is suspended due to the actions of the people. Delays in victory and relief could result from our shortcomings, as hinted in one of Imām al-Mahdī's عجل الله تعالى فرجه الشريف letters:

> If our Shīʿah, may God grant them success, had unitedly remained obedient on the covenant with resolute hearts then the blessing to meet us would not have been postponed and they would have seen us with true recognition. Nothing holds us back from them except that which reaches us (of their actions) that we dislike and that which we do not consider proper for them.[324]

[324] Ṭabrisī, Shaykh Aḥmad b. ʿAlī Ṭabrisī, *al-Iḥtijāj ʿalā Ahl al-Lijāj*, Vol. 2, p. 499.

This is a reproach from our Imām ﷺ that should stir concern in the hearts of those who love him.

36. Emotional Connection

Our Imām ﷺ is not just a distant figure; he is very much alive and aware of our actions, sharing in our pains, hoping for our aspirations, and praying for us. Yet, there are times when believers seem indifferent to his presence. Our relationship with the Imām often falls short of the respect his exalted status deserves. Although he and his noble forefathers share the same divine light, our relationship with our Imām ﷺ should be one of unwavering devotion to the living leader who oversees the affairs of his Shīʿah and followers.

It is widely understood that merely acknowledging the Imām's existence is insufficient. We need to embrace the emotional connection described by his father, Imām al-ʿAskarī ﷺ, when addressing him:

> And know that the hearts of the obedient and sincere turn towards you like birds to their nests.[325]

If someone genuinely feels this bond in their heart, without any pretense, then they can truly consider themselves among the sincere.

---

325 Ṣadūq, Shaykh Muḥammad b. ʿAlī, *Kamāl al-Dīn wa Tamām al-Niʿmah*, Vol. 2, p. 448.

37. A Private Moment with the Imām

If you want to have a special connection with the Imām, know that practical faith brings you closer to him. The more you practice faith, the nearer you are to your Imām. Therefore, it is a good idea for those seeking this closeness to set aside some private time to speak with their Imām. Ask for his compassionate gaze, which can save you from getting caught up in desires and distractions. The Imām is the vigilant eye of God, the attentive ear, the helping hand, the listener, who responds to our salutations and is fully aware of what is happening with people.

When this connection deepens for a believer, they will treasure these private moments. It is like having a heart-to-heart with someone right in front of you, and you will uncover things that are hidden from others.

38. Conversing with the Imām

From time to time, try to converse with Imām al-Mahdī in a heartfelt and spontaneous manner. For example, during Ḥajj, as you bid farewell to the Sacred House, express your feelings:

> O God, I have come to Your house as a pilgrim, and though the Imām has also been here during pilgrimage, I have not felt his presence or heard his voice. Here I am bidding farewell to Your house, without experiencing his care!

Address your Imām by saying:

> It is hard for me to see all creatures, but I cannot see you!

If you read Du'ā' al-'Ahd every day, without receiving a response or attention, say addressing the Imām:

> How long will I wander, seeking you, my master? How long?

Even in a gathering of people, say:

> Is there any helper with whom I may lament and bewail as much as I wish?

Try to enter his heart by mentioning the tragedies of his grandfather, Imām al-Ḥusayn عليه السلام, especially in secluded moments away from distractions. For instance, if you stand under the dome of Imām al-Ḥusayn عليه السلام, greet him with the greeting attributed to Imām al-Mahdī عجل الله تعالى فرجه الشريف. Say:

> Peace be upon the grey hair that was dyed with blood, peace be upon the cheek that struck the dust, peace be upon the butchered body.

39. Divine Retribution

We mourn Imām al-Ḥusayn عليه السلام for the immense tragedies he endured. On one hand, he faced unimaginable calamities, and on the other hand, justice was not served to the rulers of the oppressors. The divine path intended by God ﷻ for the Ummah was not fulfilled. Even after Imām al-Ḥusayn's martyrdom, the subsequent Imāms continued to endure oppression. Revolutions like the one led by Mukhtār and others, while they brought justice by punishing the killers of Imām al-Ḥusayn ؑ, the line of injustice remained unchanged.

Imām al-Ḥusayn ؑ rose to seek reform within his grandfather's Ummah, to establish divine justice across the lands. However, his goal was not realized and will only be achieved by his son, Imām al-Mahdī عج, whom we lament for in Duʿāʾ al-Nudbah, saying,

> Where is the seeker of justice for the one slain in Karbalāʾ?

40. Reasons for Wishing to Meet the Imām

People wish to meet the Imām عج for various reasons. Some wish to meet him to seek his assistance during times of hardship or illness. Others long for the meeting out of a deep yearning for him. However, the highest aspiration, surpassing all others, is to meet him while he establishes his authority on Earth and delivers humanity from injustice, oppression, and corruption. These are the sentiments echoed in supplications like Duʿāʾ Zamān al-Ghaybah, where believers ask:

> O God, I beseech You to allow me to see the Representative, apparent and prevalent[326]

Those who prioritize the concerns of the Ummah over their worries and genuinely pray for this from God ﷻ will likely be among those gathered under the Imām's banner. They may even be among those whom God ﷻ will resurrect from their graves to stand at the forefront, fighting alongside the Imām عجل الله تعالى فرجه الشريف.

41. The Involuntary Remembrance of the Beloved

A telltale sign of true love is the constant thought and mention of the beloved, whether there is a special occasion or not. When love grows strong and fills the heart to the brim, words about the beloved naturally spill from the tongue. This is the overpowering remembrance that cannot be stopped, even when the person is preoccupied with life's distractions. As eloquently expressed by the author of *Mikyāl al-Makārim*:

> Love, even if it is a hidden matter of the heart, leaves visible traces and branches that spread. It is like a tree with countless branches, each bearing blossoms. Some of its effects are visible on the tongue, while others manifest in other physical organs. Just as one cannot prevent a tree from displaying its flowers, one cannot

[326] Ṣadūq, Shaykh Muḥammad b. ʿAlī, *Kamāl al-Dīn wa Tamām al-Niʿmah*, Vol. 2, p. 512.

prevent a true lover from displaying the effects of their love.[327]

42. Distressing News

Some individuals hear the sorrowful news circulating among Muslims without feeling the appropriate level of distress proportional to the gravity of the events. However, believers are often sensitive souls, deeply affected by the suffering of others. Whenever they hear sad news about fellow beings, especially the oppressed, they earnestly pray to God ﷻ for relief. The Qur'ān mentions the story of Hābīl (Abel), who was unjustly killed, emphasizing the gravity of such acts. Considering this, how must it feel when someone is murdered within the sacred confines of a mosque or the shrines of the Imāms عليهم السلام, as happens in our time?

This is the reality our current Imām عجل الله تعالى فرجه الشريف faces, as he expresses,

> We hear of things that displease us.[328]

It is known that what he dislikes sometimes stems from the relentless enemies, and at times from his supporters who

---

[327] Iṣfahānī, Sayyid Muḥammad Taqī Mūsawī, *Mikyāl al-Makārim*, Vol. 1, p. 291.

[328] Ṭabrisī, Shaykh Aḥmad b. 'Alī Ṭabrisī, *al-Iḥtijāj 'alā Ahl al-Lijāj*, Vol. 2, p. 499.

harm him with their reprehensible actions. This affects him deeply because he does not expect such behavior from them.

43. Supporting the Vulnerable

One remarkable trait of our current Imām ﷻ is his unwavering support for all those in need, regardless of their beliefs. This arises from his compassionate nature, which extends to all oppressed individuals worldwide. As mentioned in the Duʿāʾ:

> He is the supporter of those who cannot find any supporter save You[329]

It is essential to note that the term oppressed here transcends religious and cultural boundaries. Additionally, Imām al-Mahdī's ﷻ message encompasses the entire globe, to achieve justice for all. If people knew of his deep empathy and commitment to global justice, they would not only seek him out but also rally behind him. Seeking liberation from oppression is a fundamental human instinct. Many who claimed to seek revolution against oppressors were exploiting this appealing title to attract the oppressed.

Therefore, it is incumbent upon the believer to take inspiration from their Imām ﷻ in feeling this profound

[329] Majlisī, ʿAllāmah Muḥammad Bāqir, *Biḥār al-Anwār*, Vol. 53, p. 96.

compassion. People fall into two categories: either they are brothers to you in religion, or equals in humanity.

44. The Impact of Loss

When someone loses something precious, it often brings about a whirlwind of emotions, marked by turmoil and sorrow. This emotional turbulence is visible in their demeanor, especially for those enduring the anguish of separation from loved ones. Anxiety and worry become palpable aspects of their existence.

It is well-known that those who bear sorrow due to their Imām's عجل الله تعالى فرجه الشريف absence also carry a deep sense of longing and sadness. They are individuals deeply cherished by their Imām, and it is unimaginable that he would neglect them during his occultation.

Blessed are those who spend their nights in solitude, consumed by the ache of separation from their Imām. With tears streaming down their cheeks, they raise their hands to the sky with tearful eyes and say:

> O God, we complain to You about the departure of our Prophet, Your blessings be on him and his Household, the absence of our leader, the big numbers of our enemies, and our small number[330]

[330] Ṣadūq, Shaykh Muḥammad b. ʿAlī, *Kamāl al-Dīn wa Tamām al-Niʿmah*, Vol. 1, p. 514.

45. The Bond of Love

What strengthens the bond between us and anyone in life is the bond of love. However, love comes in different forms: there is the pretentious love, which is not genuine but rather a means to an end, like the lazy student wishing for success without putting in effort, merely wishing for it without real commitment.

Our aim should be to cultivate a deep and genuine bond with God ﷻ and the Ahl al-Bayt عليهم السلام, one that is steady and sincere rather than superficial and fleeting. But how do we achieve this level of depth and stability?

The answer lies in self-refinement and purification, aligning ourselves with the virtues of those we love. It is this personal refinement that fosters mutual attraction between devotees.

46. Supplication After Every Obligatory Prayer

It has been reported that after every obligatory prayer, a believer is granted an answered supplication. How meaningful would it be for them to use this opportunity to pray for the reappearance and relief of their Imām عجل الله فرجه الشريف! You can imagine that he might reciprocate and pray for you as well. Imagine the blessings of having him pray for you even once in your lifetime!

Certain texts highlight the significance of supplicating for relief after the dawn and noon prayers. These times hold particular importance because the doors to the heavens are open, especially at dawn when the world is still and during the hustle of midday. This allows for two distinct opportunities for supplication to converge each day. Imām aṣ-Ṣādiq ﷺ said:

> Whoever says after the Fajr prayer and after the Ẓuhr prayer:
>
> > O God, bless Muḥammad and the family of Muḥammad, and hasten their relief,
>
> will not die until he meets the Qā'im (the Mahdī).[331]

47. His Supplication in Qunūt

Reflecting on the Imām's ﷺ supplication for himself reveals profound emotional insights, urging us to connect with his blessed presence with earnestness. Among them, he asks God ﷻ to gather his companions, knowing that his reappearance hinges on their gathering and meeting. He humbly portrays himself as a captive before his Lord, demonstrating complete submission and humility. Moreover, he acknowledges that his position is solely by divine grace, distinct from the rest of creation, thus recognizing God's mercy in all circumstances.

[331] Ṭūsī, Shaykh Muḥammad b. Ḥasan, *Miṣbāḥ al-Mutahajjid wa Silāḥ al-Muta'abbid*, Vol. 1, p. 368.

Furthermore, he seeks permission to establish justice in His land, and finally, he implores God ﷻ to fulfill the promise, as he has been awaiting this command since his birth.

So let us contemplate these sentiments in his supplication during qunūt, where he says:

> O He who never breaks His promise! Fulfill what You have promised me, and gather for me my companions and grant them patience. Aid me against Your enemies and the enemies of Your Messenger. Do not disappoint my supplication, for I am Your servant, the son of Your servant, the son of Your handmaid; I am under Your control. My Master, You who have bestowed this station upon me and favored me with it over many of Your creatures, I ask You to send blessings upon Muḥammad and the family of Muḥammad, and fulfill for me what You have promised me. Surely, You are the Truthful, and You never fail to fulfill Your promise, and You have power over all things.[332]

48. The Qunūt of Amīr al-Mu'minīn

The Commander of the Faithful ؏, known as the father of the Imāms and the close friend of prophethood, held deep concern within his heart for his son, Imām al-Mahdī ؏, to the extent that he complained to God ﷻ about his

---

[332] Majlisī, ʿAllāmah Muḥammad Bāqir, *Biḥār al-Anwār*, Vol. 82, p. 235.

absence. His heart ached at the mention of the trials that plagued his era and the blessed period of occultation. However, he placed his hope for relief from all trials, old and new, in the reappearance of his son, whom he described as the embodiment of justice and the true leader. He would say in his supplication:

> O God! The eyes are fixed on You, feet are trembling, hands are lifted, and necks are stretched. The tongues call you, and the secrets of the acts of Your creatures are clear to You. O our Lord, You judge between us and our nation with truth, as You are the best of the judges. O God, I complain to You of the absence of our Prophet and the Ghaibat of our Imām and the paucity of our numbers and the abundance of our enemies, and the display of enmity toward us and the incidence of mischief from them on us. So, please grant him success through the justice that You show. And make the rightful Imām that we recognize, reappear, O God, Āmīn, O Lord of the worlds[333]

It is narrated that Imām aṣ-Ṣādiq ﵇ advised his followers to recite this supplication in the qunūt of their prayers, following the words of Faraj.

---

333 Ṭabrisī, Mīrzā Ḥusayn Nūrī, *Mustadrak al-Wasā'il wa-Mustanbaṭ al-Masā'il*, Vol. 4, p. 404.

49. Not Feeling Gracious

Some individuals, when they increase their supplication to their Imām, engage in actions esteemed during the occultation, or endure significant hardship while advocating for the path of the Ahl al-Bayt ﷺ, may unintentionally feel a sense of graciousness over their Lord, and that what they did is a favor to the Imām and earned them merit with him. However, our connection with the Imām ﷺ mirrors our connection with God ﷻ, as it is He who has blessed us with guidance to faith and sent us a messenger from among ourselves...

If anyone experiences such an unintended sentiment, they should promptly seek forgiveness and apologize. This feeling might lead to distancing from the Imām ﷺ, who said:

> Pray a lot for the hastening of my reappearance, as in it will be your relief.[334]

> Awaiting the reappearance and the relief brings relief in itself[335]

[334] Ṣadūq, Shaykh Muḥammad b. ʿAlī, *Kamāl al-Dīn wa Tamām al-Niʿmah*, Vol. 2, p. 458.

[335] Ṭūsī, Shaykh Muḥammad b. Ḥasan, *Kitāb al-Ghaybah*, p. 459.

50. Supplication on Friday Eve

Thursday night holds significant importance in the week, a time when believers seize the opportunity to present their most urgent supplications before God ﷻ, especially during its blessed hours. Among the foremost requests to remember during this time is the hastening of the Imām's reappearance عجل الله تعالى فرجه الشريف and asking for the downfall of his adversaries, thus affirming allegiance to the Imām while dissociating from his enemies.

Shaykh al-Ṭūsī included in his summary of *Miṣbāḥ al-Mutahajjid wa Silāḥ al-Muta'abbid* when mentioning the importance of performing religious duties on Friday Eve for believers to say:

> O God, bless Muḥammad and the progeny of Muḥammad and hasten their relief. And destroy their enemies, from the Jinns and humans; from the first and the last.

A hundred times or as many times as possible.[336]

What is notable in this statement and similar ones is that expediting the relief is linked to the entirety of the Ahl al-Bayt عليهم السلام, as indicated by the phrase "and hasten their relief." Furthermore, it broadens the scope of adversaries to include the jinn, as their leaders are troubled by the

---

[336] Ṭūsī, Shaykh Muḥammad b. Ḥasan, *Miṣbāḥ al-Mutahajjid wa Silāḥ al-Muta'abbid*, Vol. 1, p. 265.

approaching time of reappearance, knowing it will thwart their schemes as well.

51. Praying for him When Crying

When a sincere believer, eagerly anticipating the reappearance of their Imām عجّل الله تعالى فرجه الشريف, is overcome by profound emotional sensitivity, they rush to invoke prayers for their Imām's reappearance before beseeching for their own needs. They acknowledge the immense right of their Imām, prioritizing his cause over their desires. Thus, they eagerly await moments and circumstances that are conducive to answered prayers, in order to intensify their supplications for the noble relief of their Imām. It should never be assumed that the Imām is too dignified to be prayed for by a neglectful follower.

There is a narration where someone asked Imām aṣ-Ṣādiq عليه السلام:

> A person pretends to cry during the obligatory prayer until they weep.

Imām aṣ-Ṣādiq عليه السلام responded:

> It is a delight, by God. When that happens, remember me in that state.[337]

---

[337] al-Ḥurr al-ʿĀmilī, Shaykh Muḥammad, *Wasāʾil al-Shīʿah*, Vol. 7, p. 247.

So what is the difference between Imām aṣ-Ṣādiq and his son Imām al-Mahdī 🕮 regarding the validity of praying for them?

52. His Prayer by The Ka'bah

One of the greatest hopes of our Imām 🕮 during the occultation is the realization of his noble relief and the fulfillment of what God 🕮 has specifically designated for him among all the successors of the prophets. He certainly seizes every opportunity to pray for this noble cause. The evidence for this is what a narrator asked Muḥammad b. 'Uthmān al-'Amrī, saying:

Have you seen the master of this affair?

He replied:

Yes, and the last time I saw him, he was near the Holy House of God praying:

O my Lord, fulfill the promise that You made to me.[338]

Similarly, what is also narrated:

'Abdullāh b. Ja'far al-Ḥumayri informed us, saying:

I heard Muḥammad b. 'Uthmān al-'Amrī saying:

---

[338] Ṣadūq, Shaykh Muḥammad b. 'Alī, *Kamāl al-Dīn wa Tamām al-Ni'mah*, Vol. 2, p. 428.

> I saw His Eminence ﷽ holding the curtain of the Kaʿbah below the spout and praying:
>
> > O my Lord, take revenge on my enemies.[339]

At times, the Imām prays for the fulfillment of the promise, and at other times, for vengeance against his enemies. It is fitting for his followers to follow his example when they visit the Kaʿbah.

53. Prayer During Ziyārah

When we visit the holy shrines of the Imāms, it is essential to keep praying for the Imām's reappearance at the top of our minds. This should be our utmost priority, never to be overlooked. During these visits, we ask for the divine promise to be fulfilled, knowing that this fulfillment can only be realized through their awaited son, Imām al-Mahdī.

We find evidence of this in the narration of Abū Ḥamzah ath-Thumālī from Imām aṣ-Ṣādiq, where he said in a part of that Ziyārah after praying for Imām al-Ḥusayn:

> And you send blessings on all the Imāms as you send salutations on al-Ḥusayn. Then say,

[339] Ibid., p. 440.

> O God! Complete Your words through them, fulfill Your promise through them, destroy Your enemy and their enemy through them[340]

In another instance, Imām aṣ-Ṣādiq عليه السلام says:

> Then place your head on the grave of Imām al-Ḥusayn عليه السلام and say:
>
> > O God, Lord of al-Ḥusayn, cure the heart of al-Ḥusayn عليه السلام. O God, Lord of al-Ḥusayn, seek justice for the blood of al-Ḥusayn[341]

Regarding this, the author of *Mikyāl al-Makārim* says:

> The reason is quite apparent since it is Imām al-Mahdī عجل الله تعالى فرجه الشريف who will avenge the blood of Imām al-Ḥusayn عليه السلام and cure his heart by taking revenge from his enemies and murderers.[342]

54. The Prayer of ar-Riḍā for al-Mahdī عليه السلام

Our Imām al-Mahdī عجل الله تعالى فرجه الشريف held a special place in the hearts of all the Imāms of the Ahl al-Bayt عليهم السلام. They dedicated heartfelt prayers to him, as if they were living through the

---

[340] al-Qummī, Ibn Qūlawayh, *Kāmil al-Zīyārāt*, p. 232.

[341] Ibid., p. 238.

[342] Iṣfahānī, Sayyid Muḥammad Taqī Mūsawī, *Mikyāl al-Makārim*, Vol. 2, p. 256.

time of his occultation. One of the most moving expressions of this devotion comes from Imām ʿAlī ar-Riḍā عليه السلام, who urged his followers to pray for Imām al-Mahdī عجل الله تعالى فرجه الشريف by saying:

> O God, bestow on him that which You have bestowed on those who established justice among the followers of the prophets. O God, ramify our splits through him, sew the rip through him, eradicate oppression through him, manifest justice through him, reform the Earth by his staying, and support him with victory, assist him with awe, strengthen his supporters, humiliate those who wish to put him down, and destroy whoever cheated him. Eliminate the despotic unbelievers, their pillars and supporters through Him, crush the heads of misguidance and the founders of innovation through Him, and also eliminate those who sought to end the Sunnah of Your Prophet and those who intensify falsehood through Him. Degrade the arrogant through him and eliminate the unbelievers and all the apostates from the east, west, land, sea, plains, mountains of the Earth through him till there shall be no abode for them. O God, You then purify Your nation from them, and give relief to Your servants from them, honor the believers through the Imām, revive the customs of Your messengers through him, make him the scholar of the Prophets' wisdom[343]

---

[343] Ṭūsī, Shaykh Muḥammad b. Ḥasan, *Miṣbāḥ al-Mutahajjid wa Silāḥ al-Mutaʿabbid*, Vol. 1, p. 409.

55. Intense Longing

According to the teachings of the Ahl al-Bayt ﷺ, each of us must cultivate a profound longing for our Imām ﷺ. This longing should be so intense that one yearns for their sorrows to be eased by meeting him, even though the path to seeing him, like with his forefathers or special envoys, is currently blocked during the occultation.

This text captures these profound sentiments. One of whom expressed their intense longing to see the Imām ﷺ was Abū Ja'far Muḥammad b. 'Uthmān al-'Amrī. He complained of his yearning to meet the Imām ﷺ, to which he was asked:

> Do you truly desire to see him with such longing?

He replied:

> Yes.

Al-'Amrī said:

> May God ﷻ reward you for your eagerness and grant you the honor of seeing Him easily, O Abū 'Abdullāh. Do not pray for seeing Him and being in His company, as these are important divine matters, and it is better to accept them. But pay attention to his Ziyārah[344]

---

[344] Majlisī, 'Allāmah Muḥammad Bāqir, *Biḥār al-Anwār*, Vol. 53, p. 174.

The author of *Mikyāl al-Makārim* provides insightful commentary on this matter. He explains:

> It is evident that having an eagerness to see the Imām is commendable, as it is a part of loving him, as implied in the statement:
>
> > May God reward you for your eagerness.
>
> There is a great reward for this, as mentioned in a tradition of Imām aṣ-Ṣādiq ﷷ.
>
> However, advising against praying specifically for a sighting refers to the accessibility of seeing him like the previous Imāms, where one could meet them at will. Nevertheless, seeking to see the Imām is not strictly forbidden; rather, it is among the religious duties, and many have been blessed with this honor[345]

56. ʿĪd of Sorrows

It is important to understand that for the family of Muḥammad ﷺ, every ʿĪd brings a renewed sense of sorrow. This stems from the memory of the position that was unjustly taken from them, a position ordained by God ﷻ and communicated by the Prophet ﷺ to the people on the Day of Ghadīr.

---

[345] Iṣfahānī, Sayyid Muḥammad Taqī Mūsawī, *Mikyāl al-Makārim*, Vol. 2, p. 145.

Our Imām Zayn al-'Ābidīn ☙ highlighted this sentiment in his prayers on Fridays and 'Īd days:

> O God, this station belongs to Your vicegerents, Your chosen, while the places of Your trusted ones in the elevated degree which You have singled out for them have been forcibly stripped[346]

Interestingly, he did not mention this in his sermons on the two 'Īds, although it would have been fitting. However, the oppressors prevented him from doing so. Instead, he expressed this grievance in his prayers, emphasizing the bitterness of this usurpation, especially as he witnessed firsthand the injustices inflicted upon his father, Imām al-Ḥusayn ☙. This expression suggests that there will come a day when justice prevails over the usurpers.

57. Presenting Needs to The Imām

The optimal relationship between the awaited Imām ☙ and those who await him is akin to the relationship of a son to his father, just as the relationship was between his forefathers and their followers in their time. The connection to them is greater than that of parenthood and offspring, for a father may not always be able to fulfill all of his son's desires, but our Imām ☙ can do so with the permission of God ☙.

---

346 Imām Zayn al-'Ābidīn ☙, *al-Ṣaḥīfah al-Sajjādiyyah*, p. 236.

A beautiful narration regarding this says:

> I wrote to Imām Abū al-Ḥasan ﷺ saying that a person loves to express to their Imām what they wish to express to their Lord. He said,
>
> > Then write: If you have a need, move your lips, for the answer will come to you.[347]

This narration suggests that if the believer has the Imām's approval, they do not need lengthy words to communicate. Sometimes, a simple movement of the lips is enough to convey their needs and emotions.

58. Praying for The Manifestation of His Authority

In our prayers, there is a phrase that deeply moves those awaiting their Imām, as expressed in the supplication:

> O God, I beseech You to allow me to see the Representative, apparent and prevalent[348]

They envision their Imām facing challenges, his authority unrecognized, and his guidance unheeded. But in reality, he

---

[347] Sayyid b. Ṭāwūs, *Kashf al-Muḥajjah li-Thamarat al-Muhjah*, p. 211.

[348] Ṣadūq, Shaykh Muḥammad b. ʿAlī, *Kamāl al-Dīn wa Tamām al-Niʿmah*, Vol. 2, p. 512.

is God's ﷻ extended arm, the bridge between heaven and Earth. Imām aṣ-Ṣādiq ؑ once said:

> Verily, God the Mighty and High, made us the best of creation, and molded us from the best of molds. He made us His Eye through which He sees His Servants. He made us the Tongue with which He speaks to His Creation. He made us the Outspread Hand of Mercy over His Servants.[349]

These insights fuel the fervent prayers for God ﷻ to reveal His vicegerent as such. However, let these prayers, like all supplications, be filled with eagerness and resolve.

Consider Prophet Yaʿqūb ؑ, who, despite knowing his son Yūsuf's fate, was overwhelmed with grief, as described by God ﷻ:

﴿وَتَوَلَّىٰ عَنۡهُمۡ وَقَالَ يَٰٓأَسَفَىٰ عَلَىٰ يُوسُفَ وَٱبۡيَضَّتۡ
عَيۡنَاهُ مِنَ ٱلۡحُزۡنِ فَهُوَ كَظِيمٞ﴾

﴿*wa-tawallā ʿanhum wa-qāla yā-ʾasafā ʿalā yūsufa wa-byaḍḍat ʿaynāhu mina l-ḥuzni fa-huwa kaẓīm*[un]﴾

[349] Fayḍ Kāshānī, Mullā Muḥammad b. Murtaḍā, *al-Wāfī*, Vol. 1, p. 419.

﴾And he turned away from them and said, 'Alas for Yūsuf!' His eyes had turned white with grief, and he choked with suppressed agony﴿[350]

We are not suggesting one must supplicate as intensely for the Imām's return as Prophet Ya'qūb ﷺ did. Yet, they should reflect the desperation of someone facing dire circumstances. Imagine yourself unjustly imprisoned, stripped of wealth and honor – how would you plead with God ﷻ to restore your freedom and dignity? Let this be the spirit of our prayers for the Imām ﷺ to be like one's state in this trial.

59. Compassion of the Infallible

The compassion of the Imām ﷺ towards us is something beyond our comprehension. As will be elucidated in the text, the Imāms fall ill and feel sorrow for our illness and sorrow. There is no wonder in that, because they are embodiments of the profound divine mercy, and their compassion for us surpasses that of our fathers and mothers. This is because their guardianship over us extends into eternity. The following beautiful story reflects a glimpse of their compassion.

A man by the name of Rumaylah said,

---

[350] Sūrat Yūsuf, Verse 84.

I fell seriously ill during the reign of Amīr al-Mu'minīn. I felt deeply distressed and said to myself on Friday,

> I do not know of anything better than to pour water over myself and pray behind Amīr al-Mu'minīn.

So, I did just that. When Amīr al-Mu'minīn ascended the pulpit in the mosque, my illness returned. When Amīr al-Mu'minīn finished and returned to the palace, I followed him in. He said,

> O Rumaylah, I saw you struggling while standing.

I replied,

> Yes,

and narrated to him the incident that had occurred to me, and that I was compelled to pray behind him. He ﷺ then said:

> O Rumaylah, no believer falls ill but that we feel his illness, nor does he sorrow but that we share in his sorrow, nor does he supplicate but that we join him in his supplication, nor does he remain silent but that we pray for him.

So, I said to him,

> O Commander of the Faithful ﷺ, may I be your ransom, this applies to those with you in the palace. What if it were in the remote corners of the land?

He replied,

> O Rumaylah, no believer is absent from our awareness, whether in the east or the west.[351]

60. His Prayers for His Helpers

The care of the Imām عجل الله تعالى فرجه الشريف for his awaiters is not limited to the time of the reappearance. Indeed, he prays for his helpers during the occultation, asking God ﷻ to support them in defending the faith and to grant them victory over their enemies. We know that the Imām's supplications are always answered. One such prayer attributed to Imām al-Mahdī عجل الله تعالى فرجه الشريف is:

> make those who follow me helpers to support Your religion, striving in Your path, and grant us victory over those who wish evil upon me and them[352]

---

[351] Majlisī, ʿAllāmah Muḥammad Bāqir, *Biḥār al-Anwār*, Vol. 26, p. 140.

[352] Sayyid b. Ṭāwūs, *Muhaj ad-Daʿawāt wa Manhaj al-ʿIbādāt*, p. 301.

This prayer shows the divine support that God ﷻ bestows upon the Imām's followers throughout the occultation, a support that surpasses human comprehension. Without this divine assistance, their adversaries would have overwhelmed them, and adversities would have befallen them, as mentioned in other texts.

61. The Position of Fatherhood

Among the feelings that the awaiting believer must inevitably carry during the time of occultation is a strong connection akin to that of a father with their Imām عجل الله تعالى فرجه الشريف. While the biological father is the reason for one's existence in this transient world, the spiritual father, embodied by the Imām عجل الله تعالى فرجه الشريف, is essential for attaining eternal happiness.

Whoever wrongs their Imām عجل الله تعالى فرجه الشريف has indeed disregarded all the respect and obedience due to biological fathers. However, the spiritual father, the Imām, holds even greater rights, a loftier status, and deserves more kindness than the biological father. The Prophet ﷺ alluded to this, saying:

> I and ʿAlī عليه السلام are two fathers of this Ummah and our right on them is much higher than that of their parents who gave birth to them because we will free them from Hell-fire if they obey us and we will lead them to Paradise which is the place to dwell and we will release

> them from the slavery of desires and join them with the best free persons.[353]

62. An Emotional Expression

Some portrayals of Imām al-Mahdī ﷻ stir deep feelings, like the words of Imām al-Kāẓim ﷺ when asked about Imām al-Mahdī ﷻ:

> He is that one who is wandering, lonely, remote, and hidden from his family who would be the avenger of his father.[354]

Inspired by this, awaiting believers strive to reflect his situation: they try to be a refuge for those who love him, to counter his state of "wandering"; they offer companionship towards his Shīʿah, to counter his "loneliness"; they alleviate the isolation felt by their brethren, opposing his "remoteness"; they show kindness to their family, contrasting him being "hidden from his family"; and finally they share in consoling him in grieving the tragedy of his grandfather, as he is the avenger of his forefathers.

It is widely understood that the most effective way to connect with someone is by sharing in their joys and

---

[353] Majlisī, ʿAllāmah Muḥammad Bāqir, *Biḥār al-Anwār*, Vol. 23, p. 259.

[354] Ṣadūq, Shaykh Muḥammad b. ʿAlī, *Kamāl al-Dīn wa Tamām al-Niʿmah*, Vol. 2, p. 361.

sorrows. And who is closer to our Imām than Imām al-Ḥusayn ﷺ, and those who sacrificed alongside him? And what sorrow compares to that of his family and children being taken captive?

63. Two Qualities of the Awaiters

The awaiting believer whom the Imām approves of possesses two fundamental qualities. Firstly, it is the sincere and profound love, where their tears flow freely in his absence. This sentiment was captured by Imām aṣ-Ṣādiq ﷺ when he said:

> And the eyes of the believers will shed tears for him[355]

Secondly, it is their steadfast and unwavering faith, untouched by the doubts raised by their enemies during the occultation or by the various misleading movements. Imām aṣ-Ṣādiq ﷺ also referred to this when he said:

> At that time, twelve standards will arise and all of them will be alike, thus it will not be known which is the standard of truth. I began to weep upon hearing this, so the Imām said,
>
>> O Abī ʿAbdullāh, why do you weep?

[355] Kulaynī, Shaykh Muḥammad b. Yaʿqūb, *al-Kāfī*, Vol. 2, p. 146.

I replied:

> Master, why shouldn't I weep when you say that twelve standards will arise and all of them will be alike? Thus, how do we know which is the standard of truth?

He replied,

> O Abī 'Abdullāh, have you seen the sun?

I said:

> Yes.

Imām said:

> I swear by God, our matter (*wilāyah*) is clearer than the sun.[356]

In a comprehensive expression, the sincere awaiter combines both emotion and reason, which together form the bonds of connection with the Imām of the Time عجل الله فرجه الشريف.

64. Affiliation to His Banner

One of the key elements that strengthens our emotional connection to the Imām of the Time عجل الله فرجه الشريف is the belief that we will be gathered under his banner. It is widely

356 Ibid.

understood that he only accepts those he is pleased with under his banner on that challenging day. It is hard to imagine any of the infallible Imāms from the Ahl al-Bayt ﷣ welcoming someone rejected by the Imām of their time.

Being associated with his banner in this life means more than just being recognized as his supporter; it means being counted among those who strive under his banner, even if one passes away before his reappearance. This concept is reflected in the narration attributed to Imām aṣ-Ṣādiq ﵇ when al-Fuḍayl asked about the meaning of the verse:

﴿يَوْمَ نَدْعُو كُلَّ أُنَاسٍ بِإِمَامِهِمْ﴾

﴾*yawma nadʿū kulla unāsin bi-ʾimāmihim*﴿

﴾*The day We shall summon every group of people with their imām**﴿[357]

Imām aṣ-Ṣādiq ﵇ answered:

> O Fuḍayl, know your Imām because if you know your Imām, it does not harm you whether this matter (the appearance of al-Qāʾim) comes soon or late. He, who knows his Imām and dies before the appearance of al-Qāʾim, is like one who will be in the camp of al-Qāʾim

[357] Sūrat al-Isrāʾ, Verse 71.

* That is, leader.

> or like one who will be under the banner of al-Qā'im.[358]

65. Gentleness in Interaction

The Imām ﷺ, just like his predecessors, displays the utmost gentleness and compassion in his dealings with his followers. When comforting his deputy Muḥammad b. 'Uthmān for the loss of his father, he expressed:

> We grieve just as you grieve. It [his death] has left you bereft just as it has left us bereft.[359]

This expression of shared grief reveals the Imām's deep emotional connection to those who served him. The reason behind this bond is further hinted at in his message, where he describes him as:

> He was always dedicated to their [the Imāms'] cause and diligent in what would take him near God ﷻ, and the Imāms.[360]

This serves as a lesson for the believers awaiting the Imām's ﷺ reappearance, urging them to heed the Imām's indication regarding the secret of acceptance, which lies in

[358] Kulaynī, Shaykh Muḥammad b. Ya'qūb, *al-Kāfī*, Vol. 2, p. 250.

[359] Ṭūsī, Shaykh Muḥammad b. Ḥasan, *Kitāb al-Ghaybah*, p. 361.

[360] Ṣadūq, Shaykh Muḥammad b. 'Alī, *Kamāl al-Dīn wa Tamām al-Ni'mah*, Vol. 2, p. 510.

diligence and effort. It is worth noting the prayer the Imām offered for his ambassador, saying:

> May He be your Guardian, Protector and Guide, and God is sufficient for you.[361]

This prayer closely resembles the content of Duʿāʾ al-Faraj, which we recite for our Imām عليه السلام. Indeed, how fortunate is the one for whom the Imām of their time prays with such words!

66. The Imām is the one in Dire Need

When an ordinary person faces tough times, God عزّ وجلّ answers their prayers, as promised in His book, especially for those considered among the elite believers. God عزّ وجلّ never turns away the pleas of those who seek His help. But in this regard, the one most desperately in need of all creation is Imām al-Mahdī عجّل الله تعالى فرجه الشريف; for with him, the needs of all converge, as he is the ultimate refuge for this Ummah in every aspect.

It has been reported from Imām aṣ-Ṣādiq عليه السلام regarding the verse:

﴿أَمَّن يُجِيبُ الْمُضْطَرَّ إِذا دَعاهُ وَيَكْشِفُ السّوءَ وَيَجْعَلُكُمْ خُلَفاءَ الأَرضِ﴾

[361] Ṭūsī, Shaykh Muḥammad b. Ḥasan, *Kitāb al-Ghaybah*, p. 361.

﴾am-man yujību l-muḍṭarra idhā daʿāhu wa-yakshifu s-sūʾa wa-yajʿalukum khulafāʾa l-ʾarḍi﴿

﴾Is He who answers the call of the distressed [person] when he invokes Him and removes his distress, and makes you the earth's successors?﴿[362]

He ﷺ said:

> This verse was revealed about the Qāʾim of the family of Muḥammad ﷺ I swear to God that he is *the distressed [person]* who will perform two units of prayer by Maqaam of Ibrāhīm and then will beseech God. God will answer his prayers and will remove the distress and make him the successor in the Earth.[363]

67. The Comprehensive Duʿāʾ

In some of the Imām al-Mahdī's ﷺ letters, some teachings can be applied by anyone, even if they were originally intended for a specific person. One such instance was when someone asked the Imām ﷺ for a prayer covering all aspects of life, both in this world and the hereafter. The reply came:

---

[362] Sūrat an-Naml, Verse 62.

[363] Majlisī, ʿAllāmah Muḥammad Bāqir, *Mirʾāt al-ʿUqūl fī Sharḥ Akhbār Āl al-Rasūl*, Vol. 25, p. 201.

May God ﷻ bring together for you and your brothers all the goodness of this world and the hereafter.[364]

During the month of Rajab, we recite a similar prayer, asking:

Grant me, through my request to you, all the goodness of this world and the hereafter.[365]

There is no harm if a believer persistently seeks this from their Imām ﷹ throughout their life. If granted, they will lack nothing in terms of worldly or spiritual needs thereafter.

68. Compassion for the Awaiters

The Imām ﷹ clarifies the reason for his attention to the Ummah by saying:

If I had no affection for you and had not desired mercy and goodness for you, I would not have said anything to you[366]

This underscores the importance of mutual love, as fairness dictates. He further explains that his focus is drawn to what

---

[364] Ṭūsī, Shaykh Muḥammad b. Ḥasan, *Kitāb al-Ghaybah*, p. 378.

[365] Sayyid b. Ṭāwūs, *Iqbāl al-Aʿmāl*, Vol. 2, p. 644.

[366] Ṭūsī, Shaykh Muḥammad b. Ḥasan, *Kitāb al-Ghaybah*, p. 286.

prevents him from addressing the issue, namely, the trial of the oppressors. He explains:

> It is by way of trial and divine test for us that a misguided oppressor, without any right, has become a prisoner of his selfish desires and usurped the right of others.[367]

Hence, those who sense the Imām's ﷻ special care during the occultation should cherish this blessing, as the attention of one engaged in such significant matters carries immeasurable value!

69. Feeling for their Tragedies

One of the most evident signs of loyalty to Ahl al-Bayt, the Imāms عليهم السلام, is being moved by their sufferings. It is well-known that their deaths are marked by martyrdom, as documented in history. Therefore, the awaiting believer awaits the memories of their martyrdom to share the grief of their Imām ﷻ during his affliction. There is no doubt that he is the most affected during these occasions, given his knowledge of their esteemed positions and the reality of what befell them. Indeed, what reaches us through narrations and historical texts does not fully reflect the reality of what happened to them.

---

367 Majlisī, ʿAllāmah Muḥammad Bāqir, *Biḥār al-Anwār*, Vol. 53, p. 179.

In this regard, Imām aṣ-Ṣādiq ﷺ reportedly said:

> Whoever sheds a tear for us, whether it be for the blood of ours that was shed, or for a right of ours that was violated, or for the honor of ours that was tarnished, or for any one of our Shīʿah, God will reward them for it making Paradise their abode for ages[368]

70. The Aspiration for Participation

The desire to participate with Imām al-Mahdī ﷺ in restoring the religion to its rightful path was prevalent in the hearts of those close to the Imāms of the Ahl al-Bayt ﷺ to a remarkable degree. One of them addressed Imām aṣ-Ṣādiq ﷺ with the following words:

> May I be sacrificed for you, O son of the Messenger of God. I have been waiting for your Qāʾim for a hundred years, saying:
>
> > This month and this year,
>
> and my years have increased, my bones have become brittle, and my end is near. Yet, I do not see in you what I love. I see you killed and scattered, while your enemies soar with wings. So why shouldn't I cry?

---

[368] Mufīd, Shaykh Muḥammad, *al-Amālī*, p. 175.

Then, tears filled the eyes of Abū Abdillah ﷺ. He said,

> O Shaykh, If God prolongs your life until you witness our Qā'im, you will be with us in the highest company, and if death comes to you before then, you will come on the Day of Resurrection with the weight of Muḥammad ﷺ, and we are his weight.

He ﷺ said:

> I am leaving among you two weighty things, and if you hold fast to them, you will never go astray: the Book of God and my family, the people of my household.

The elder said,

> I do not worry after hearing this news.[369]

71. The Imām's Compassion for our Needs

The Imām ﷺ is among the most compassionate of beings, deeply affected by the sufferings of his Shī'ah, especially when they turn to him for help. So, why not approach your Imām just as believers of the past sought help and refuge in their Imām?

[369] Majlisī, 'Allāmah Muḥammad Bāqir, *Biḥār al-Anwār*, Vol. 36, p. 409.

This account sheds light on the nature of this relationship. It is narrated that Imām aṣ-Ṣādiq ﵇ was once approached by an elderly man who greeted him and said:

> O son of the Messenger of God, I love you, the Ahl al-Bayt, and I disassociate from your enemies. I have been afflicted with severe hardship, and I have come to seek refuge in the house of God from what I endure.

Then, he wept and threw himself at the feet of Imām aṣ-Ṣādiq ﵇, kissing his head and feet, while Imām aṣ-Ṣādiq ﵇ stepped back from him, showing mercy and shedding tears, then said:

> Your brother (in faith) has come to you seeking refuge in you, so raise your hands.

Imām aṣ-Ṣādiq ﵇ raised his hands, and we raised ours. Then he ﵇ said:

> O God, You created this soul from pure clay, and You made from it Your friends and the friends of Your friends. If You wish to remove afflictions from it, You can do so. O God, we seek refuge in Your Sacred House, in which everything finds security. O God, we seek refuge through us. I ask You, O You who veiled Himself with His light from His creation, I ask You, by the right of Muḥammad, ʿAlī, Fāṭimah, al-Ḥasan, and al-Ḥusayn, the ultimate relief for every distressed, longing, grieving, and afflicted person, to grant them

> security from what they fear, to wipe away from their clay what has been decreed upon it of affliction, and to relieve their distress, O Most Merciful of the Merciful.[370]

72. Prayers for the Awaiters

One of the greatest sources of blessings for those who await, as well as all believers throughout history, is the prayers offered by the Imām of each era for his followers. This involves asking God to bless them and grant them goodness, using the same words we recite when sending blessings upon them. Here, Imām Zayn al-ʿĀbidīn ﷺ is seen praying for the general followers of the Imāms:

> O God, and bless the friends [of the Imāms], the confessors of their station, the keepers to their course, the pursuers of their tracks, the clingers to their handhold, the adherents to their guardianship, the followers of their Imāmate, the submitters to their command, the strivers to obey them, the awaiters of their days, the directors of their eyes toward them, with blessings blessed, pure, growing, fresh, and fragrant![371]

Two important points stand out in this passage: Firstly, seeking blessings for followers is tied to their acknowledgment of the Imāms' esteemed status and their

---

[370] Ibid., Vol. 47, p. 122.

[371] Imām Zayn al-ʿĀbidīn ﷺ, *al-Ṣaḥīfah al-Sajjādīyyah*, p. 220.

commitment to following their teachings. This ensures that those who seek the Imāms' favor truly deserve it. Secondly, the mention of the specific group of awaiters, who turn to the Imāms with this divine blessing, highlights the special place these awaiters hold in the hearts of the Imāms.

73. The Approach of His Grandfather

Our Imām will employ a powerful method to evoke emotions, following in the footsteps of his grandfather, Imām al-Ḥusayn, when enemies confronted him on the day of ʿĀshūrāʾ. Firstly, he will remind people of his close connection to the Prophet, highlighting his adherence to the Prophet's teachings and his noble character, as well as his position within the esteemed household. Secondly, he will emphasize the injustices he and his followers suffered, as well as those awaiting him during the period of occultation.

Therefore, for those who are moved by knowledge and understanding, it is sufficient to read his words:

> Whoever argues with me about the Book of God, I am the worthiest of the Book of God. Whoever argues with me about the Sunnah of the Messenger of God, I am the worthiest of the Sunnah of the Messenger of

> God. I urge everyone who hears my speech today to inform them of its absence.[372]

For those whose emotions and desire to alleviate oppression from the Prophet ﷺ and his family are strong, it is enough to read the Imām's words:

> I ask you with the right of God, the right of His messenger, and with my right, for I have a right of kinship to the messenger of God, to support us and to protect us from those who have wronged us. We have been wronged, offended, expelled from our homes, separated from our families, deprived of our rights, and the evil people have distorted our honor and virtues. For the sake of God, do not fail us. Support us, may God support you![373]

74. Intense Longing for Him:

A distinctive trait of devoted Awaiters is their deep yearning to connect with their Imām عجل الله تعالى فرجه الشريف. Alongside this longing is an insatiable hunger to learn the tenets of their religion as he so chooses. Some would embark on arduous journeys driven by this dua pursuit of longing and learning. As we know, God ﷻ does not overlook the righteous deeds. Consider the tale of one such determined individual:

[372] Nuʿmānī, Muḥammad b. Ibrāhīm, *Kitāb al-Ghaybah*, p. 281.

[373] Ibid.

I took a paper and wrote down forty-odd questions that were difficult for me and said to myself that I must hand it over to the representative of Imām al-Ḥasan al-ʿAskarī ﷺ (that is, Aḥmad b. Isḥāq, who resided in Qum).

But when I went to him I learnt that he had left on a journey. I departed in his pursuit. I caught up with him at some point, and when we shook hands, he said,

> I trust it is positive matters that bring you after me?

I replied,

> Longing first, then the habit of seeking answers.

Aḥmad b. Isḥāq said to me:

> Let us go together to Sāmarrāʾ and ask our master, al-Ḥasan b. ʿAlī ﷺ, about this.

So I accompanied him to Sāmarrāʾ until we reached the house of our master, and I asked for permission to enter, which was granted. We then went inside.

Aḥmad b. Isḥāq had a leather bag that he had concealed inside his Tiberian cloak. The bag contained 160 purses containing gold and silver coins. Each purse was sealed with the sender's seal. When our eyes fell upon the elegant face of His Eminence, Abū Muḥammad al-Ḥasan b. ʿAlī ﷺ, we saw that his face

> was like a full moon, and a child was sitting in his lap. He was very beautiful, like a Jupiter star with nice locks of hair.[374]

Reflect on the saying

> Longing first, then the habit of seeking answers,

where both drove individuals to undertake perilous journeys, as they sought to meet the Imām during his house arrest.

75. The Imām's Compassion Towards His Followers

A remarkable trait of the Imām is his meticulous concern for even the smallest details concerning his followers. If we were to see this unveiled, we would surely be astonished. It is quite likely that the Imām would pray to divert someone from a path they are set on, knowing it is not in their best interest. Or he may subtly guide their hearts away from it, in line with the saying:

> I have known God through the nullifying of resolutions and thwarting of aspirations.

---

[374] Ṣadūq, Shaykh Muḥammad b. ʿAlī, *Kamāl al-Dīn wa Tamām al-Niʿmah*, Vol. 2, p. 456.

To illustrate this, let us look at a letter from Imām al-Mahdī عجل الله تعالى فرجه الشريف to Abū Jaʿfar b. Nubakht, who intended to perform Ḥajj. Abū Jaʿfar recounted:

> I intended to go for Ḥajj and made preparations for this purpose. A message from the Imām came,
>
>> We dislike that; however, it is your decision.
>
> I became anxious and sad. I wrote,
>
>> I remain submissive and obedient. However, I am sad for missing the Ḥajj.
>
> The answer came:
>
>> Grieve not, for you will perform Ḥajj next year.
>
> Next year, I sought permission, and the answer came in positive. I wrote,
>
>> I see Muḥammad b. al-ʿAbbās appropriate as my peer to run my affairs. I am confident of his religiosity and trustworthiness.
>
> The answer came,
>
>> Al-Asadi is the best peer. If he comes, do not choose anyone over him.

Al-Asadi came and I appointed him as my peer.[375]

76. He is Not Too Distant from Us

Some might think that during the period of occultation, the Imām ﷺ is distant, secluded in his sacred realm, seemingly unaffected by the struggles of the Ummah. However, in his qunut during the early stages of the occultation, the Imām revealed that the situation had reached an extreme, necessitating the divine wrath in response to the actions of the oppressors. This highlights the importance of praying for divine justice against the enemies of the religion. Here is a portion of his prayer:

And You said:

﴿فَلَمّا آسَفونا انتقَمنا مِنهُم﴾

﴾fa-lammā 'āsafūnā ntaqamnā minhum﴿

﴾So when they roused Our wrath, We took vengeance on them﴿[376]

Indeed, the end is within reach, and we are angered by Your anger, We are steadfast in supporting the truth, eager for Your command to come, We await the

---

[375] Majlisī, 'Allāmah Muḥammad Bāqir, *Biḥār al-Anwār*, Vol. 51, p. 308.

[376] Sūrat az-Zukhruf, Verse 55.

> fulfillment of Your promise, eagerly anticipating its realization, And we expect the fulfillment of Your threat upon Your enemies.[377]

The sincere awaiter should indeed feel a deep longing for truth within themselves, and they should aspire to fulfill the Imām's desires in order to assist him in enduring the pain he experiences.

77. His Prayers for his Supporters

One of Imām al-Mahdī's عجل الله تعالى فرجه الشريف notable traits during his occultation is his frequent prayers for his supporters. This is to acknowledge their right first, because some of what they endure during the occultation is for the sake of strengthening his cause. Secondly, to reinforce and support them, which is a prerequisite for expediting his reappearance. The matter of his reappearance is contingent upon the gathering of their numbers and ranks.

In one such prayer, the Imām عجل الله تعالى فرجه الشريف says:

> When You grant permission for my appearance, strengthen me with Your soldiers, and make those who follow me supporters of Your religion, striving in Your

[377] Majlisī, ʿAllāmah Muḥammad Bāqir, *Biḥār al-Anwār*, Vol. 82, p. 233.

> cause, and victorious over those who wish harm upon me and them[378]

Imām al-Mahdī's ﷺ prayers for God ﷻ to fortify his supporters extend throughout both the period of occultation and reappearance, because the goal in both is the same: supporting the religion.

78. The Depth of Relationship

Examining closely how followers interacted with their Imām during the minor occultation period provides insight into the depth of their relationship. It shows how the Imām ﷺ becomes a sanctuary, addressing their concerns, including even the most personal ones, such as marital disputes. Take the story of a man known as al-Zurārah and his wife, for example. He recalls:

> I intended in my heart not to disclose the condition of my wife (mother of ʿAbbās) to anyone. She and I had many differences, and she was very angry at me, while I was greatly fond of her. I said in my heart that I will ask him for a Duʿāʾ to remedy this problem that had been troubling me much.

Feeling the need for divine intervention, he requested the deputy to write a letter to the Imām ﷺ, asking for

[378] al-Kafʿamī, Ibrāhīm b. ʿAlī, *Miṣbāḥ Kafʿamī*, p. 219.

a du'ā' to relieve his distress without detailing the issue. The response from the Imām then arrived:

> As for the man from Zurārah and the condition between the husband and wife, may God rectify their relationship.

He was astonished that the Imām was aware of his inner turmoil. Yet, the deputy reassured him, asking,

> Do you doubt the Imām's capabilities?

al-Zurārah then recounts how his problem was resolved:

> We returned to Kūfah and I went to my house. My wife, who had been angry at me and was living with her family, came and sought my pleasure and apologized to me. She remained very agreeable to me and never disagreed with me until death separated us.[379]

79. The Imāms' Longing for him

Imām al-Mahdī عجل الله تعالى فرجه الشريف was the center of attention for all the infallibles, evident in their supplications and narrations, and even through expressing their eagerness to see him and witness the establishment of his noble reign. The

---

[379] Ṭūsī, Shaykh Muḥammad b. Ḥasan, *Kitāb al-Ghaybah*, p. 303.

Commander of the believers ﷺ mentions his son, Imām al-Mahdī ﷺ, describing his state as he moves from Wādī as-Salām towards al-Sahlah in order to establish the foundations of his rule.

Reflecting on this narration, it is evident that the Imām ﷺ exhibits the utmost reliance on God ﷻ, saying:

> You are my haven when the wide courses fail to carry me, and the Earth becomes narrow for me despite its vastness. O God, You created me while You are needless of my creation, and were it not for Your support, I would have been among the overwhelmed.

The he mentions the overwhelming Divine Greatness, saying:

> O God, You are the supporter of every solitary believer and the humiliator of every stubborn tyrant. O He for whom the kings place the yoke of humiliation upon their necks, and they are fearful of His Authority[380]

Lastly, he voices his needs, praying for the fulfillment of the divine promise, hoping it unfolds that very night, at that very moment.

---

[380] Majlisī, ʻAllāmah Muḥammad Bāqir, *Biḥār al-Anwār*, Vol. 52, p. 391.

www.ingramcontent.com/pod-product-compliance
Lightning Source LLC
Chambersburg PA
CBHW021700120626
46545CB00004B/1334